PRAISE FOR *THE SPIRIT*

'Might be the most important book...'
Guardian (UK)

'Fascinating and deeply provoking . . . *The Spirit Level does*
contain a powerful political message. It is impossible to read it
and not to be impressed by how often greater equality appears to
be the answer, whatever happens to be the question. It provides a
connection between what otherwise look like disparate social
problems.'
David Runciman, *London Review of Books* (UK)

'A compass to rebuild our societies . . . A shining vision.'
Johann Hari, *Independent* (UK)

'A crucial contribution to the ideological argument . . . It provides
a vital part of the intellectual manifesto on which
the battle for a better society can be fought.'
Roy Hattersley, *New Statesman* (UK)

'I recognize in this book a truth that most of us know in our
bones. A fair society is an essential part of our wellbeing.'
Colette Douglas Home, *Glasgow Herald*

'Compelling and shocking. All free marketers should
be made to memorize it from cover to cover.'
Yasmin Alibhai-Brown, *Independent* (UK)

'An impressive body of evidence, presented in an
easily digestible form . . . It raises some big questions.'
Will Kymlicka, *Globe and Mail* (Canada)

'Brave and imaginative . . . A far-reaching analysis.'
Michael Sargent, *Nature*

'My bet to become the manifesto for the next ten years.'
Richard Gillis, *Irish Times*

'A groundbreaking work and one that deserves the widest
possible readership.' Iain Ferguson, *Socialist Review* (UK)

'Powerful.' John Kay, *Financial Times* (UK)

'Surprising . . . Upends the traditional debate about income inequality.' Peter Wilson, *The Australian*

'This is a book with a big idea, big enough to change political thinking . . . In half a page [*The Spirit Level*] tells you more about the pain of inequality than any play or novel could.' John Carey, *Sunday Times* (UK)

'The connection [between income inequality and dysfunctional societies] is spelt out with stark clarity in Richard Wilkinson and Kate Pickett's remarkable new book, *The Spirit Level*. Income inequality, they show beyond any doubt, is not just bad for those at the bottom but for everyone.' Will Hutton, *Observer* (UK)

'Richard Wilkinson and Kate Pickett put forward compelling evidence that income inequalities are at the root of a wide range of health and social problems in society.' Niall Crowley, *Irish Times Weekend Review*

'The evidence, here painstakingly marshaled, is hard to dispute.' *Economist* (UK)

'Many [*New Statesman*] readers will be inspired as I am by a new book, *The Spirit Level* . . . Wilkinson and Pickett compare not only different countries, but also the 50 US states. They show that greater equality benefits not just the poor, but all occupational groups . . . [*The Spirit Level* has] lots of graphs but no jargon.' Peter Wilby, *New Statesman* (UK)

'In this fascinating sociological study, the authors do an excellent job of presenting the research, analyzing nuances, and offering policy suggestions for creating more equal and sustainable societies. For all readers, specialized or not, with an interest in understanding the dynamics today between economic and social conditions.' *Library Journal*

RICHARD WILKINSON AND KATE PICKETT

The Spirit Level

Why Greater Equality Makes Societies Stronger

BLOOMSBURY PRESS
NEW YORK • BERLIN • LONDON • SYDNEY

Published by Bloomsbury Press, New York

All papers used by Bloomsbury Press are natural, recyclable products made from
wood grown in well-managed forests. The manufacturing processes conform to
the environmental regulations of the country of origin.

LIBRARY OF CONGRESS CATALOGING-IN-PUBLICATION DATA

Wilkinson, Richard G.
The spirit level : why greater equality makes societies stronger /
Richard Wilkinson and Kate Pickett.—1st American ed.
p. cm.
Includes bibliographical references and index.
ISBN 978-1-60819-036-2 (hardcover : alk. paper)
1. Equality. 2. Social mobility. 3. Quality of life. 4. Social policy. I. Pickett, Kate. II. Title.

HM821.W55 2009
306.01—dc22
2009030428

First published in Great Britain by Allen Lane,
a division of the Penguin Group, in 2009
First published in the United States by Bloomsbury Press in 2010
This paperback edition published in 2011

Paperback ISBN: 978-1-60819-341-7

1 3 5 7 9 10 8 6 4 2

Typeset by Rowland Phototypesetting Ltd, Bury St Edmunds, Suffolk
Printed in the United States of America by Quad/Graphics, Fairfield, Pennsylvania

For our parents
Don and Marion Chapman
George and Mary Guillemard

Contents

PART THREE

A Better Society

Foreword

ROBERT B. REICH

Professor of Public Policy, University of California
Former U.S. Secretary of Labor

Most American families are worse off today than they were three decades ago. The Great Recession of 2008–2009 destroyed the value of their homes, undermined their savings, and too often left them without jobs. But even before the Great Recession began, most Americans had gained little from the economic expansion that began almost three decades before. Today, the Great Recession notwithstanding, the U.S. economy is far larger than it was in 1980. But where has all the wealth gone? Mostly to the very top. The latest data shows that by 2007, America's top 1 percent of earners received 23 percent of the nation's total income—almost triple their 8 percent share in 1980.

This rapid trend toward inequality in America marks a significant reversal of the move toward income equality that began in the early part of the twentieth century and culminated during the middle decades of the century.

Yet inequality has not loomed large as a political issue. Even Barack Obama's modest proposal to return income tax rates to where they stood in the 1990s prompted his 2008 Republican opponents to call him a socialist who wanted to spread the wealth. Once president, Obama's even more modest proposal to limit the income tax deductions of the wealthy in order to pay for health care for all met fierce resistance from a Democratically controlled Congress.

If politicians have failed to grapple with the issue of inequality, few scholars have done better. Philosophers have had little to say on the subject. Some who would tax the rich to help the poor frame their arguments as utilitarian. Taking a hundred dollars from a rich person and giving it to a poor person would diminish the rich person's happiness only slightly, they argue, but greatly increase the happiness of the poor person. Others ground their arguments in terms of hypothetical consent. John Rawls defends redistribution on the grounds that most people would be in favor of it if they had no idea what their income would otherwise be.

Nor have economists, whom we might expect to focus attention on such a dramatic trend, expressed much concern about widening inequality. For the most part, economists concern themselves with efficiency and growth. In fact, some of them argue that wide inequality is a necessary, if not inevitable, consequence of a growing economy. A few worry that it cuts off opportunities among the children of the poor for productive lives—but whether to distribute wealth more equally, or what might be gained from doing so, is a topic all but ignored by today's economic researchers.

It has taken two experts from the field of public health to deliver a major study of the effects of inequality on society. Though Richard Wilkinson and Kate Pickett are British, their research explores the United States in depth, and their work is an important contribution to the debate our country needs.

The Spirit Level looks at the negative social effects of wide inequality— among them, more physical and mental illness not only among those at the lower ranks, but even those at the top of the scale. The authors find, not surprisingly, that where there are great disparities in wealth, there are heightened levels of social distrust. They argue convincingly that wide inequality is bad for a society, and that more equal societies tend to do better on many measures of social health and wealth.

But if wide inequality is socially dysfunctional, then why are certain countries, such as the United States, becoming so unequal? Largely because of the increasing gains to be had by being just a bit better than other competitors in a system becoming ever more competitive.

Consider executive pay. During the 1950s and '60s, CEOs of major American companies took home about 25 to 30 times the wages of the typical worker. After the 1970s, the two pay scales diverged. In 1980, the big-company CEO took home roughly 40 times; by 1990, it was 100 times. By 2007, just before the Great Recession, CEO pay packages had ballooned to about 350 times what the typical worker earned. Recent supports suggest that the upward trajectory of executive pay, temporarily stopped by the economic meltdown, is on the verge of continuing. To make the comparison especially vivid, in 1968 the CEO of General Motors—then the largest company in the United States—took home around 66 times the pay and benefits of the typical GM worker at the time. In 2005, the CEO of Wal-Mart—by then the largest U.S. company—took home 900 times the pay and benefits of the typical Wal-Mart worker.

What explains this trajectory? Have top executives become greedier? Have corporate boards grown less responsible? Are CEOs more crooked? Are investors more docile? Is Wall Street more tractable? There's no evidence to support any of these theories. Here's a simpler explanation: Forty years ago, everyone's pay in a big company—even pay at the top—was affected by bargains struck among big business, big labor, and, indirectly, government. Big companies and their unions directly negotiated pay scales for hourly workers, while white-collar workers understood that their pay grades were indirectly affected. Large corporations resembled civil service bureaucracies. Top executives in these huge companies had to maintain the good will of organized labor. They also had to maintain good relationships with public officials in order to be free to set wages and prices; to obtain regulatory permissions on fares, rates, or licenses; and to continue to secure government contracts. It would have been unseemly of them to draw very high salaries.

Since then, competition has intensified. With ever greater ease, rival companies can get access to similar low-cost suppliers from all over the world. They can streamline their operations with the same information technology their competitors use; they can cut their labor force and substitute similar software, culled from many of the same vendors. They can just as readily outsource hourly jobs abroad. They can get capital for new investment on much the same terms. They can gain access to distribution channels that are no less efficient, some of them even identical (Wal-Mart or other big-box retailers). They can attract shareholders by showing even slightly better performance, or the promise of it.

The dilemma facing so many companies is therefore how to beat rivals. Even a small advantage can make a huge difference to the bottom line. In economic terms, CEOs have become less like top bureaucrats and more like Hollywood celebrities or star athletes, who take a share of the house. Hollywood's most popular celebrities now pull in around 15 percent of whatever the studios take in at the box office, and athletes are also getting a growing portion of sales. As the New Yorker's James Surowiecki has reminded us, Mickey Mantle earned $60,000 in 1957. Carlos Beltran made $15 million in 2005. Even adjusting for inflation, Beltran got 40 times as much as Mantle. Clark Gable earned $100,000 a picture in the 1940s, which translates into roughly $800,000 today. Tom Hanks, by contrast, makes closer to $20 million per film. Movie studios and baseball teams find it profitable to pay these breathtaking sums because they're still relatively small compared to the money these stars bring in and the profits they generate. Today's big companies are paying their CEOs mammoth sums for much the same reason.

In the world of finance, the numbers are yet greater. Top investment bankers and traders take home even more than CEOs or most Hollywood stars. For the managers of twenty-six major hedge funds, the *average* take-home pay in 2005 was $363 million, a 45 percent increase over their average earnings the year before. The Wall Street meltdown took its toll on some of these hedge funds and their managers, but by the end of 2009 many were back.

This economic explanation for these startling levels of pay does not justify them socially or morally. It only means that in our roles as *consumers* and *investors* we implicitly think CEOs, star athletes, and Hollywood celebrities are worth it. As *citizens*, though, most of us disapprove. Polls continue to show that a great majority of Americans believes CEOs are overpaid, and that inequality of income and wealth is a large problem.

In short, our nation's wealth is becoming even more concentrated at the top. It has become the financial equivalent of hydrodynamics: Large streams of income create even larger pools of wealth. The family of Wal-Mart founder Sam Walton has a combined fortune estimated to be about $90 billion. In 2005, Bill Gates was worth $46 billion; Warren Buffet, $44 billion. By contrast, the combined wealth of the bottom 40 percent of the United States population that year—some 120 million people—was estimated to be around $95 billion. Here again, the Great Recession of 2008–2009 took a toll; some of these billionaires' fortunes were whittled down by 20 to 40 percent. But even then, they remained immense.

As citizens, we may feel that inequality on this scale cannot possibly be good for us, and Wilkinson and Pickett supply the evidence that confirms our gut sense of unease. Such inequality undermines the trust, solidarity, and mutuality on which responsibilities of citizenship depend. It creates a new aristocracy whose privileges perpetuate themselves over generations (one of the striking findings in these pages is that America now has less social mobility than many poorer countries). And it breeds cynicism among the rest of us.

This is not to say that the superrich are at fault. By and large, "the market" is generating these outlandish results. But the market is a creation of public policies. And public policies, as the authors make clear, can reorganize the market to reverse these trends. *The Spirit Level* shows why the effort to do so is a vital one for the health of our society.

Berkeley, California
July 2009

Preface

People usually exaggerate the importance of their own work and we worry about claiming too much. But this book is not just another set of nostrums and prejudices about how to put the world to rights. The work we describe here comes out of a very long period of research (over fifty person-years between us) devoted, initially, to trying to understand the causes of the big differences in life expectancy – the 'health inequalities' – between people at different levels in the social hierarchy in modern societies. The focal problem initially was to understand why health gets worse at every step down the social ladder, so that the poor are less healthy than those in the middle, who in turn are less healthy than those further up.

Like others who work on the social determinants of health, our training in epidemiology means that our methods are those used to trace the causes of diseases in populations – trying to find out why one group of people gets a particular disease while another group doesn't, or to explain why some disease is becoming more common. The same methods can, however, also be used to understand the causes of other kinds of problems – not just health.

Just as the term 'evidence-based medicine' is used to describe current efforts to ensure that medical treatment is based on the best scientific evidence of what works and what does not, we thought of calling this book 'Evidence-based Politics'. The research which underpins what we describe comes from a great many research teams in different universities and research organizations. Replicable methods have been used to study observable and objective outcomes, and peer-reviewed research reports have been published in academic, scientific journals.

This does not mean that there is no guesswork. Results always have to be interpreted, but there are usually good reasons for favouring one interpretation over another. Initial theories and expectations are often called into question by later research findings which make it necessary to think again. We would like to take you on the journey we have travelled, signposted by crucial bits of evidence and leaving out only the various culs-de-sac and wrong turnings that wasted so much time, to arrive at a better understanding of how we believe it is possible to improve the quality of life for everyone in modern societies. We shall set out the evidence and our reasons for interpreting it the way we do, so that you can judge for yourself.

At an intuitive level people have always recognized that inequality is socially corrosive. But there seemed little reason to think that levels of inequality in developed societies differed enough to expect any measurable effects. The reasons which first led one of us to look for effects seem now largely irrelevant to the striking picture which has emerged. Many discoveries owe as much to luck as judgement.

The reason why the picture we present has not been put together until now is probably that much of the data has only become available in recent years. With internationally comparable information not only on incomes and income distribution but also on different health and social problems, it could only have been a matter of time before someone came up with findings like ours. The emerging data have allowed us, and other researchers, to analyse how societies differ, to discover how one factor is related to another, and to test theories more rigorously.

It is easy to imagine that discoveries are more rapidly accepted in the natural than in the social sciences – as if physical theories are somehow less controversial than theories about the social world. But the history of the natural sciences is littered with painful personal disputes, which started off as theoretical disagreements but often lasted for the rest of people's lives. Controversies in the natural sciences are usually confined to the experts: most people do not have strong views on rival theories in particle physics. But they do have views on how society works. Social theories are partly theories about ourselves; indeed, they might almost be regarded as part of our self-awareness or self-consciousness of societies. While natural scientists do not have to convince individual cells or atoms to accept their theories, social theorists are up against a plethora of individual views and powerful vested interests.

In 1847, Ignaz Semmelweiss discovered that if doctors washed their hands before attending women in childbirth it dramatically reduced deaths from puerperal fever. But before his work could have much benefit he had to persuade people – principally his medical colleagues – to change their behaviour. His real battle was not his initial discovery but what followed from it. His views were ridiculed and he was driven eventually to insanity and suicide. Much of the medical profession did not take his work seriously until Louis Pasteur and Joseph Lister had developed the germ theory of disease, which explained why hygiene was important.

We live in a pessimistic period. As well as being worried by the likely consequences of global warming, it is easy to feel that many societies are, despite their material success, increasingly burdened by their social failings. And now, as if to add to our woes, we have the economic recession and its aftermath of high unemployment. But the knowledge that we cannot carry on as we have, that change is necessary, is perhaps grounds for optimism: maybe we do, at last, have the chance to make a better world. The extraordinarily positive reception of the hardback editon of this book confirms that there is a widespread appetite for change and a desire to find positive solutions to our problems.

We have made only minor changes to this edition. Details of the statistical sources, methods and results, from which we thought most readers would want to be spared, are now provided in an appendix for those with a taste for data. Chapter 13, which is substantially about causation, has been slightly reorganized and strengthened. We have also expanded our discussion of what has made societies substantially more or less equal in the past. Because we conclude that these changes have been driven by changes in political attitudes, we think it is a mistake to discuss policy as if it were a matter of finding the right technical fix. As there are really hundreds of ways that societies can become more equal if they choose to, we have not nailed our colours to one or other set of policies. What we need is not so much a clever solution as a society which recognizes the benefits of greater equality. If correct, the theory and evidence set out in this book tells us how to make substantial improvements in the quality of life for the vast majority of the population. Yet unless it is possible to change the way most people see the societies they live in, the theory will be stillborn. Public opinion will only support the necessary political changes if something like the perspective we outline in this book permeates the public mind. We have therefore set up a not-for-profit organization called The Equality Trust (described at the end of this book) to make the kind of evidence set out in the following pages better known and to suggest that there is a way out of the woods for us all.

Acknowledgements

We are grateful to Danny Dorling, Stuart Proffitt and Alison Quick for their careful reading and many helpful comments on our manuscript. We also thank Molly Scott Cato for her comments on Chapter 15, Majid Ezzati for kindly sending us his corrected estimates of body mass index for US states, and Stephen Bezruchka for helpful discussions.

We are also grateful to the Joseph Rowntree Charitable Trust, especially Stephen Pittam, for supporting our efforts to disseminate this research via The Equality Trust; and Kathryn Busby and Bill Kerry whose hard work has made it a going concern.

Richard Wilkinson would like to thank the University of Nottingham and his former colleagues in the Division of Epidemiology and Public Health for the freedom which allowed him to devote his time to the research which went into this book. Kate Pickett thanks the University of York and her colleagues for their generous support.

Figures 3.1 and 3.2 are reproduced by kind permission of Jean Twenge. We are grateful to Cambridge University Press for permission to reproduce Figures 4.3 and 10.1. Figure 6.1 is reproduced with permission from BMJ Publishing group; Figure 6.7 with permission from Bryan Christie Design, LLC; and Figure 15.3 with permission from the *Economic Journal*. All other Figures are our own, and can be freely reproduced with acknowledgement.

The cartoons on pp. 16, 32, 64, 104, 118, 130, 146, 158, 172, 194, 214 and 230 are from www.CartoonStock.com. Grateful acknowledgement is given to them and to the following for permission to reproduce cartoons: p. 2, copyright © Andy Singer, 2007, politicalcartoons.com; p. 48, copyright © *The New Yorker*

Note on Graphs

FACTS FROM FIGURES: HOW TO LOOK AT THE GRAPHS IN THIS BOOK

Most of the graphs that we use in this book are charts linking income inequality to different health and social problems. They show relationships, either: (1) internationally, comparing rich countries or (2) in the USA, comparing different states.

In all of these graphs, we put income inequality along the horizontal line at the bottom (the x-axis), so societies with low levels of inequality are to the left, and societies with high levels of inequality are towards the right of the graph.

The different health and social outcomes are shown on the vertical line (the y-axis) on the left side of the graph.

On most of the graphs, there are two features. First there is a scatter of points, either of rich countries, or of US states, so that readers can see exactly how each society compares to others. Second, there is a line, called a *regression line*, which shows the 'best fit' relationship between income inequality and the outcome on that graph. This line is not chosen by us, but is calculated by statistical software to give the line which best fits the trend through the data points. It is also possible to calculate how unlikely it is that the pattern we see could result from chance alone. We have only included a best fit line through the points if the relationship would be very unlikely to occur by chance. When a graph has no best fit line it means that there is no evidence of a relationship.

If the line slopes steeply upwards from left to right, it shows that the health or social outcome becomes more common in more unequal societies. This pattern tends to occur with problems that we think of as bad, such as violence:

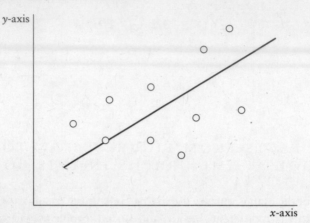

If the line slopes steeply downwards from left to right, it shows that the health or social outcome is much less common in more unequal societies. We see this pattern for things that we think of as good, such as trust:

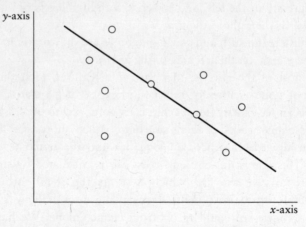

A wider scatter of points on the graph means that there are other important influences on the outcome. It may not mean that inequality is not a powerful influence, simply that other factors matter as well:

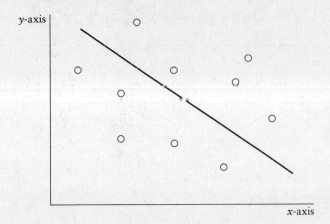

A narrow scattering of points means that there is a very close relationship between inequality and the outcome and that inequality is an excellent predictor of the outcome:

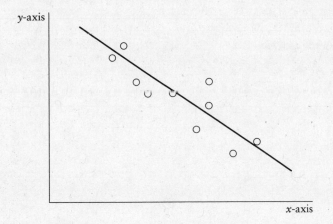

Further details of our methods can be found at: www. equalitytrust.org.uk

PART ONE

Material Success,
Social Failure

I

The end of an era

I care for riches, to make gifts to friends, or lead a sick
man back to health with ease and plenty. Else small aid
is wealth for daily gladness; once a man be done with
hunger, rich and poor are all as one.   Euripides, *Electra*

It is a remarkable paradox that, at the pinnacle of human material
and technical achievement, we find ourselves anxiety-ridden, prone
to depression, worried about how others see us, unsure of our
friendships, driven to consume and with little or no community life.
Lacking the relaxed social contact and emotional satisfaction we all
need, we seek comfort in over-eating, obsessive shopping and spending, or become prey to excessive alcohol, psychoactive medicines and
illegal drugs.

How is it that we have created so much mental and emotional
suffering despite levels of wealth and comfort unprecedented in
human history? Often what we feel is missing is little more than
time enjoying the company of friends, yet even that can seem beyond
us. We talk as if our lives were a constant battle for psychological
survival, struggling against stress and emotional exhaustion, but the
truth is that the luxury and extravagance of our lives is so great that
it threatens the planet.

Research from the Harwood Institute for Public Innovation
(commissioned by the Merck Family Foundation) in the USA shows
that people feel that 'materialism' somehow comes between them
and the satisfaction of their social needs. A report entitled *Yearning
for Balance*, based on a nationwide survey of Americans, concluded

3

that they were 'deeply ambivalent about wealth and material gain'.[1]* A large majority of people wanted society to 'move away from greed and excess toward a way of life more centred on values, community, and family'. But they also felt that these priorities were not shared by most of their fellow Americans, who, they believed, had become 'increasingly atomized, selfish, and irresponsible'. As a result they often felt isolated. However, the report says, that when brought together in focus groups to discuss these issues, people were 'surprised and excited to find that others share[d] their views'. Rather than uniting us with others in a common cause, the unease we feel about the loss of social values and the way we are drawn into the pursuit of material gain is often experienced as if it were a purely private ambivalence which cuts us off from others.

Mainstream politics no longer taps into these issues and has abandoned the attempt to provide a shared vision capable of inspiring us to create a better society. As voters, we have lost sight of any collective belief that society could be different. Instead of a better society, the only thing almost everyone strives for is to better their own position – as individuals – within the existing society.

The contrast between the material success and social failure of many rich countries is an important signpost. It suggests that, if we are to gain further improvements in the real quality of life, we need to shift attention from material standards and economic growth to ways of improving the psychological and social wellbeing of whole societies. However, as soon as anything psychological is mentioned, discussion tends to focus almost exclusively on individual remedies and treatments. Political thinking seems to run into the sand.

It is now possible to piece together a new, compelling and coherent picture of how we can release societies from the grip of so much dysfunctional behaviour. A proper understanding of what is going on could transform politics and the quality of life for all of us. It would change our experience of the world around us, change what we vote for, and change what we demand from our politicians.

In this book we show that the quality of social relations in a society is built on material foundations. The scale of income differ-

*Superscripts refer to numbered references listed at the end of the book.

ences has a powerful effect on how we relate to each other. Rather than blaming parents, religion, values, education or the penal system, we will show that the scale of inequality provides a powerful policy lever on the psychological wellbeing of all of us. Just as it once took studies of weight gain in babies to show that interacting with a loving care-giver is crucial to child development, so it has taken studies of death rates and of income distribution to show the social needs of adults and to demonstrate how societies can meet them.

Long before the financial crisis which gathered pace in the later part of 2008, British politicians commenting on the decline of community or the rise of various forms of anti-social behaviour, would sometimes refer to our 'broken society'. The financial collapse shifted attention to the broken economy, and while the broken society was sometimes blamed on the behaviour of the poor, the broken economy was widely attributed to the rich. Stimulated by the prospects of ever bigger salaries and bonuses, those in charge of some of the most trusted financial institutions threw caution to the wind and built houses of cards which could stand only within the protection of a thin speculative bubble. But the truth is that both the broken society and the broken economy resulted from the growth of inequality.

WHERE THE EVIDENCE LEADS

We shall start by outlining the evidence which shows that we have got close to the end of what economic growth can do for us. For thousands of years the best way of improving the quality of human life was to raise material living standards. When the wolf was never far from the door, good times were simply times of plenty. But for the vast majority of people in affluent countries the difficulties of life are no longer about filling our stomachs, having clean water and keeping warm. Most of us now wish we could eat less rather than more. And, for the first time in history, the poor are – on average – fatter than the rich. Economic growth, for so long the great engine of progress, has, in the rich countries, largely finished its work. Not only have measures of wellbeing and happiness ceased to rise with economic growth but, as affluent societies have grown richer, there have been long-term rises in rates of anxiety, depression and numerous other social problems. The populations of rich countries have got to the end of a long historical journey.

The course of the journey we have made can be seen in Figure 1.1. It shows the trends in life expectancy in relation to Gross National Income per head in countries at various stages of economic development. Among poorer countries, life expectancy increases rapidly during the early stages of economic development, but then, starting among the middle-income countries, the rate of improvement slows down. As living standards rise and countries get richer and richer, the relationship between economic growth and life expectancy weakens. Eventually it disappears entirely and the rising curve in Figure 1.1 becomes horizontal – showing that for rich countries to get richer adds nothing further to their life expectancy. That has already happened in the richest thirty or so countries – nearest the top right-hand corner of Figure 1.1.

The reason why the curve in Figure 1.1 levels out is not because we have reached the limits of life expectancy. Even the richest countries go on enjoying substantial improvements in health as time goes by. What has changed is that the improvements have ceased to be related to average living standards. With every ten years that passes, life expectancy among the rich countries increases by between two and three years. This happens regardless of economic growth, so that a country as rich as the USA no longer does better than Greece or New Zealand, although they are not much more than half as rich. Rather than moving out along the curve in Figure 1.1, what happens as time goes by is that the curve shifts upwards: the same levels of income are associated with higher life expectancy. Looking at the data, you cannot help but conclude that as countries get richer, further increases in average living standards do less and less for health.

While good health and longevity are important, there are other components of the quality of life. But just as the relationship between health and economic growth has levelled off, so too has the relationship with happiness. Like health, how happy people are rises in the early stages of economic growth and then levels off. This

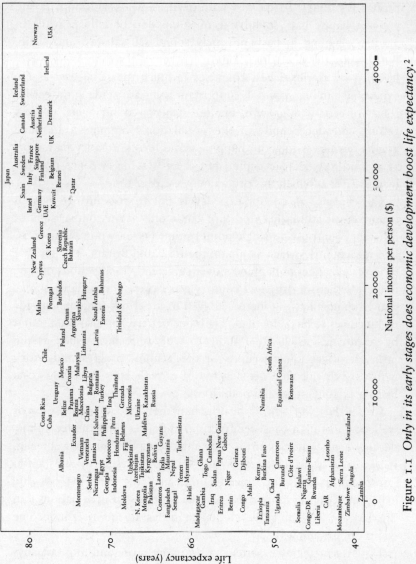

Figure 1.1 *Only in its early stages does economic development boost life expectancy.*[2]

is a point made strongly by the economist, Richard Layard, in his book on happiness.[3] Figures on happiness in different countries are probably strongly affected by culture. In some societies not saying you are happy may sound like an admission of failure, while in another claiming to be happy may sound self-satisfied and smug. But, despite the difficulties, Figure 1.2 shows the 'happiness curve' levelling off in the richest countries in much the same way as life expectancy. In both cases the important gains are made in the earlier stages of economic growth, but the richer a country gets, the less getting still richer adds to the population's happiness. In these graphs the curves for both happiness and life expectancy flatten off at around $25,000 per capita, but there is some evidence that the income level at which this occurs may rise over time.[4]

The evidence that happiness levels fail to rise further as rich countries get still richer does not come only from comparisons of different countries at a single point in time (as shown in Figure 1.2). In a few countries, such as Japan, the USA and Britain, it is possible to look at changes in happiness over sufficiently long periods of time to see whether they rise as a country gets richer. The evidence shows that happiness has not increased even over periods long enough for real incomes to have doubled. The same pattern has also been found by researchers using other indicators of wellbeing – such as the 'measure of economic welfare' or the 'genuine progress indicator', which try to calculate net benefits of growth after removing costs like traffic congestion and pollution.

So whether we look at health, happiness or other measures of wellbeing there is a consistent picture. In poorer countries, economic development continues to be very important for human wellbeing. Increases in their material living standards result in substantial improvements both in objective measures of wellbeing like life expectancy, and in subjective ones like happiness. But as nations join the ranks of the affluent developed countries, further rises in income count for less and less.

This is a predictable pattern. As you get more and more of anything, each addition to what you have – whether loaves of bread or cars – contributes less and less to your wellbeing. If you are hungry, a loaf of bread is everything, but when your hunger is satisfied, many

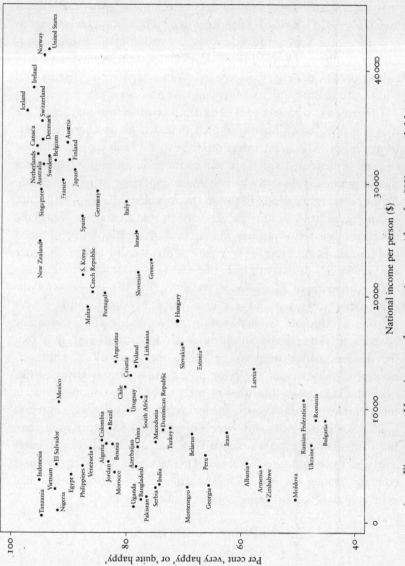

Figure 1.2 *Happiness and average incomes (data for UK unavailable).*[5]

more loaves don't particularly help you and might become a nuisance as they go stale.

Sooner or later in the long history of economic growth, countries inevitably reach a level of affluence where 'diminishing returns' set in and additional income buys less and less additional health, happiness or wellbeing. A number of developed countries have now had almost continuous rises in average incomes for over 150 years and additional wealth is not as beneficial as it once was.

The trends in different causes of death confirm this interpretation. It is the diseases of poverty which first decline as countries start to get richer. The great infectious diseases – such as tuberculosis, cholera or measles – which are still common in the poorest countries today, gradually cease to be the most important causes of death. As they disappear, we are left with the so-called diseases of affluence – the degenerative cardiovascular diseases and cancers. While the infectious diseases of poverty are particularly common in childhood and frequently kill even in the prime of life, the diseases of affluence are very largely diseases of later life.

One other piece of evidence confirms that the reason why the curves in Figures 1.1 and 1.2 level off is because countries have reached a threshold of material living standards after which the benefits of further economic growth are less substantial. It is that the diseases which used to be called the 'diseases of affluence' became the diseases of the poor in affluent societies. Diseases like heart disease, stroke and obesity used to be more common among the rich. Heart disease was regarded as a businessman's disease and it used to be the rich who were fat and the poor who were thin. But from about the 1950s onwards, in one developed country after another, these patterns reversed. Diseases which had been most common among the better-off in each society reversed their social distribution to become more common among the poor.

THE ENVIRONMENTAL
LIMITS TO GROWTH

At the same time as the rich countries reach the end of the real benefits of economic growth, we have also had to recognize the problems of global warming and the environmental limits to growth. The dramatic reductions in carbon emissions needed to prevent runaway climate change and rises in sea levels may mean that even present levels of consumption are unsustainable – particularly if living standards in the poorer, developing, world are to rise as they need to. In Chapter 15 we shall discuss the ways in which the perspective outlined in this book fits in with policies designed to reduce global warming.

INCOME DIFFERENCES WITHIN
AND BETWEEN SOCIETIES

We are the first generation to have to find new answers to the question of how we can make further improvements to the real quality of human life. What should we turn to if not to economic growth? One of the most powerful clues to the answer to this question comes from the fact that we are affected very differently by the income differences *within* our own society from the way we are affected by the differences in average income *between* one rich society and another.

In Chapters 4–12 we focus on a series of health and social problems like violence, mental illness, teenage births and educational failure, which within each country are all more common among the poor than the rich. As a result, it often looks as if the effect of higher incomes and living standards is to lift people out of these problems. However, when we make comparisons between different societies, we find that these social problems have little or no relation to levels of *average* incomes in a society.

Take health as an example. Instead of looking at life expectancy across both rich and poor countries as in Figure 1.1, look just at the richest countries. Figure 1.3 shows just the rich countries and confirms that among them some countries can be almost twice as rich as others without any benefit to life expectancy. Yet *within* any of them death rates are closely and systematically related to income. Figure 1.4 shows the relation between death rates and income levels within the USA. The death rates are for people in zip code areas classified by the typical household income of the area in which they live. On the right are the richer zip code areas with lower death rates, and on the left are the poorer ones with higher death rates. Although we use American data to illustrate this, similar health gradients, of varying steepness, run across almost every society. Higher incomes are related to lower death rates at every level in society. Note that this is not simply a matter of the poor having worse health than everyone else. What is so striking about Figure 1.4 is how regular the health gradient is right across society – it is a gradient which affects us all.

Within each country, people's health and happiness are related to

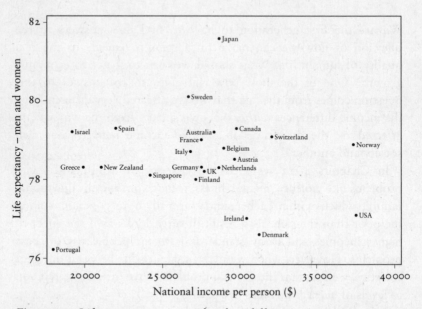

Figure 1.3 *Life expectancy is unrelated to differences in average income between rich countries.*[6]

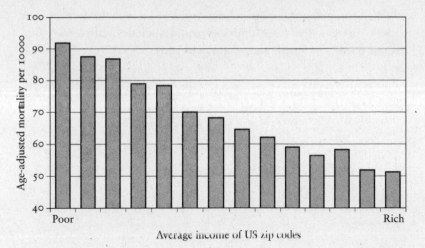

Figure 1.4 *Death rates are closely related to differences in income* within *societies.*[7]

their incomes. Richer people tend, on average, to be healthier and happier than poorer people in the same society. But comparing rich countries it makes no difference whether on average people in one society are almost twice as rich as people in another.

What sense can we make of this paradox – that differences in average income or living standards between whole populations or countries don't matter at all, but income differences within those same populations matter very much indeed? There are two plausible explanations. One is that what matters in rich countries may not be your actual income level and living standard, but how you compare with other people in the same society. Perhaps average standards don't matter and what does is simply whether you are doing better or worse than other people – where you come in the social pecking order.

The other possibility is that the social gradient in health shown in Figure 1.4 results not from the effects of relative income or social status on health, but from the effects of social mobility, sorting the healthy from the unhealthy. Perhaps the healthy tend to move up the social ladder and the unhealthy end up at the bottom.

This issue will be resolved in the next chapter. We shall see whether compressing, or stretching out, the income differences in a society matters. Do more and less equal societies suffer the same overall burden of health and social problems?

2

Poverty or inequality?

> Poverty is not a certain small amount of goods, nor is it
> just a relation between means and ends; above all it is a
> relation between people. Poverty is a social status ... It has
> grown ... as an invidious distinction between classes ...
> Marshall Sahlins, *Stone Age Economics*

HOW MUCH INEQUALITY?

In the last chapter we saw that economic growth and increases in
average incomes have ceased to contribute much to wellbeing in the
rich countries. But we also saw that within societies health and social
problems remain strongly associated with incomes. In this chapter
we will see whether the amount of income inequality in a society
makes any difference.

Figure 2.1 shows how the size of income differences varies from
one developed country to another. At the top are the most equal
countries and at the bottom are the most unequal. The length of the
horizontal bars shows how much richer the richest 20 per cent of
the population is in each country compared to the poorest 20 per
cent. Within countries such as Japan and some of the Scandinavian
countries at the top of the chart, the richest 20 per cent are less than
four times as rich as the poorest 20 per cent. At the bottom of the
chart are countries in which these differences are at least twice as
big, including two in which the richest 20 per cent get about nine
times as much as the poorest. Among the most unequal are
Singapore, USA, Portugal and the United Kingdom. (The figures are

'Miss Smith, buy up the rights to the Bible and get that part changed about the rich man and the eye of the needle.'

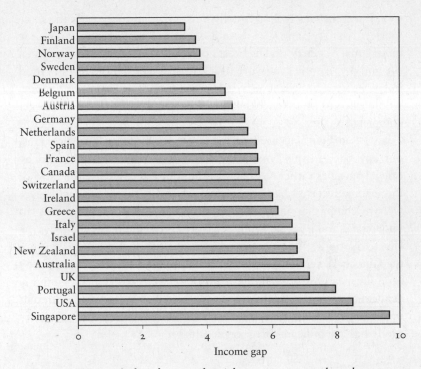

Figure 2.1 *How much richer are the richest 20 per cent than the poorest 20 per cent in each country?*[2]

for household income, after taxes and benefits, adjusted for the number of people in each household.)

There are lots of ways of measuring income inequality and they are all so closely related to each other that it doesn't usually make much difference which you use. Instead of the top and bottom 20 per cent, we could compare the top and bottom 10 or 30 per cent. Or we could have looked at the proportion of all incomes which go to the poorer half of the population. Typically, the poorest half of the population get something like 20 or 25 per cent of all incomes and the richest half get the remaining 75 or 80 per cent. Other more sophisticated measures include one called the Gini coefficient. It measures inequality across the whole society rather than simply comparing the extremes. If all income went to one person (maximum inequality) and everyone else got nothing, the Gini coefficient would be equal to 1. If income was shared equally and everyone got exactly the same (perfect equality), the Gini would equal 0. The lower its value, the more equal a society is. The most common values tend to be between 0.3 and 0.5. Another measure of inequality is called the Robin Hood Index because it tells you what proportion of a society's income would have to be taken from the rich and given to the poor to get complete equality.

To avoid being accused of picking and choosing our measures, our approach in this book has been to take measures provided by official agencies rather than calculating our own. We use the ratio of the income received by the top to the bottom 20 per cent whenever we are comparing inequality in different countries: it is easy to understand and it is one of the measures provided ready-made by the United Nations. When comparing inequality in US states, we use the Gini coefficient: it is the most common measure, it is favoured by economists and it is available from the US Census Bureau. In many academic research papers we and others have used two different inequality measures in order to show that the choice of measures rarely has a significant effect on results.

DOES THE AMOUNT OF INEQUALITY MAKE A DIFFERENCE?

Having got to the end of what economic growth can do for the quality of life and facing the problems of environmental damage, what difference do the inequalities shown in Figure 2.1 make?

It has been known for some years that poor health and violence are more common in more unequal societies. However, in the course of our research we became aware that almost all problems which are more common at the bottom of the social ladder are more common in more unequal societies. It is not just ill-health and violence, but also, as we will show in later chapters, a host of other social problems. Almost all of them contribute to the widespread concern that modern societies are, despite their affluence, social failures.

To see whether these problems were more common in more unequal countries, we collected internationally comparable data on health and as many social problems as we could find reliable figures for. The list we ended up with included:

- level of trust
- mental illness (including drug and alcohol addiction)
- life expectancy and infant mortality
- obesity
- children's educational performance
- teenage births
- homicides
- imprisonment rates
- social mobility (not available for US states)

Occasionally what appear to be relationships between different things may arise spuriously or by chance. In order to be confident that our findings were sound we also collected data for the same health and social problems – or as near as we could get to the same – for each of the fifty states of the USA. This allowed us to check whether or not problems were consistently related to inequality in these two independent settings. As Lyndon Johnson said, 'America is not merely a nation, but a nation of nations.'

To present the overall picture, we have combined all the health and social problem data for each country, and separately for each US state, to form an Index of Health and Social Problems for each country and US state. Each item in the indexes carries the same weight – so, for example, the score for mental health has as much influence on a society's overall score as the homicide rate or the teenage birth rate. The result is an index showing how common all these health and social problems are in each country and each US state. Things such as life expectancy are reverse scored, so that on every measure higher scores reflect worse outcomes. When looking at the Figures, the higher the score on the Index of Health and Social Problems, the worse things are. (For information on how we selected countries shown in the graphs we present in this book, please see the Appendix.)

We start by showing, in Figure 2.2, that there is a very strong tendency for ill-health and social problems to occur less frequently in

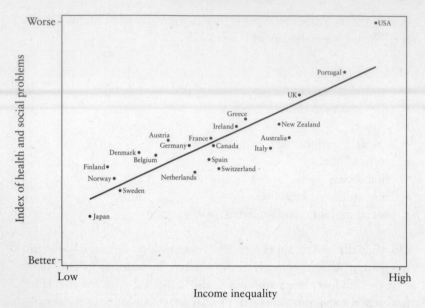

Figure 2.2 *Health and social problems are closely related to inequality among rich countries.*

the more equal countries. With increasing inequality (to the right on the horizontal axis), the higher is the score on our Index of Health and Social Problems. Health and social problems are indeed more common in countries with bigger income inequalities. The two are extraordinarily closely related – chance alone would almost never produce a scatter in which countries lined up like this.

To emphasize that the prevalence of poor health and social problems in whole societies really is related to inequality rather than to average living standards, we show in Figure 2.3 the same index of health and social problems but this time in relation to average incomes (National Income per person). It shows that there is no similarly clear trend towards better outcomes in richer countries. This confirms what we saw in Figures 1.1 and 1.2 in the first chapter. However, as well as knowing that health and social problems are more common among the less well-off within each society (as shown in Figure 1.4), we now know that the overall burden of these problems is much higher in more unequal societies.

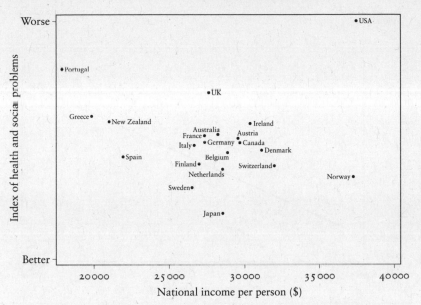

Figure 2.3 *Health and social problems are only weakly related to national average income among rich countries.*

To check whether these results are not just some odd fluke, let us see whether similar patterns also occur when we look at the fifty states of the USA. We were able to find data on almost exactly the same health and social problems for US states as we used in our international index. Figure 2.4 shows that the Index of Health and Social Problems is strongly related to the amount of inequality in each state, while Figure 2.5 shows that there is no clear relation between it and average income levels. The evidence from the USA confirms the international picture. The position of the US in the international graph (Figure 2.2) shows that the high average income level in the US as a whole does nothing to reduce its health and social problems relative to other countries.

We should note that part of the reason why our index combining data for ten different health and social problems is so closely related to inequality is that combining them tends to emphasize what they have in common and downplays what they do not. In Chapters 4–12 we will examine whether each problem – taken on its own – is

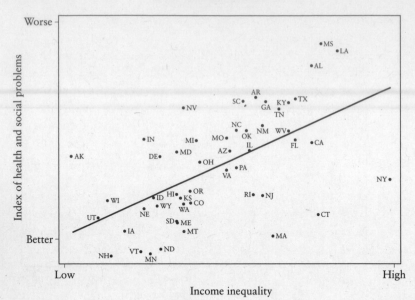

Figure 2.4 *Health and social problems are related to inequality in US states.*

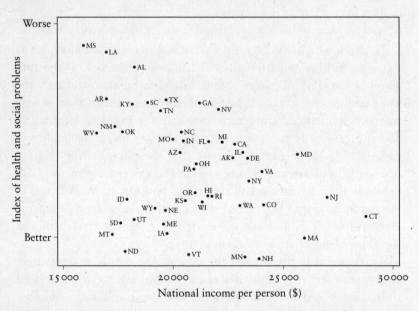

Figure 2.5 *Health and social problems are only weakly related to average income in US states.*

related to inequality and will discuss the various reasons why they might be caused by inequality.

This evidence cannot be dismissed as some statistical trick done with smoke and mirrors. What the close fit shown in Figure 2.2 suggests is that a common element related to the prevalence of all these health and social problems is indeed the amount of inequality in each country. All the data come from the most reputable sources – from the World Bank, the World Health Organization, the United Nations and the Organization for Economic Cooperation and Development (OECD), and others.

Could these relationships be the result of some unrepresentative selection of problems? To answer this we also used the 'Index of child wellbeing in rich countries' compiled by the United Nations Children's Fund (UNICEF). It combines forty different indicators covering many different aspects of child wellbeing. (We removed the measure of child relative poverty from it because it is, by definition, closely related to inequality.) Figure 2.6 shows that child wellbeing is

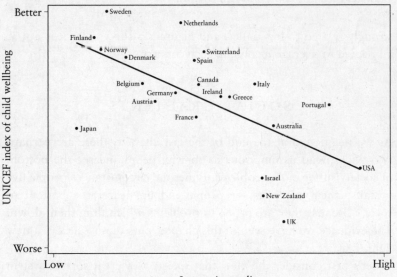

Figure 2.6 *The UNICEF index of child wellbeing in rich countries is related to inequality.*

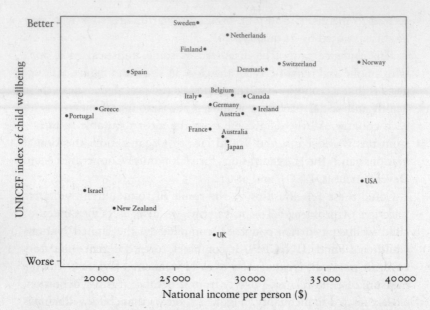

Figure 2.7 *The UNICEF index of child wellbeing is not related to Gross National Income per head in rich countries.*

strongly related to inequality, and Figure 2.7 shows that it is not at all related to average income in each country.

SOCIAL GRADIENTS

As we mentioned at the end of the last chapter, there are perhaps two widespread assumptions as to why people nearer the bottom of society suffer more problems. Either the circumstances people live in cause their problems, or people end up nearer the bottom of society because they are prone to problems which drag them down. The evidence we have seen in this chapter puts these issues in a new light.

Let's first consider the view that society is a great sorting system with people moving up or down the social ladder according to their personal characteristics and vulnerabilities. While things such as having poor health, doing badly at school or having a baby when still a teenager all load the dice against your chances of getting up the social ladder, sorting alone does nothing to explain why more unequal societies have more of all these problems than less unequal ones. Social mobility may partly explain whether problems congregate at the bottom, but not why more unequal societies have more problems overall.

The view that social problems are caused directly by poor *material* conditions such as bad housing, poor diets, lack of educational opportunities and so on implies that richer developed societies would do better than the others. But this is a long way from the truth: some of the richest countries do worst.

It is remarkable that these measures of health and social problems in the two different settings, and of child wellbeing among rich countries, all tell so much the same story. The problems in rich countries are not caused by the society not being rich enough (or even by being too rich) but by the scale of material differences between people within each society being too big. What matters is where we stand in relation to others in our own society.

Of course a small proportion of the least well-off people even in the richest countries sometimes find themselves without enough money for food. However, surveys of the 12.6 per cent of Americans living below the federal poverty line (an absolute income level rather than a relative standard such as half the average income) show that 80 per cent of them have air-conditioning, almost 75 per cent own at least one car or truck and around 33 per cent have a computer, a dishwasher or a second car. What this means is that when people lack money for essentials such as food, it is usually a reflection of the strength of their desire to live up to the prevailing standards. You may, for instance, feel it more important to maintain appearances by spending on clothes while stinting on food. We knew of a young man who was unemployed and had spent a month's income on a new mobile phone because he said girls ignored people who hadn't got the right stuff. As Adam Smith emphasized, it is important to be able to present oneself creditably in society without the shame and stigma of apparent poverty.

However, just as the gradient in health ran right across society from top to bottom, the pressures of inequality and of wanting to keep up are not confined to a small minority who are poor. Instead, the effects are – as we shall see – widespread in the population.

DIFFERENT PROBLEMS – COMMON ROOTS

The health and social problems which we have found to be related to inequality tend to be treated by policy makers as if they were quite separate from one another, each needing separate services and remedies. We pay doctors and nurses to treat ill-health, police and prisons to deal with crime, remedial teachers and educational psychologists to tackle educational problems, and social workers, drug rehabilitation units, psychiatric services and health promotion experts to deal with a host of other problems. These services are all expensive, and none of them is more than partially effective. For instance, differences in the quality of medical care have less effect on people's life expectancy than social differences in their risks of getting some life-threatening disease in the first place. And even when the various services are successful in stopping someone re-offending, in curing a cancer, getting someone off drugs or dealing with educational failure, we know that our societies are endlessly recreating these problems in each new generation. Meanwhile, all these problems are most common in the most deprived areas of our society and are many times more common in more unequal societies.

WHAT DOES INCOME INEQUALITY TELL US?

Before proceeding, in the following chapters, to look at how the scale of income differences may be related to other problems, we should say a few words about what we think income differences tell us about a society. Human beings have lived in every kind of society, from the most egalitarian prehistoric hunting and gathering societies, to the most plutocratic dictatorships. Although modern market democracies fall into neither of those extremes, it is reasonable to assume that there are differences in how hierarchical they are. We believe that this is what income inequality is measuring. Where income differences are bigger, social distances are bigger and social stratification more important.

It would be nice to have lots of different indicators of the scale of hierarchy in different countries – to be able to compare inequalities not only in income, but also in wealth, education and power. It would also be interesting to see how they are related to social distances, to indicators of status like people's choice of clothes, music and films, or to the importance of hierarchy and position. While additional measures which can be compared between countries might become available in the future, at the moment we must rely simply on income inequality. But what is perhaps surprising is how much this measure tells us even on its own.

There are two important reasons for interpreting income inequality in this way. The first pointer is that only the health and social problems which have strong social class gradients – becoming more common further down the social hierarchy – are more common in more unequal societies. This seems to be a general phenomenon: the steeper the social gradient a problem has within society, the more strongly it will be related to inequality.[8] This not only applies to each problem – to teenage birth rates or to children doing badly at school, for example – it looks as if it also applies to sex differences in the same problem. The reason why women's obesity rates turn out – as we shall see – to be more closely related to inequality than men's, seems to be that the social gradient in obesity is steeper among women than men. Health problems such as breast cancer, which are not usually more common among the less well off, are unrelated to inequality.[9]

The other pointer which suggests that income inequality reflects how hierarchical societies are, became clear when we reviewed nearly 170 academic papers reporting different pieces of research on the relationship between income inequality and health.[10] The size of the areas over which researchers had measured inequality varied substantially. Some had calculated how much inequality there was in local neighbourhoods and looked to see if it was related to average death rates in those neighbourhoods. Others had used whole towns and cities as the units in which inequality and health were measured. Still others had looked at regions and states, or done international studies comparing whole countries. When we reviewed all this research, a clear pattern emerged. While there was overwhelming evidence that inequality was related to health when both were measured in large areas (regions, states or whole countries), the findings were much more mixed when inequality was measured in small local areas.

This makes perfect sense if we think about why health tends to be worse in more deprived local areas. What marks out the neighbourhoods with poor health – where life expectancy may be as much as ten years shorter than in the healthiest neighbourhoods – is not of course the inequality within them. It is instead that they are unequal – or deprived – in relation to the rest of society. What matters is the extent of inequality right across society.

We concluded that, rather than telling us about some previously unknown influence on health (or social problems), the scale of income differences in a society was telling us about the social hierarchy across which gradients in so many social outcomes occur. Because gradients in health and social problems reflect social status differences in culture and behaviour, it looks as if material inequality is probably central to those differences.

We should perhaps regard the scale of material inequalities in a society as providing the skeleton, or framework, round which class and cultural differences are formed. Over time, crude differences in wealth gradually become overlaid by differences in clothing, aesthetic taste, education, sense of self and all the other markers of class identity. Think, for instance, of how the comparatively recent emergence of huge income differences in Russia will come to affect its class structure. When the children of the new Russian oligarchs have grown up in grand houses, attended private schools and travelled the world, they will have developed all the cultural trappings of an upper class. A British Conservative politician was famously described by another as someone who 'had to buy his own furniture'. Although there has always been prejudice against the nouveau riche, wealth does not remain new for ever: once the furniture is inherited it becomes old money. Even as far back as the eighteenth century, when people thought that birth and breeding were what defined the upper echelons of society, if you lost your fortune you might maintain status briefly as 'genteel poor', but after a generation or so there would be little to distinguish you from the rest of the poor. Moreover, as Jane Austen shows in both *Mansfield Park* and *Sense and Sensibility*, the consequences – whatever your birth – of marrying for love rather than money could be serious. Whether material wealth is made or lost, you cannot long remain 'a person of substance' without it. And it is surely because material differences provide the framework round which social distinctions develop that people have often regarded inequality as socially divisive.

QUALITY OF LIFE FOR ALL AND NATIONAL STANDARDS OF PERFORMANCE

Having come to the end of what higher material living standards can offer us, we are the first generation to have to find other ways of improving the real quality of life. The evidence shows that reducing inequality is the best way of improving the quality of the social environment, and so the real quality of life, for all of us. As we shall see in Chapter 13, this includes the better-off.

It is clear that greater equality, as well as improving the wellbeing of the whole population, is also the key to national standards of achievement and how countries perform in lots of different fields. When health inequalities first came to prominence on the public health agenda in the early 1980s, people would sometimes ask why there was so much fuss about inequalities. They argued that the task of people working in public health was to raise overall standards of health as fast as possible. In relation to that, it was suggested that health inequalities were a side issue of little relevance. We can now see that the situation may be almost the opposite of that. National standards of health, and of other important outcomes which we shall discuss in later chapters, are substantially determined by the amount of inequality in a society. If you want to know why one country does better or worse than another, the first thing to look at is the extent of inequality. There is not one policy for reducing inequality in health or the educational performance of school children, and another for raising national standards of performance. Reducing inequality is the best way of doing both. And if, for instance, a country wants higher average levels of educational achievement among its school children, it must address the underlying inequality which creates a steeper social gradient in educational achievement.

DEVELOPING COUNTRIES

Before leaving this topic, we should emphasize that although inequality also matters in developing countries, it may do so for a different mix of reasons. In the rich countries, it is now the symbolic importance of wealth and possessions that matters. What purchases say about status and identity is often more important than the goods themselves. Put crudely, second-rate goods are assumed to reflect second-rate people.

Possessions are markers of status everywhere, but in poorer societies, where necessities are a much larger part of consumption, the reasons why more equal societies do better may have less to do with status issues and more to do with fewer people being denied access to food, clean water and shelter. It is only among the very richest countries that health and wellbeing are no longer related to Gross National Income per person. In poorer countries it is still essential to raise living standards and it is most important among the poorest. In those societies a more equal distribution of resources will mean fewer people will be living in shanty towns, with dirty water and food insecurity, or trying to scrape a living from inadequate land-holdings.

In the next chapter we will look in a little more detail at why people in the developed world are so sensitive to inequality that it can exert such a major effect on the psychological and social wellbeing of modern populations.

3

How inequality gets under the skin

'Tis very certain that each man carries in his eye the exact
indication of his rank in the immense scale of men, and we
are always learning to read it.

Ralph Waldo Emerson, *The Conduct of Life*

How is it that we are affected as strongly by inequality and our
position within society as the data in the last chapter suggest? Before
exploring – as we shall in the next nine chapters – the relations
between inequality and a wide range of social problems, including
those in our Index of Health and Social Problems, we want to
suggest why human beings might be so sensitive to inequality.

As inequality is an aspect of the broad structure of societies, explanations of its effects involve showing how individuals are affected
by the social structure. It is individuals – not the societies themselves
– who have poor health, are violent or become teenage mothers.
Although individuals do not have an income distribution, they do
have a relative income, social status or class position in the wider
society. So in this chapter we will show the ways in which our
individual sensitivity to the wider society explains why living in
more unequal societies might have such profound effects.

To understand our vulnerability to inequality means discussing
some of our common psychological characteristics. Too often when
we speak or write about these issues, people misinterpret our
purpose. We are not suggesting that the problem is a matter of
individual psychology, or that it is really people's sensitivity, rather
than the scale of inequality, that should be changed. The solution to

problems caused by inequality is not mass psychotherapy aimed at making everyone less vulnerable. The best way of responding to the harm done by high levels of inequality would be to reduce inequality itself. Rather than requiring anti-anxiety drugs in the water supply or mass psychotherapy, what is most exciting about the picture we present is that it shows that reducing inequality would increase the wellbeing and quality of life for all of us. Far from being inevitable and unstoppable, the sense of deterioration in social wellbeing and the quality of social relations in society *is* reversible. Understanding the effects of inequality means that we suddenly have a policy handle on the wellbeing of whole societies.

The powerful mechanisms which make people sensitive to inequality cannot be understood in terms either of social structure or of individual psychology alone. Individual psychology and societal inequality relate to each other like lock and key. One reason why the effects of inequality have not been properly understood before is because of a failure to understand the relationship between them.

THE RISE IN ANXIETY

Given the unprecedented material comfort and physical convenience of modern societies, it might seem sensible to be sceptical of the way everyone talks of stress, as if life was barely survivable. However, Jean Twenge, a psychologist at San Diego State University, has put together impressive evidence that we really are much more anxious than we used to be. By reviewing the large number of studies of anxiety levels in the population carried out at different dates, she has documented very clear trends. She found 269 broadly comparable studies measuring anxiety levels in the USA at various times between 1952 and 1993.[11] Together the surveys covered over 52,000 individuals. What they showed was a continuous upward trend throughout this forty-year period. Her results for men and women are shown in Figure 3.1. Each dot in the graph shows the average level of anxiety found in a study recorded against the date it was undertaken. The rising trend across so many studies is unmistakable. Whether she looked at college students or at children, Twenge found the same

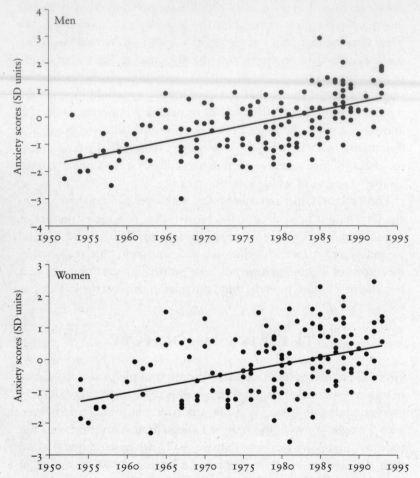

Figure 3.1 *Rise in anxiety levels among US college students 1952–93. Data from 269 samples covering 52,000 individuals.*[15] *(Reproduced with kind permission from Jean M. Twenge.)*

pattern: the average college student at the end of the period was more anxious than 85 per cent of the population at the beginning of it and, even more staggering, by the late 1980s the average American child was more anxious than child psychiatric patients in the 1950s.

This evidence comes from the administration of standardized

anxiety measures to samples of the population. It cannot be explained away by saying that people have become more aware of anxiety. The worsening trend also fits what we know has been happening in related conditions such as depression. Depression and anxiety are closely connected: people who suffer from one often suffer from the other, and psychiatrists sometimes treat the two conditions in similar ways. There are now large numbers of studies showing substantial increases in rates of depression in developed countries. Some studies have looked at change over the last half century or so by comparing the experience of one generation with another, while taking care to avoid pitfalls such as an increased awareness leading to more frequent reporting of depression.[12] Others have compared rates in studies which have followed up representative samples of the population born in different years. In Britain, for example, depression measured among people in their mid-20s was found to be twice as common in a study of 10,000 or so people born in 1970 as it had been in a similar study carried out earlier of people in their mid-20s born in 1958.[13]

Reviews of research conclude that people in many developed countries have experienced substantial rises in anxiety and depression. Among adolescents, these have been accompanied by increases in the frequency of behavioural problems, including crime, alcohol and drugs.[12, 14] They 'affected males and females, in all social classes and all family types'.[13]

It is important to understand what these rises in anxiety are about before their relevance to inequality becomes clear. We are not suggesting that they were triggered by increased inequality. That possibility can be discounted because the rises in anxiety and depression seem to start well before the increases in inequality which in many countries took place during the last quarter of the twentieth century. (It is possible, however, that the trends between the 1970s and 1990s may have been aggravated by increased inequality.)

SELF-ESTEEM AND SOCIAL INSECURITY

An important clue to what lies behind the mental health trends comes from evidence that they were accompanied by a surprising rise in what at first was thought to be self-esteem. When compared over time, in much the same way as the trends in anxiety are shown in Figure 3.1, standard measures of self-esteem also showed a very clear long-term upward trend. It looked as if, despite the rising anxiety levels, people were also taking a more positive view of themselves over time. They were, for instance, more likely to say they felt proud of themselves; they were more likely to agree with statements such as 'I am a person of worth'; and they seemed to have put aside self-doubts and feelings that they were 'useless' or 'no good at all'. Twenge says that in the 1950s only 12 per cent of teenagers agreed with the statement 'I am an important person', but by the late 1980s this proportion had risen to 80 per cent.

So what could have been going on? People becoming much more self-confident doesn't seem to fit with them also becoming much more anxious and depressed. The answer turns out to be a picture of increasing anxieties about how we are seen and what others think of us which has, in turn, produced a kind of defensive attempt to shore up our confidence in the face of those insecurities. The defence involves a kind of self-promoting, insecure egotism which is easily mistaken for high self-esteem. This might seem like a difficult set of issues to pin down, particularly as we are talking about general trends in whole populations. But let us look briefly at the evidence which has accumulated since the self-esteem movement of the 1980s, which shows what has been happening.

Over the years, many research groups looking at individual differences in self-esteem at a point in time (rather than at trends in population averages over time) began to notice two categories of people who came out with high scores. In one category, high self-esteem went with positive outcomes and was associated with happiness, confidence, being able to accept criticism, an ability to make friends, and so on. But as well as positive outcomes, studies repeatedly found that there was another group who scored well on self-esteem measures. They were people who showed tendencies to violence, to racism, who were insensitive to others and were bad at personal relationships.

The task was then to develop psychological tests which could distinguish between people with a healthy and those with an unhealthy kind of self-esteem. The healthier kind seemed to centre on a fairly well-founded sense of confidence, with a reasonably accurate view of one's strengths in different situations and an ability to recognize one's weaknesses. The other seemed to be primarily defensive and involved a denial of weaknesses, a kind of internal attempt to talk oneself up and maintain a positive sense of oneself in the face of threats to self-esteem. It was (and is) therefore fragile, like whistling in the dark, and reacts badly to criticism. People with insecure high self-esteem tend to be insensitive to others and to show an excessive preoccupation with themselves, with success, and with their image and appearance in the eyes of others. This unhealthy high self-esteem is often called 'threatened egotism', 'insecure high self-esteem', or 'narcissism'. During the comparatively short time over which data are available to compare trends in narcissism without getting it mixed up with real self-esteem, Twenge has shown a rising trend. She found that by 2006, two-thirds of American college students scored above what had been the average narcissism score in 1982. The recognition that what we have seen is the rise of an insecure narcissism – particularly among young people – rather than a rise in genuine self-esteem now seems widely accepted.

THREATS TO THE SOCIAL SELF

So the picture of self-esteem rising along with anxiety levels isn't true. It is now fairly clear that the rises in anxiety have been accompanied by rising narcissism and that the two have common roots. Both are caused by an increase in what has been called 'social evaluative threat'. There are now good pointers to the main sources of stress in modern societies. As living with high levels of stress is now recognized as harmful to health, researchers have spent a lot of time trying to understand both how the body responds to stress and what the most important sources of stress are in society at large. Much of the research has been focused on a central stress hormone called cortisol which can be easily measured in saliva or blood. Its release is triggered by the brain and it serves to prepare us physiologically for dealing with potential threats and emergencies. There have now been numerous experiments in which volunteers have been invited to come into a laboratory to have their salivary cortisol levels measured while being exposed to some situation or task designed to be stressful. Different experiments have used different stressors: some have tried asking volunteers to do a series of arithmetic problems – sometimes publicly comparing results with those of others – some have exposed them to loud noises or asked them to write about an unpleasant experience, or filmed them while doing a task. Because so many different kinds of stressor have been used in these experiments, Sally Dickerson and Margaret Kemeny, both psychologists at the University of California, Los Angeles, realized that they could use the results of all these experiments to see what kinds of stressors most reliably caused people's cortisol levels to rise.[16]

They collected findings from 208 published reports of experiments in which people's cortisol levels were measured while they were exposed to an experimental stressor. They classified all the different kinds of stressor used in experiments and found that: 'tasks that included a social-evaluative threat (such as threats to self-esteem or social status), in which others could negatively judge performance, particularly when the outcome of the performance was uncontrollable, provoked larger and more reliable cortisol changes than stressors without these particular threats' (p. 377). Indeed, they suggested that 'Human beings are driven to preserve the social self and are vigilant to threats that may jeopardize their social esteem or status' (p. 357). Social evaluative threats were those which created the possibility for loss of esteem. They typically involved the presence of an evaluative audience in the experiment, a potential for negative social comparison such as scoring worse than someone else, or having your performance videoed or recorded, so creating the potential for later evaluation. The highest cortisol responses came when a social evaluative threat was combined with a task in which participants could not avoid failure – for instance because the task was designed to be impossible, or because there was too little time, or they were simply told they were failing however they performed.

The finding that social evaluative threats are the stressors which get to us most powerfully fits well with the evidence of rising anxiety accompanied by a narcissistic defence of an insecure self-image. As Dickerson and Kemeny say, the 'social self' which we try to defend 'reflects one's esteem and status, and is largely based on others' perception of one's worth' (p. 357).

A quite separate strand of health research corroborates and fills out this picture. One of the most important recent developments in our understanding of the factors exerting a major influence on health in rich countries has been the recognition of the importance of psychological stress. We will outline in Chapter 6 how frequent and/or prolonged stress affects the body, influencing many physio-logical systems, including the immune and cardiovascular systems. But what matters to us in this chapter is that the most powerful sources of stress affecting health seem to fall into three intensely social categories: low social status, lack of friends, and stress in early life. All have been shown, in many well-controlled studies, to be seriously detrimental to health and longevity.

Much the most plausible interpretation of why these keep cropping up as markers for stress in modern societies is that they all affect – or reflect – the extent to which we do or do not feel at ease and confident with each other. Insecurities which can come from a stressful early life have some similarities with the insecurities which can come from low social status, and each can exacerbate the effects of the other. Friendship has a protective effect because we feel more secure and at ease with friends. Friends make you feel appreciated, they find you good company, enjoy your conversation – they like you. If, in contrast, we lack friends and feel avoided by others, then few of us are thick-skinned enough not to fall prey to self-doubts, to worries that people find us unattractive and boring, that they think we are stupid or socially inept.

PRIDE, SHAME AND STATUS

The psychoanalyst Alfred Adler said 'To be human means to feel inferior.' Perhaps he should have said 'To be human means being highly sensitive about being regarded as inferior.' Our sensitivity to such feelings makes it easy to understand the contrasting effects of high and low social status on confidence. How people see you matters. While it is of course possible to be upper-class and still feel totally inadequate, or to be lower-class and full of confidence, in general the further up the social ladder you are, the more help the world seems to give you in keeping the self-doubts at bay. If the social hierarchy is seen – as it often is – as if it were a ranking of the human race by ability, then the outward signs of success or failure (the better jobs, higher incomes, education, housing, car and clothes) all make a difference.

It's hard to disregard social status because it comes so close to defining our worth and how much we are valued. To do well for yourself or to be successful is almost synonymous with moving up the social ladder. Higher status almost always carries connotations of being better, superior, more successful and more able. If you don't want to feel small, incapable, looked down on or inferior, it is not quite essential to avoid low social status, but the further up the social ladder you are, the easier it becomes to feel a sense of pride, dignity and self-confidence. Social comparisons increasingly show you in a positive light – whether they are comparisons of wealth, education, job status, where you live, holidays, or any other markers of success.

Not only do advertisers play on our sensitivity to social comparisons, knowing we will tend to buy things which enhance how we are seen, but, as we shall see in Chapter 10, one of the most common causes of violence, and one which plays a large part in explaining why violence is more common in more unequal societies, is that it is often triggered by loss of face and humiliation when people feel looked down on and disrespected. By playing on our fears of being seen as of less worth, advertisers may even contribute to the level of violence in a society.

It was Thomas Scheff, emeritus professor of sociology at the University of California, Santa Barbara, who said that shame was *the* social emotion.[17] He meant almost exactly what Dickerson and Kemeny were referring to when they found that the most likely kinds of stressors to raise levels of stress hormones were 'social evaluative threats'. By 'shame' he meant the range of emotions to do with feeling foolish, stupid, ridiculous, inadequate, defective, incompetent, awkward, exposed, vulnerable and insecure. Shame and its opposite, pride, are rooted in the processes through which we internalize how we imagine others see us. Scheff called shame *the* social emotion because pride and shame provide the social evaluative feedback as we experience ourselves as if through others' eyes. Pride is the pleasure and shame the pain through which we are socialized, so that we learn, from early childhood onwards, to behave in socially acceptable ways. Nor of course does it stop in childhood: our sensitivity to shame continues to provide the basis for conformity throughout adult life. People often find even the smallest infringement of social norms in the presence of others causes so much embarrassment that they are left wishing they could just disappear, or that the ground would swallow them up.

Although the Dickerson and Kemeny study found that it was exposure to social evaluative threats which most reliably raised levels of stress hormones, that does not tell us how frequently people suffer from such anxieties. Are they a very common part of everyday life, or only occasional? An answer to that question comes from the health research showing that low social status, lack of friends, and a difficult early childhood are the most important markers of psychosocial stress in modern societies. If our interpretation of these three factors is right, it suggests that these kinds of social anxiety and insecurity are the most common sources of stress in modern societies. Helen Lewis, a psychoanalyst who drew people's attention to shame emotions, thought she saw very frequent behavioural indications of shame or embarrassment – perhaps not much more than we would call a momentary feeling of awkwardness or self-consciousness – when her patients gave an embarrassed laugh or hesitated at particular points while speaking in a way suggesting slight nervousness.[18]

FROM COMMUNITY
TO MASS SOCIETY

Why have these social anxieties increased so dramatically over the last half century – as Twenge's studies showing rising levels of anxiety and fragile, narcissistic egos suggest they have? Why does the social evaluative threat seem so great? A plausible explanation is the break-up of the settled communities of the past. People used to grow up knowing, and being known by, many of the same people all their lives. Although geographical mobility had been increasing for several generations, the last half century has seen a particularly rapid rise. At the beginning of this period it was still common for people – in rural and urban areas alike – never to have travelled much beyond the boundaries of their immediate city or village community. Married brothers and sisters, parents and grandparents, tended to remain living nearby and the community consisted of people who had often known each other for much of their lives. But now that so many people move from where they grew up, knowledge of neighbours tends to be superficial or non-existent. People's sense of identity used to be embedded in the community to which they belonged, in people's real knowledge of each other, but now it is cast adrift in the anonymity of mass society. Familiar faces have been replaced by a constant flux of strangers. As a result, who we are, identity itself, is endlessly open to question.

The problem is shown even in the difficulty we have in distinguishing between the concept of the 'esteem' in which we may or may not be held by others, and our own self-esteem. The evidence of our sensitivity to 'social evaluative threat', coupled with Twenge's evidence of long-term rises in anxiety and narcissism, suggests that we may – by the standards of any previous society – have become highly self-conscious, obsessed with how we appear to others, worried that we might come across as unattractive, boring, stupid or whatever, and constantly trying to manage the impressions we make. And at the core of our interactions with strangers is our concern at the social judgements and evaluations they might make: how do they rate us, did we give a good account of ourselves? This vulnerability is part of the modern psychological condition and feeds directly into consumerism.

It is well known that these problems are particularly difficult for adolescents. While their sense of themselves is most uncertain, they have to cope in schools of a thousand or more of their peers. It is hardly surprising that peer pressure becomes such a powerful force in their lives, that so many are dissatisfied with what they look like, or succumb to depression and self-harm.

INEQUALITY INCREASES EVALUATION ANXIETIES

Although the rises in anxiety that seem to centre on social evaluation pre-date the rise in inequality, it is not difficult to see how rising inequality and social status differences may impact on them. Rather than being entirely separate spheres, how much status and wealth people achieve – from unskilled low-paid work to success, money and pre-eminence – affects not only their sense of themselves, but also how positively they are seen even by friends and family. Our need to feel valued and capable human beings means we crave positive feedback and often react with anger even to implied criticism. Social status carries the strongest messages of superiority and inferiority, and social mobility is widely seen as a process by which people are sorted by ability. Indeed, in job applications and promotions, where discrimination by age, sex, race or religion is prohibited, it is the task of the interview panel to discriminate between individuals exclusively by ability – just as long as they don't make inferences from gender or skin colour, etc.

Greater inequality seems to heighten people's social evaluation anxieties by increasing the importance of social status. Instead of accepting each other as equals on the basis of our common humanity as we might in more equal settings, getting the measure of each other becomes more important as status differences widen. We come to see social position as a more important feature of a person's identity. Between strangers it may often be the dominant feature. As Ralph Waldo Emerson, the nineteenth-century American philosopher, said,

''Tis very certain that each man carries in his eye the exact indication of his rank in the immense scale of men, and we are always learning to read it.'[19] Indeed, psychological experiments suggest that we make judgements of each other's social status within the first few seconds of meeting.[20] No wonder first impressions count, and no wonder we feel social evaluation anxieties!

If inequalities are bigger, so that some people seem to count for almost everything and others for practically nothing, where each one of us is placed becomes more important. Greater inequality is likely to be accompanied by increased status competition and increased status anxiety. It is not simply that where the stakes are higher each of us worries more about where he or she comes. It is also that we are likely to pay more attention to social status in how we assess each other. Surveys have found that when choosing prospective marriage partners, people in more unequal countries put less emphasis on romantic considerations and more on criteria such as financial prospects, status and ambition, than do people in less unequal societies.[21]

SELF-PROMOTION REPLACES SELF-DEPRECATION AND MODESTY

Comparing Japan with the USA, that is, the most equal with almost the most unequal of the rich market democracies (see Figure 2.1), research has revealed a stark contrast between the way people see and present themselves to others in the two countries. In Japan, people choose a much more self-deprecating and self-critical way of presenting themselves, which contrasts sharply with the much more self-enhancing style in the USA. While Americans are more likely to attribute individual successes to their own abilities and their failures to external factors, the Japanese tend to do just the opposite.[22] More than twenty studies in Japan have failed to find any evidence of the more self-serving pattern of attributions common in the USA. In Japan people tended to pass their successes off as if they were more a reflection of luck than of judgement, while suggesting their failures are probably attributable to their own lack of ability. This Japanese pattern was also found in Taiwan and China.

Rather than getting too caught up in psychological terminology, we would do well to see these patterns as differences in how far people value personal modesty, preferring to maintain social bonds by not using their successes to build themselves up as more able than others. As greater inequality increases status competition and social evaluative threat, egos have to be propped up by self-promoting and self-enhancing strategies. Modesty easily becomes a casualty of inequality: we become outwardly tougher and harder in the face of greater exposure to social evaluation anxieties, but inwardly – as the literature on narcissism suggests – probably more vulnerable, less able to take criticism, less good at personal relationships and less able to recognize our own faults.

LIBERTY, EQUALITY AND FRATERNITY

The demand for 'liberty, equality and fraternity' during the French Revolution shows just how long the issues we have been discussing here have been recognized. The slogan focused attention on the dimensions of social relations which matter most if we are to create a better society and make a difference to the real quality of our lives. 'Liberty' meant not being subservient or beholden to the feudal nobility and landed aristocracy. It was liberty from the feudal shackles of inferiority. Similarly, 'fraternity' reflects a desire for greater mutuality and reciprocity in social relations. We raise the same issues when we talk about community, social cohesion or solidarity. Their importance to human wellbeing is demonstrated repeatedly in research which shows how beneficial friendship and involvement in community life is to health. 'Equality' comes into the picture as a precondition for getting the other two right. Not only do large inequalities produce all the problems associated with social differences and the divisive class prejudices which go with them, but, as later chapters show, it also weakens community life, reduces trust, and increases violence.

PART TWO

The Costs of Inequality

4

Community life and
social relations

Among the new objects that attracted my attention during
my stay in the United States, none struck me with greater
force than the equality of conditions. I easily perceived the
enormous influence that this primary fact exercises on the
workings of the society.

Alexis de Tocqueville, *Democracy in America*

In August 2005 Hurricane Katrina hit the Gulf Coast of the southern
United States, devastating cities in Mississippi and Louisiana, overwhelming flood protection systems, and leaving 80 per cent of the
city of New Orleans under water. A mandatory evacuation order
was issued for the city the day before the storm hit, but by that
time most public transport had shut down and fuel and rental cars
were unavailable. The city government set up 'refuges of last resort'
for people who couldn't get out of New Orleans, including the
Superdome, a vast sports arena, which ended up sheltering around
26,000 people, despite sections of its roof being ripped off by the
storm. At least 1,836 people were killed by the hurricane, and
another 700 people were missing and unaccounted for.

What captured the attention of the world's media in the aftermath
of the storm as much as the physical devastation – the flattened
houses, flooded streets, collapsed highways and battered oil rigs –
was what seemed like the complete breakdown of civilization in
the city. There were numerous arrests and shoot-outs throughout
the week following the hurricane. Television news screens showed
desperate residents begging for help, for baby food, for medicine,

and then switched to images of troops, cruising the flooded streets in boats – not evacuating people, not bringing them supplies, but, fully armed with automatic weapons, looking for looters.

This response to the chaos in New Orleans led to widespread criticism and condemnation within the US. Many alleged that the lack of trust between law enforcement and military forces on the one hand and the mostly poor, black citizens of New Orleans on the other, reflected deeper issues of race and class. During a widely televised benefit concert for victims of the hurricane, musician Kanye West, burst out: 'I hate the way they portray us in the media. You see a white family, it says, "They're looking for food." You see a black family, it says, "They're looting."' As troops were mobilized to go into the city, Louisiana Governor Kathleen Blanco said: 'They have M16s and are locked and loaded. These troops know how to shoot and kill and I expect they will.'

The lack of trust on display during the rescue efforts in New Orleans was also roundly condemned internationally. Countries around the world offered aid and assistance, while their news coverage was filled with criticism. We can contrast the way in which troops in New Orleans seemed to be used primarily to control the population, with the rapid deployment of unarmed soldiers in rescue and relief missions in China after the devastating earthquake of 2008, a response widely applauded by the international community.

THE EQUALITY OF CONDITIONS

A very different vision of America is offered by one of its earliest observers. Alexis de Tocqueville travelled throughout the United States in 1831.[23] He met presidents and ex-presidents, mayors, senators and judges, as well as ordinary citizens, and everywhere he went he was impressed by the 'equality of conditions' (p. 11), 'the blending of social ranks and the abolition of privileges' – the way that society was 'one single mass' (p. 725) (at least for whites). He wrote that 'Americans of all ages, conditions, and all dispositions constantly unite together' (p. 596), that 'strangers readily congregate in the same places and find neither danger nor advantage in telling each other freely what they think', their manner being 'natural, open and unreserved' (p. 656). And de Tocqueville points out the ways in which Americans support one another in times of trouble:

Should some unforeseen accident occur on the public highway, people run from all sides to help the victim; should some family fall foul of an unexpected disaster, a thousand strangers willingly open their purses ... (p. 661)

De Tocqueville believed that the equality of conditions he observed had helped to develop and maintain trust among Americans.

WHAT'S TRUST GOT TO DO WITH IT?

But does inequality corrode trust and divide people – government from citizens, rich from poor, minority from majority? This chapter shows that the quality of social relations deteriorates in less equal societies.

Inequality, not surprisingly, is a powerful social divider, perhaps because we all tend to use differences in living standards as markers of status differences. We tend to choose our friends from among our near equals and have little to do with those much richer or much poorer. And when we have less to do with other kinds of people, it's harder for us to trust them. Our position in the social hierarchy affects who we see as part of the in-group and who as out-group – us and them – so affecting our ability to identify with and empathize with other people. Later in the book, we'll show that inequality not only has an impact on how much we look down on others because they have less than we do, but also affects other kinds of discrimination, such as racism and sexism, with attitudes sometimes justified by statements like 'they just don't live like us'.

De Tocqueville understood this point. A lifelong opponent of slavery, he wrote about the exclusion of both African-Americans and Native Americans from the liberty and equality enjoyed by other Americans.[23] Slavery, he thought, could only be maintained because African-Americans were viewed as 'other', so much so that 'the

European is to other races what man himself is to the animals' (p. 371). Empathy is only felt for those we view as equals, 'the same feeling for one another does not exist between the different classes' (p. 650). Prejudice, thought de Tocqueville, was 'an imaginary inequality' which followed the 'real inequality produced by wealth and the law' (p. 400).

Early socialists and others believed that material inequality was an obstacle to a wider human harmony, to a universal human brotherhood, sisterhood or comradeship. The data we present in this chapter suggest that this intuition was sound: inequality is divisive, and even small differences seem to make an important difference.

INCOME INEQUALITY AND TRUST

Figures 4.1 and 4.2 show that levels of trust between members of the public are lower in countries and states where income differences

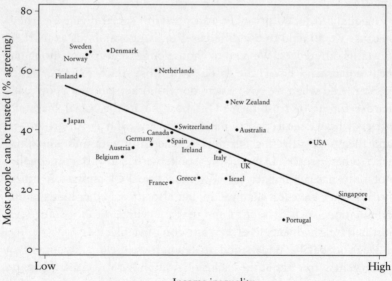

Figure 4.1 *The percentage of people agreeing that 'most people can be trusted' is higher in more equal countries.*

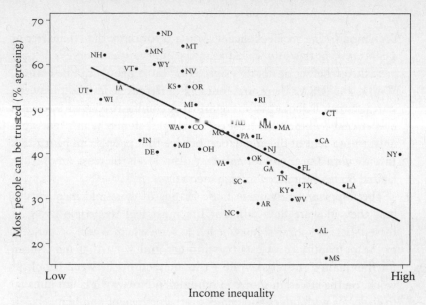

Figure 4.2 *In more equal states more people agree that 'most people can be trusted'. (Data available for only forty-one US states.)*

are larger. These relationships are strong enough that we can be confident that they are not due to chance. The international data on trust in Figure 4.1 come from the European and World Values Survey, a study designed to allow international comparisons of values and norms. In each country, random samples of the population were asked whether or not they agreed with the statement: 'Most people can be trusted.' The differences between countries are large. People trust each other most in the Scandinavian countries and the Netherlands; Sweden has the highest levels of trust, with 66 per cent of people feeling that they can trust others. The lowest level of trust is seen in Portugal, where only 10 per cent of the population believe that others can be trusted. So just within these rich, market democracies, there are more than sixfold differences in levels of trust, and, as the graph shows, high levels of trust are linked to low levels of inequality.

The data on trust within the USA, shown in Figure 4.2, are taken from the federal government's *General Social Survey*, which has been monitoring social change in America for more than a quarter of a century.[24] In this survey, just as in the international surveys, people are asked whether or not they agree that most people can be trusted. Within the USA, there are fourfold differences in trust between states. North Dakota has a level of trust similar to that of Sweden – 67 per cent feel they can trust other people – whereas in Mississippi only 17 per cent of the population believe that people can be trusted. Just as with the international data, low levels of trust among the United States are related to high inequality.

The important message in these graphs of trust and inequality is that they indicate how different life must feel to people living in these different societies. Imagine living somewhere where 90 per cent of the population mistrusts one another and what that must mean for the quality of everyday life – the interactions between people at work, on the street, in shops, in schools. In Norway it is not unusual to see cafés with tables and chairs on the pavement and blankets left out for people to use if they feel chilly while having a coffee. Nobody worries about customers or passers-by stealing the blankets. Many people feel nostalgic for time past, when they could leave their doors unlocked, and trusted that a lost wallet would be handed in. Of all large US cities, New Orleans is one of the most unequal. This was the background to the tensions and mistrust in the scenes of chaos after Hurricane Katrina that we described above.

CHICKEN OR EGG?

In the USA, trust has fallen from a high of 60 per cent in 1960, to a low of less than 40 per cent by 2004.[24] But does inequality create low levels of trust, or does mistrust create inequality? Which comes first? Political scientist Robert Putnam of Harvard University, in his book *Bowling Alone*, shows how inequality is related to 'social capital', by which he means the sum total of people's involvement in community life.[25] He says:

Community and equality are mutually reinforcing . . . Social capital and economic equality moved in tandem through most of the twentieth century. In terms of the distribution of wealth and income, America in the 1950s and 1960s was more egalitarian than it had been in more than a century ... those same decades were also the high point of social connectedness and civic engagement. Record highs in equality and social capital coincided ... Conversely, the last third of the twentieth century was a time of growing inequality *and* eroding social capital ... The timing of the two trends is striking: Sometime around 1965–70 America reversed course and started becoming both less just economically and less well connected socially and politically. (p. 359)

In another article, Putnam says:

the causal arrows are likely to run in both directions, with citizens in high social capital states likely to do more to reduce inequalities, and inequalities themselves likely to be socially divisive.[26]

Taking a more definite stance in his book, *The Moral Foundations of Trust,* Eric Uslaner, a political scientist at the University of Maryland, believes that it is inequality that affects trust, not the other way round.[27] If we live in societies with more social capital, then we know more people as friends and neighbours and that might increase our trust of people we know, people we feel are like us. But Uslaner points out that the kind of trust that is being measured in surveys such as the European and World Values Survey is trust of strangers, of people we don't know, people who are often not like us. Using a wealth of data from different sources, he shows that people who trust others are optimists, with a strong sense of control over their lives. The kind of parenting that people receive also affects their trust of other people.

In a study with his colleague Bo Rothstein, Uslaner shows, using a statistical test for causality, that inequality affects trust, but that there is 'no direct effect of trust on inequality; rather, the causal direction starts with inequality'.[28, p. 45] Uslaner says that 'trust cannot thrive in an unequal world' and that income inequality is the 'prime mover' of trust, with a stronger impact on trust than rates of unemployment, inflation or economic growth.[27] It is not average levels of economic wellbeing that create trust, but economic equality. Uslaner's graph showing that trust has declined in the USA during a

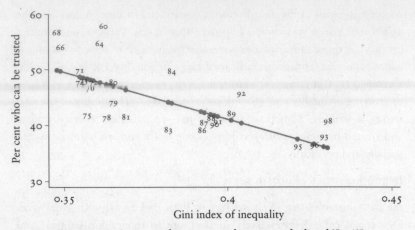

Figure 4.3 *As inequality increased, so trust declined.*[27, p. 187]

period in which inequality rapidly increased, is shown in Figure 4.3. The numbers on the graph show for each year (1960–98) the relation between the level of trust and inequality in that year.

Changes in inequality and trust go together over the years. With greater inequality, people are less caring of one another, there is less mutuality in relationships, people have to fend for themselves and get what they can – so, inevitably, there is less trust. Mistrust and inequality reinforce each other. As de Tocqueville pointed out, we are less likely to empathize with those not seen as equals; material differences serve to divide us socially.

TRUST MATTERS

Both Putnam and Uslaner make the point that trust leads to co-operation. Uslaner shows that, in the USA, people who trust others are more likely to donate time and money to helping other people. 'Trusters' also tend to believe in a common culture, that America is held together by shared values, that everybody should be treated with respect and tolerance. They are also supportive of the legal order.

Trust affects the wellbeing of individuals, as well as the wellbeing of civic society. High levels of trust mean that people feel secure, they have less to worry about, they see others as co-operative rather than competitive. A number of convincing studies in the USA have linked trust to health – people with high levels of trust live longer.[29] In fact, people who trust others benefit from living in communities with generally high levels of trust, whereas people who are less trusting of others fare worse in such neighbourhoods.[30]

Trust, or lack of it, meant the difference between life and death for some people caught up in the chaotic aftermath of Hurricane Katrina. Trust was also crucial for survival in the Chicago heatwave of 1995. Sociologist Eric Klinenberg, in his book about the heat-wave,[31] showed how poor African-Americans, living in areas with low levels of trust and high levels of crime, were too frightened to open their windows or doors, or leave their homes to go to local cooling centres established by the city authorities. Neighbours didn't check on neighbours, and hundreds of elderly and vulnerable people died. In equally poor Hispanic neighbourhoods, characterized by high levels of trust and active community life, the risk of death was much lower.

RAIDERS AND MAVERICKS

Perhaps another marker of corroded social relations and lack of trust among people was the rapid rise in the popularity of the Sport Utility Vehicle (SUV) through the 1980s and 1990s. These vehicles are known in the UK by the derogatory term 'Chelsea tractors' – Chelsea being a rich area of London, the name draws attention to the silliness of driving rugged off-road vehicles in busy urban areas. But the vehicles themselves have names that evoke images of hunters and outdoorsmen – Outlander, Pathfinder, Cherokee, Wrangler, etc. Others evoke an even tougher image, of soldiers and warriors, with names like Trooper, Defender, Shogun, Raider and Commander. These are vehicles for the 'urban jungle', not the real thing.

Not only did the popularity of SUVs suggest a preoccupation with looking tough, it also reflected growing mistrust, and the need to feel safe from others. Josh Lauer, in his paper, 'Driven to extremes',

asked why military ruggedness became prized above speed or sleek-
ness, and what the rise of the SUV said about American society.[32]
He concluded that the trend reflected American attitudes towards
crime and violence, an admiration for rugged individualism and the
importance of shutting oneself off from contact with others mis
trust. These are not large vehicles born from a co-operative public-
spiritedness and a desire to give lifts to hitch-hikers – hitch-hiking
started to decline just as inequality started to rise in the 1970s. As
one anthropologist has observed, people attempt to shield themselves from the threats of a harsh and untrusting society 'by riding in
SUVs, which look armoured, and by trying to appear as intimidat-
ing as possible to potential attackers'.[33] Pollster Michael Adams,
writing about the contrasting values of the USA and Canada,
pointed out that minivans outsell SUVs in Canada by two to one –
the ratio is reversed in America (and Canada is of course more equal
than America).[34] Accompanying the rise in SUVs were other signs of
Americans' increasing uneasiness and fear of one another: growing
numbers of gated communities,[35] and increasing sales of home security systems.[32] In more recent years, due to the steeply rising cost of
filling their fuel tanks, sales of SUVs have declined, but people still
want that rugged image – sales of smaller, tough-looking 'cross-over'
vehicles continue to rise.

WOMEN'S STATUS

In several respects, more unequal societies seem more masculine, at
least in terms of the stereotypes. When we put this to the test, we
found that just as levels of trust and social relations are affected by
inequality, so too is the status of women.

In the USA, the Institute for Women's Policy Research produces
measures of the status of women. Using these measures, researchers
at Harvard University showed that women's status was linked to
state-level income inequality.[36] Three of the measures are: women's
political participation, women's employment and earnings, and
women's social and economic autonomy. When we combine these
measures for each US state and relate them to state levels of income

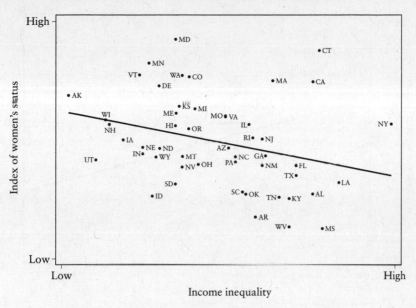

Figure 4.4 *Women's status and inequality in US states.*

inequality, we also find that women's status is significantly worse in more unequal states, although this is not a particularly strong relationship (Figure 4.4). The fairly wide scatter of points around the line on the graph shows that factors besides inequality affect women's status. Nevertheless, there is a tendency that cannot be put down to chance, for fewer women to vote or hold political office, for women to earn less, and fewer women to complete college degrees in more unequal states.

Internationally we find the same thing, and we show this relationship in Figure 4.5. Combining measures of the percentage of women in the legislature, the male–female income gap, and the percentage of women completing higher education to make an index of women's status, we find that more equal countries do significantly better.

Japan is conspicuous among the most equal countries in that women's status is lower than we would expect given its level of inequality; Italy also has worse women's status than expected, and Sweden does better. As with the scattering of points on the American graph above, this shows that other factors are also influencing

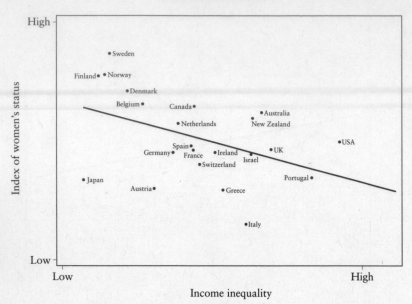

Figure 4.5 *Women's status and inequality in rich countries.*

women's status. In both Japan and Italy women have traditionally had lower status than men, whereas Sweden has a long tradition of women's rights and empowerment. But again, the link between income inequality and women's status cannot be explained by chance alone, and there is a tendency for women's status to be better in more equal countries.

Epidemiologists have found that in US states where women's status is higher, both men and women have lower death rates,[36] and women's status seems to matter for all women, whether rich or poor.[37]

TRUST BEYOND BORDERS

Not surprisingly, just as individuals who trust other people are more likely to give to charity, more equal countries are also more generous to poorer countries. The United Nations' target for spending on foreign development aid is 0.7 per cent of Gross National Income.

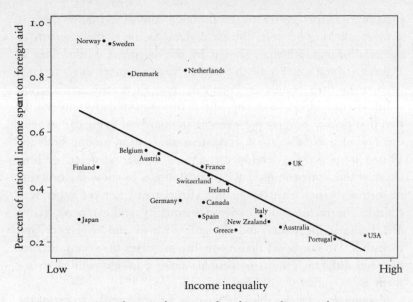

Figure 4.6 *Spending on foreign aid and inequality in rich countries.*

Only Norway, Sweden, Denmark and the Netherlands meet that target – indeed, they are generous beyond what the United Nations expects – and, as we show in Figure 4.6 using data from the OECD,[38] more unequal countries spend significantly lower percentages of their income on foreign aid. Japan and the UK might be seen as outliers on this graph. Perhaps Japan's lower than expected spending on aid reflects its withdrawal from the international stage following the Second World War, and the UK's higher than expected spending reflects historical, colonial ties to many developing countries.

WHAT WE HAVE LEARNED

In this chapter, we have shown that levels of social trust are connected to income inequality, but of course showing a correlation is not the same thing as showing causality.

There are several reasons why we believe that equality is the precondition for greater trust (although almost certainly there is a feedback loop between the two). One factor is the strength of the relationship, which is shown by the steepness of the lines in Figures 4.1 and 4.2. People in Sweden are much more likely to trust each other than people in Portugal. Any alternative explanation would need to be just as strong, and in our own statistical models we find that neither poverty nor average standards of living can explain our findings. We also see a consistent association among both the United States and the developed countries. Earlier we described how Uslaner and Rothstein used a statistical model to show the ordering of inequality and trust: inequality affects trust, not the other way round. The relationships between inequality and women's status and between inequality and foreign aid also add coherence and plausibility to our belief that inequality increases the social distance between different groups of people, making us less willing to see them as 'us' rather than 'them'.

In summary, we can think of trust as an important marker of the ways in which greater material equality can help to create a cohesive, co-operative community, to the benefit of all.

5

Mental health and drug use

It is no measure of health to be well adjusted to a profoundly sick society.   Krishnamurti

MENTAL ILLNESS IN THE UK AND USA

Children's mental health now makes the front pages of newspapers, Britain's *Daily Mail* for example, under banner headlines such as 'THE DISTURBED GENERATION'. A million British children – one in ten between the ages of 5 and 16 – are estimated to be mentally ill.[39] It has been suggested that in any secondary school with 1,000 students, 50 will be severely depressed, 100 will be distressed, 10–20 will be suffering from obsessive-compulsive disorder and between 5–10 girls will have an eating disorder.[40] This is backed up by a 2008 report from the Good Childhood Inquiry, an independent inquiry commissioned by the Children's Society.[41] After surveying thousands of children, they report that increasing numbers of children have mental health problems, over a quarter regularly feeling depressed, mostly as a result of family breakdown and peer pressure.

In the USA, 6 per cent of children have been diagnosed with Attention Deficit Hyperactivity Disorder, a behavioural syndrome characterized by serious distractibility, impulsivity and restlessness.[42] In a national survey, almost 10 per cent of children aged 3–17 had moderate or severe difficulties in 'the areas of emotions, concentration, behaviour, or being able to get along with other people'.[43]

And how are adults doing in these same two societies? In the UK,

"We're all on the same wavelength. Everyone's
on an anti-depressant!"

in a national survey conducted in 2000, 23 per cent of adults had either a neurotic disorder, a psychotic disorder, or were addicted to alcohol or drugs, 4 per cent of adults having more than one disorder.[44] In 2005, doctors in England alone wrote 29 million prescriptions for anti-depressant drugs, costing over £400 million to the National Health Service.[45] In the USA, one in four adults have been mentally ill in the past year and almost a quarter of these episodes were severe; over their lifetime more than half will suffer from a mental illness.[46] In 2003, the USA spent $100 billion on mental health treatments.[47]

MENTAL WELLBEING

Before we turn to comparisons of mental illness in other societies, it's worth asking – what is a healthy mind?

MIND, the National Association for Mental Health in the UK, publishes a pamphlet called 'How to Improve Your Mental Well-being'. It begins with the premise that:

Good mental health isn't something you have, but something you do. To be mentally healthy you must value and accept yourself.[48]

It concludes that people who are mentally well are able to look after themselves, see themselves as valuable people and judge themselves by reasonable, rather than unrealistic, standards. People who don't value themselves become frightened of rejection; they keep others at a distance, and get trapped in a vicious circle of loneliness.

It is also important to note that although people with mental illness sometimes have changes in the levels of certain chemicals in their brains, nobody has shown that these are *causes* of depression, rather than *changes* caused by depression. Similarly, although genetic vulnerability may underlie some mental illness, this can't by itself explain the huge rises in illness in recent decades – our genes can't change that fast.

APPLES AND ORANGES?

Can we really compare levels of mental illness in different countries? Don't different cultures have different labels for mental disorders, and different standards of normality, or tolerance of differences? Aren't people in different societies more or less reluctant to admit to emotional problems, or drug use, or any stigmatized condition?

Not surprisingly, it hasn't always been easy to get comparable measures of how many people are suffering from mental illness in different countries. But this began to get easier in the 1980s, when researchers developed diagnostic interviews – sets of questions that could be asked by non-psychiatrists and non-psychologists, allowing researchers to measure on a large scale the numbers of people meeting diagnostic criteria for different mental illnessess.

In 1998, the World Health Organization set up the World Mental Health Survey Consortium in an attempt to estimate the numbers of people with mental illness in different countries, the severity of their illness and patterns of treatment. Although their methods don't entirely overcome worries about cultural differences in interpreting and responding to such questions, at least the same questions are being asked, in the same way, in different places. Among our set of rich developed countries, WHO surveys have been completed in nine: Belgium, France, Germany, Italy, Japan, Netherlands, New Zealand, Spain and the USA.[49-50] Although not strictly comparable, very similar national surveys give estimates of the proportion of the adult population with mental illness in another three countries – Australia,[51] Canada[52] and the UK.[44]

INCOME INEQUALITY AND
MENTAL ILLNESS

In Figure 5.1 we use these surveys to show the association in rich countries between income inequality and the proportion of adults who had been mentally ill in the twelve months prior to being interviewed. This is a strong relationship: a much higher percentage of

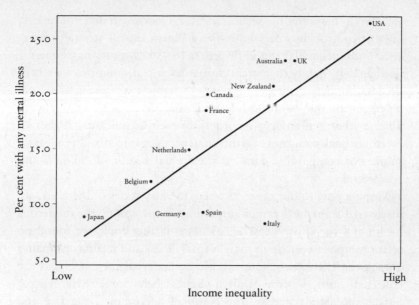

Figure 5.1 *More people suffer from mental illnesses in more unequal countries.*

the population suffer from mental illness in more unequal countries. Such a close relationship cannot be due to chance, indeed the countries line up almost perfectly, with only Italy standing out as having lower levels of mental illness than we might expect, based on its level of income inequality.

Just as we saw with levels of trust in the previous chapter, there are big differences in the proportion of people with mental illness (from 8 per cent to 26 per cent) between countries. In Germany, Italy, Japan and Spain, fewer than 1 in 10 people had been mentally ill within the previous year; in Australia, Canada, New Zealand and the UK the numbers are more than 1 in 5 people; and in the USA, as we described above, more than 1 in 4. Overall, it looks as if differences in inequality tally with more than threefold differences in the percentage of people with mental illness in different countries.

For our nine countries with data from the WHO surveys, we can also look at sub-types of mental illness, specifically anxiety disorders, mood disorders, impulse-control disorders and addictions, as well as a measure of severe mental illness. Anxiety disorders, impulse-control disorders and severe illness are all strongly correlated with inequality; mood disorders less so. We saw in Chapter 3 how anxiety has been increasing in developed countries in recent decades. Anxiety disorders represent the largest sub-group of mental illness in all our countries. Indeed, the percentage of all mental illnesses that are anxiety disorders is itself significantly higher in more unequal countries. Unfortunately, there are no international sources of comparable data on the mental health of children and adolescents.

Turning now to our other test-bed, the fifty states of the USA, we discovered something rather surprising. Alone among the numerous health and social problems we examine in this book, we found no relationship between adult male mental illness and income inequality among the US states. State-specific estimates of mental illness are collected both by the United States Behavioral Risk Factor Surveillance Study and by the National Survey on Drug Use and Health, but the lack of a relationship between income inequality and mental illness among men was consistent in both sources.

However, income inequality *is* associated with mental illness in adult women. It is not a particularly strong relationship, but too strong to be dismissed as chance. There is also a similar relationship with the mental health of children. The National Survey of Children's Health provides estimates of the percentage of children in each state with 'moderate or severe difficulties in the area of emotions, concentration, behavior, or getting along with others'.[43] Although, as for adult women, the relationship with state inequality is not particularly strong, children's mental health *is* significantly correlated with state levels of income inequality.

There are several plausible explanations for the lack of an association between the available measures of adult mental health among men and inequality. In general, problems related to inequality have steep social gradients (becoming more common lower down the social ladder).[8] Some indicators suggest that mental health in the USA does not show a consistent social gradient. Whether the explanation for this lies in methods of data collection, gender differences in reporting mental illness, the apparent resilience of ethnic minority

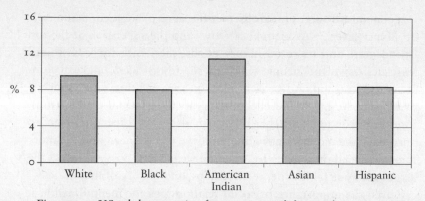

Figure 5.2 *US adults reporting frequent mental distress, 1993–2001.*[53]

populations to mental illness (see Figure 5.2), or a delay in being able to observe the effects of growing inequality, it is important to remember that, from an international perspective, levels of mental illness in the USA as a whole are exactly what we would expect, given its high overall level of inequality.

CLINGING TO THE LADDER

So why do more people tend to have mental health problems in more unequal places? Psychologist and journalist Oliver James uses an analogy with infectious disease to explain the link. The 'affluenza' virus, according to James, is a 'set of values which increase our vulnerability to emotional distress', which he believes is more common in affluent societies.[54] It entails placing a high value on acquiring money and possessions, looking good in the eyes of others and wanting to be famous. These kinds of values place us at greater risk of depression, anxiety, substance abuse and personality disorder, and are closely related to those we discussed in Chapter 3. In another recent book on the same subject, philosopher Alain de Botton describes 'status anxiety' as 'a worry so pernicious as to be capable of ruining extended stretches of our lives'. When we fail to maintain our position in the social hierarchy we are 'condemned to consider the successful with bitterness and ourselves with shame'.[55]

Economist Robert Frank observes the same phenomenon and calls it 'luxury fever'.[56] As inequality grows and the super-rich at the top spend more and more on luxury goods, the desire for such things cascades down the income scale and the rest of us struggle to compete and keep up. Advertisers play on this, making us dissatisfied with what we have, and encouraging invidious social comparisons. Another economist, Richard Layard, describes our 'addiction to income' – the more we have, the more we feel we need and the more time we spend on striving for material wealth and possessions, at the expense of our family life, relationships, and quality of life.[3]

Given the importance of social relationships for mental health, it is not surprising that societies with low levels of trust and weaker community life are also those with worse mental health.

INEQUALITY AND ILLEGAL DRUGS

Low position in the social status hierarchy is painful to most people, so it comes as no surprise to find out that the use of illegal drugs, such as cocaine, marijuana and heroin, is more common in more unequal societies.

Internationally, the United Nations Office on Drugs and Crime publishes a *World Drug Report*,[57] which contains separate data on the use of opiates (such as heroin), cocaine, cannabis, ecstasy and amphetamines. We combined these data to form a single index, giving each drug category the same weight so that the figures were not dominated by the use of any one drug. We use this index in Figure 5.3, which shows a strong tendency for drug use to be more common in more unequal countries.

Within the United States, there is also a tendency for addiction to illegal drugs and deaths from drug overdose to be higher in more unequal states.[58]

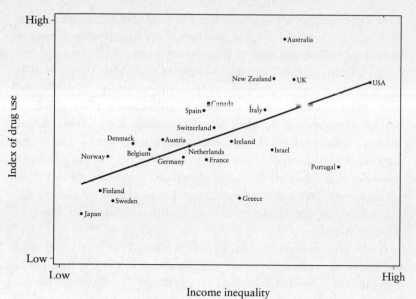

Figure 5.3 *The use of illegal drugs is more common in more unequal countries.*

MONKEY BUSINESS

The importance of social status to our mental wellbeing is reflected in the chemical behaviour of our brains. Serotonin and dopamine are among the chemicals that play important roles in the regulation of mood: in humans, low levels of dopamine and serotonin have been linked to depression and other mental disorders. Although we must be cautious in extrapolating to humans, studies in animals show that low social status affects levels of, and responses to, different chemicals in the brain.

In a clever experiment, researchers at Wake Forest School of Medicine in North Carolina took twenty macaque monkeys and housed them for a while in individual cages.[59] They next housed the animals in groups of four and observed the social hierarchies which developed in each group, noting which animals were dominant and which subordinate. They scanned the monkey's brains before and

71

after they were put into groups. Next, they taught the monkeys that they could administer cocaine to themselves by pressing a lever – they could take as much or as little as they liked.

The results of this experiment were remarkable. Monkeys that had become dominant had more dopamine activity in their brains than they had exhibited before becoming dominant, while monkeys that became subordinate when housed in groups showed no changes in their brain chemistry. The dominant monkeys took much less cocaine than the subordinate monkeys. In effect, the subordinate monkeys were medicating themselves against the impact of their low social status. This kind of experimental evidence in monkeys adds plausibility to our inference that inequality is causally related to mental illness.

At the beginning of this chapter we mentioned the huge number of prescriptions written for mood-altering drugs in the UK and USA; add these to the self-medicating users of illegal drugs and we see the pain wrought by inequality on a very large scale.

6

Physical health and life expectancy

A sad soul can kill you quicker than a germ.

John Steinbeck, *Travels with Charley*

MATERIAL AND PSYCHOSOCIAL DETERMINANTS OF HEALTH

As societies have become richer and our circumstances have changed, so the diseases we suffer from and the most important causes of health and illness have changed.

The history of public health is one of shifting ideas about the causes of disease.[60-61] In the nineteenth century, reformers began to collect statistics which showed the burden of ill-health and premature death suffered by the poor living in city slums. This led to the great reforms of the Sanitary Movement. Drainage and sewage systems, rubbish collection, public baths and decent housing, safer working conditions and improvements in food hygiene – all brought major improvements in population health, and life expectancy lengthened as people's material standards of living advanced.

As we described in Chapter 1, when infectious diseases lost their hold as the major causes of death, the industrialized world underwent a shift, known as the 'epidemiological transition', and chronic diseases, such as heart disease and cancer, replaced infections as the major causes of death and poor health. During the greater part of the twentieth century, the predominant approach to improving the health of populations was through 'lifestyle choices' and 'risk

73

"What do you mean, I have an ulcer?
I give ulcers, I don't get them!"

factors' to prevent these chronic conditions. Smoking, high-fat diets, exercise and alcohol were the focus of attention.

But in the latter part of the twentieth century, researchers began to make some surprising discoveries about the determinants of health. They had started to believe that stress was a cause of chronic disease, particularly heart disease. Heart disease was then thought of as the executive's disease, caused by the excess stress experienced by businessmen in responsible positions. The Whitehall I Study, a long-term follow-up study of male civil servants, was set up in 1967 to investigate the causes of heart disease and other chronic illnesses. Researchers expected to find the highest risk of heart disease among men in the highest status jobs; instead, they found a strong inverse association between position in the civil service hierarchy and death rates. Men in the lowest grade (messengers, doorkeepers, etc.) had a death rate three times higher than that of men in the highest grade (administrators).[62-3]

Further studies in Whitehall I, and a later study of civil servants, Whitehall II, which included women, have shown that low job status is not only related to a higher risk of heart disease: it is also related to some cancers, chronic lung disease, gastrointestinal disease, depression, suicide, sickness absence from work, back pain and self-reported health.[64-6] So was it low status itself that was causing worse health, or could these relationships be explained by differences in lifestyle between civil servants in different grades?

Those in lower grades were indeed more likely to be obese, to smoke, to have higher blood pressure and to be less physically active, but these risk factors explained only one-third of their increased risk of deaths from heart disease.[67] And of course factors such as absolute poverty and unemployment cannot explain the findings, because everybody in these studies was in paid employment. Of all the factors that the Whitehall researchers have studied over the years, job stress and people's sense of control over their work seem to make the most difference. There are now numerous studies that show the same thing, in different societies and for most kinds of ill-health – low social status has a clear impact on physical health, and not just for people at the very bottom of the social hierarchy. As well as highlighting the importance of social status, this is the other important message from the Whitehall studies. There is a social gradient in health running right across society, and where we are placed in relation to other people matters; those above us have better health, those below us have worse health, from the very bottom to the very top.[68] Understanding these health gradients means understanding why senior administrators live longer than those in professional and executive grades, as well as understanding the worse health profiles of the poor.

Besides our sense of control over our lives, other factors which make a difference to our physical health include our happiness, whether we're optimistic or pessimistic, and whether we feel hostile or aggressive towards other people. Our psychological wellbeing has a direct impact on our health, and we're less likely to feel in control, happy, optimistic, etc. if our social status is low.

It's not just our social status and psychological wellbeing that affects our health. The relationships we have with other people matter too. This idea goes back as far as the work on suicide by Émile Durkheim, one of the founding fathers of sociology, in the late nineteenth century.[69] Durkheim showed that the suicide rates of different countries and populations were related to how well people were integrated into society and whether or not societies were undergoing rapid change and turmoil. But it wasn't until the 1970s that epidemiologists began to investigate systematically how people's social networks relate to health, showing that people with fewer friends were at higher risk of death. Having friends, being married, belonging to a religious group or other association and having people who will provide support, are all protective of health.[70-71]

Social support and social networks have also been linked both to the incidence of cardiovascular disease and to recovery from heart attacks. In a striking experiment, researchers have also shown that people with friends are less likely to catch a cold when given the same measured exposure to the cold virus – in fact the more friends they had, the more resistant they were.[72] Experiments have also shown that physical wounds heal faster if people have good relationships with their intimate partners.[73]

Social status and social integration are now well established as important determinants of population health and, increasingly, researchers are also recognizing that stress in early life, in the womb as well as in infancy and early childhood, has an important influence on people's health throughout their lives.[74-5] Stress in early life affects physical growth, emotional, social and cognitive development, as well as later health and health behaviours. And the socioeconomic status of the families in which children live also determines their lifelong trajectories of health and development.[76]

Taken together, social status, social networks and stress in early childhood are what researchers label 'psychosocial factors', and these are of increasing importance in the rich, developed countries where material living standards, as we described in Chapter 1, are now high enough to have ceased to be important direct determinants of population health.

LIFE IS SHORT WHERE LIFE IS BRUTAL

Evolutionary psychologists Margo Wilson and Martin Daly were interested in whether adopting more impulsive and risky strategies was an evolved response to more stressful circumstances in which life is likely to be shorter. In more threatening circumstances, then, more reckless strategies are perhaps necessary to gain status, maximize sexual opportunities, and enjoy at least some short-term gratifications. Perhaps only in more relaxed conditions, in which a longer life is assured, can people afford to plan for a long-term future.[77] To test this hypothesis, they collected data on the murder rates for the seventy-seven community areas of Chicago, and then they collected data on death rates for those same areas, subtracting all of the deaths caused by homicide. When they put the two together, they showed a remarkably close relationship, seen in Figure 6.1 – neighbourhoods with high homicide rates were also neighbourhoods where people were dying younger from other causes as well. Something about these neighbourhoods seemed to be affecting both health and violence.

In Chapter 4 we showed how different developed countries and

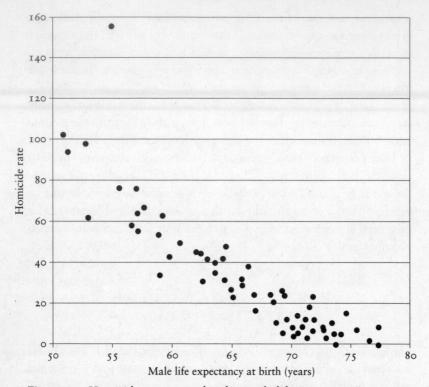

Figure 6.1 *Homicide rates are related to male life expectancy in seventy-seven neighbourhoods in Chicago. (Calculation of life expectancy included deaths from all causes* except *homicide.)*[77]

US states vary in the levels of social trust that people feel. There are sixfold differences in levels of trust between developed countries and fourfold differences among US states. We mentioned that levels of trust have been linked to population health and, in fact, research on social cohesion and social capital has mushroomed over the past ten years or so. More than forty papers on the links between health and social capital have now been published.[78]

In the United States, epidemiologist Ichiro Kawachi and his colleagues at the Harvard School of Public Health looked at death rates in thirty-nine states in which the General Social Surveys had been conducted in the late 1980s.[79] These surveys allowed them to count how many people in each state were members of voluntary organizations, such as church groups and unions. This measure of group membership turned out to be a strong predictor of deaths from all causes combined, as well as deaths from coronary heart disease, cancers, and infant deaths. The higher the group membership, the lower the death rate.

Robert Putnam looked at social capital in relation to an index of health and health care for the US states.[25] This index included information on such things as the percentage of babies born with low birthweight, the percentage of mothers receiving antenatal care, many different death rates, expenditure on health care, the number of people with AIDS and cancer, immunization rates, use of car safety belts, and numbers of hospital beds, among other factors. The health index was closely linked to social capital; states such as Minnesota and Vermont had high levels of social capital and scored high on the health index, states such as Louisiana and Nevada scored badly on both. Clearly, it's not just our individual social status that matters for health, the social connections between us matter too.

HEALTH AND WEALTH

Let's consider the health of two babies born into two different societies.

Baby A is born in one of the richest countries in the world, the USA, home to more than half of the world's billionaires. It is a country that spends somewhere between 40–50 per cent of the world's total spending on health care, although it contains less than 5 per cent of the world's population. Spending on drug treatments and high-tech scanning equipment is particularly high. Doctors in this country earn almost twice as much as doctors elsewhere and medical care is often described as the best in the world.

Baby B is born in one of the poorer of the western democracies, Greece, where average income is not much more than half that of the USA. Whereas America spends about $6,000 per person per year on health care, Greece spends less than $3,000. This is in real terms, after taking into account the different costs of medical care.

And Greece has six times fewer high-tech scanners per person than the USA.

Surely Baby B's chances of a long and healthy life are worse than Baby A's?

In fact, Baby A, born in the USA, has a life expectancy of 1.2 years less than Baby B, born in Greece. And Baby A has a 40 per cent higher risk of dying in the first year after birth than Baby B. Among developed countries, there are even bigger contrasts than the comparison we've used here: babies born in the USA are twice as likely to die in their first year than babies in Japan, and the difference in average life expectancy between the USA and Sweden is three years, between Portugal and Japan it is over five years. Some comparisons are even more shocking: in 1990, Colin McCord and Harold Freeman in the Department of Surgery at Columbia University calculated that black men in Harlem were less likely to reach the age of 65 than men in Bangladesh.[80]

Among other things, our comparison between Baby A and Baby B

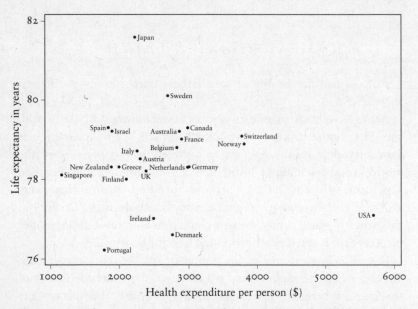

Figure 6.2 *Life expectancy is unrelated to spending on health care in rich countries (currencies converted to reflect purchasing power).*

shows that spending on health care and the availability of high-tech medical care are not related to population health. Figure 6.2 shows that, in rich countries, there is no relationship between the amount of health spending per person and life expectancy.

THE 'BIG IDEA'

If average levels of income don't matter, and spending on high-tech health care doesn't matter, what does? There are now a large number of studies of income inequality and health that compare countries, American states, or other large regions, and the majority of these studies show that more egalitarian societies tend to be healthier.[10] This vast literature was given impetus by a study by one of us, on inequality and death rates, published in the *British Medical Journal* in 1992.[81] In 1996, the editors of that journal, commenting on further studies confirming the link between income inequality and health, wrote:

The big idea is that what matters in determining mortality and health in a society is less the overall wealth of that society and more how evenly wealth is distributed. The more equally wealth is distributed the better the health of that society.[82]

Inequality is associated with lower life expectancy, higher rates of infant mortality, shorter height, poor self-reported health, low birthweight, AIDS and depression. Figures 6.3–6.6 show income inequality in relation to life expectancy for men and women, and to infant mortality – first for the rich countries, and then for the US states.

Of course, population averages hide the differences in health *within* any population, and these can be even more dramatic than the differences *between* countries. In the UK, health disparities have been a major item on the public health agenda for over twenty-five years, and the current *National Health Service Plan* states that 'No injustice is greater than the inequalities in health which scar our nation.'[83] In the late 1990s the difference in life expectancy between the lowest and highest social class groups was 7.3 years for men and

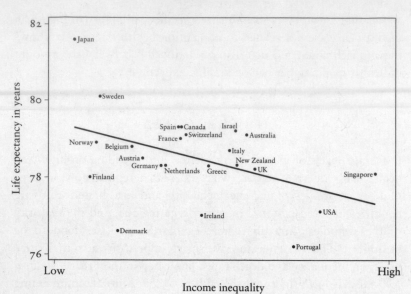

Figure 6.3 *Life expectancy is related to inequality in rich countries.*

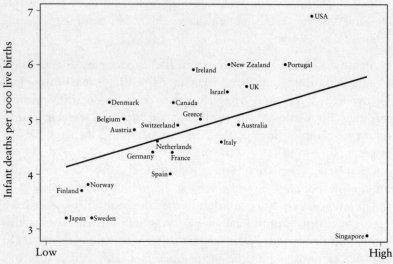

Figure 6.4 *Infant mortality is related to inequality in rich countries.*

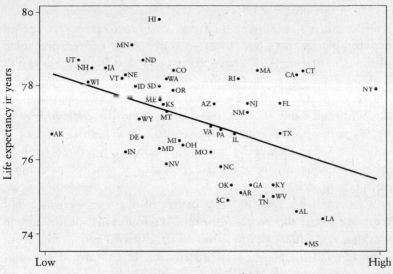

Figure 6.5 *Life expectancy is related to inequality in US states.*

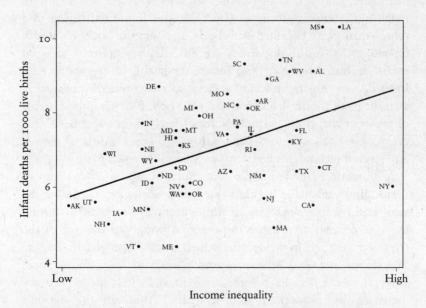

Figure 6.6 *Infant mortality is related to inequality in US states.*

7 years for women.[84] Studies in the USA often report even larger differences, such as a 28-year difference in life expectancy at age 16 between blacks and whites living in some of the poorest and some of the richest areas.[85-7] To have many years' less life because you're working-class rather than professional – no one can argue about the serious injustice that these numbers represent. Note that, as the Whitehall study showed, these gaps cannot be explained away by worse health behaviours among those lower down the social scale.[88-90] What, then, if the cost of that injustice is a three- or four-year shortening of *average* life expectancy if we live in a more unequal society?

We examined several different causes of death to see which had the biggest class differences in health. We found that deaths among working-age adults, deaths from heart disease, and deaths from homicide had the biggest class differences. In contrast, death rates from prostate cancer had small class differences and breast cancer death rates were completely unrelated to social class. Then we looked at how those different death rates were affected by income inequality, and found that those with big class differences were much more sensitive to inequality.[8] We also found that living in a more equal place benefited everybody, not just the poor. It's worth repeating that health disparities are not simply a contrast between the ill-health of the poor and the better health of everybody else. Instead, they run right across society so that even the reasonably well-off have shorter lives than the very rich. Likewise, the benefits of greater equality spread right across society, improving health for everyone – not just those at the bottom. In other words, at almost any level of income, it's better to live in a more equal place.

A dramatic example of how reductions in inequality can lead to rapid improvements in health is the experience of Britain during the two world wars.[91] Increases in life expectancy for civilians during the war decades were twice those seen throughout the rest of the twentieth century. In the decades which contain the world wars, life expectancy increased between 6 and 7 years for men and women, whereas in the decades before, between and after, life expectancy increased by between 1 and 4 years. Although the nation's nutritional status improved with rationing in the Second World War, this was not true for the First World War, and material living standards declined during both wars. However, both wartimes were characterized by full employment and considerably narrower income differences – the result of deliberate government policies to promote co-operation with the war effort. During the Second World War, for example, working-class incomes rose by 9 per cent, while incomes of the middle class fell by 7 per cent; rates of relative poverty were halved. The resulting sense of camaraderie and social cohesion not only led to better health – crime rates also fell.

UNDER OUR SKIN

So how *do* the stresses of adverse experiences in early life, of low social status and lack of social support make us unwell?[92] The belief that the mind affects the body has been around since ancient times, and modern research has enhanced our understanding of the ways in which stress increases the risk of ill-health, and pleasure and happiness promote wellbeing. The psyche affects the neural system and in turn the immune system – when we're stressed or depressed or feeling hostile, we are far more likely to develop a host of bodily ills, including heart disease, infections and more rapid ageing.[93] Stress disrupts our body's balance, interferes with what biologists call 'homeostasis' – the state we're in when everything is running smoothly and all our physiological processes are normal.

When we experience some kind of acute stress and experience something traumatic, our bodies go into the fight-or-flight response.[93] Energy stores are released, our blood vessels constrict, clotting factors are released into the bloodstream, anticipating injury, and the heart and lungs work harder. Our senses and memory are enhanced and our immune system perks up. We are primed and ready to fight or run away from whatever has caused the stress. If the emergency is over in a few minutes, this amazing response is healthy and protective, but when we go on worrying for weeks or months and stress becomes chronic, then our bodies are in a constant state of anticipation of some challenge or threat, and all those fight-or-flight responses become damaging.

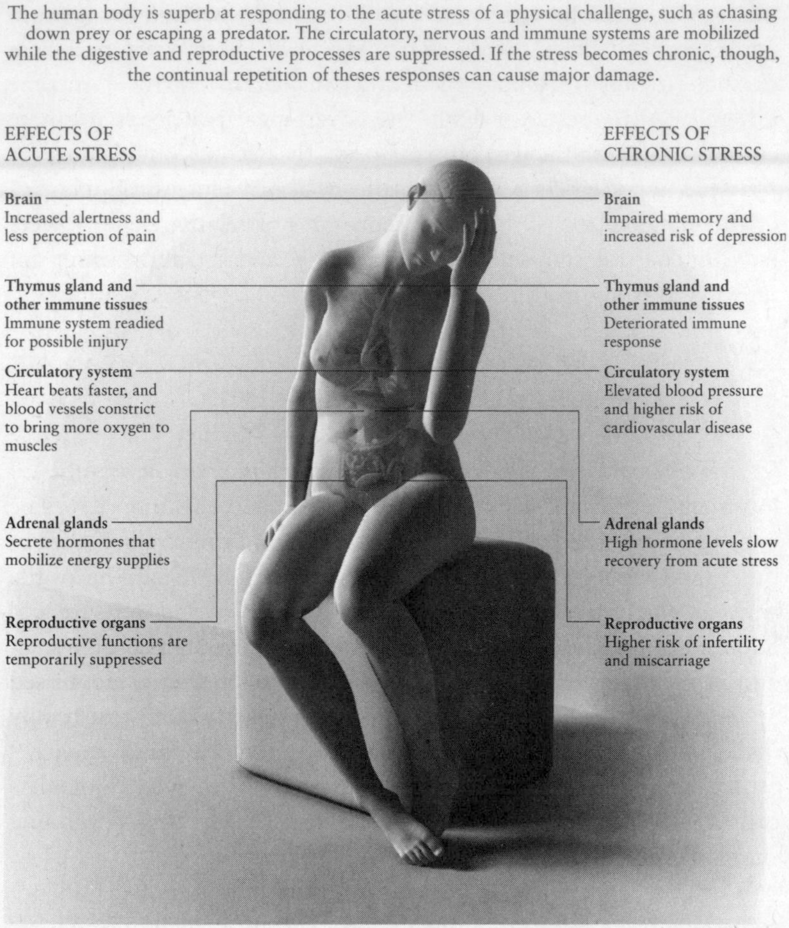

The human body is superb at responding to the acute stress of a physical challenge, such as chasing down prey or escaping a predator. The circulatory, nervous and immune systems are mobilized while the digestive and reproductive processes are suppressed. If the stress becomes chronic, though, the continual repetition of theses responses can cause major damage.

EFFECTS OF
ACUTE STRESS

EFFECTS OF
CHRONIC STRESS

Brain
Increased alertness and
less perception of pain

Brain
Impaired memory and
increased risk of depression

**Thymus gland and
other immune tissues**
Immune system readied
for possible injury

**Thymus gland and
other immune tissues**
Deteriorated immune
response

Circulatory system
Heart beats faster, and
blood vessels constrict
to bring more oxygen to
muscles

Circulatory system
Elevated blood pressure
and higher risk of
cardiovascular disease

Adrenal glands
Secrete hormones that
mobilize energy supplies

Adrenal glands
High hormone levels slow
recovery from acute stress

Reproductive organs
Reproductive functions are
temporarily suppressed

Reproductive organs
Higher risk of infertility
and miscarriage

Figure 6.7 *The biology of stress.*[92]

Chronic mobilization of energy in the form of glucose into the bloodstream can lead us to put on weight in the wrong places (central obesity) and even to diabetes; chronic constriction of blood vessels and raised levels of blood-clotting factors can lead to hypertension and heart disease. While acute momentary stress perks up our immune system, chronic continuing stress suppresses immunity and can lead to growth failure in children, ovulation failure in women, erectile dysfunction in men and digestive problems for all of us. Neurons in some areas of the brain are damaged and cognitive function declines. We have trouble sleeping. Chronic stress wears us down and wears us out.

In this chapter we've shown that there is a strong relationship between inequality and many different health outcomes, with a consistent picture in the USA and developed countries. Our belief that this is a causal relationship is enhanced by the coherent picture that emerges from research on the psychosocial determinants of health, and the social gradients in health in developed countries. Position in society matters, for health and alternative explanations, such as higher rates of smoking among the poor, don't account for these gradients. There are now a number of studies showing that income inequality affects health, even after adjusting for people's individual incomes.[94] The dramatic changes in income differences in Britain during the two world wars were followed by rapid improvements in life expectancy. Similarly, in Japan, the influence of the post-Second World War Allied occupation on demilitarization, democracy and redistribution of wealth and power led to an egalitarian economy and unrivalled improvements in population health.[95] In contrast, Russia has experienced dramatic decreases in life expectancy since the early 1990s, as it moved from a centrally planned to a market economy, accompanied by a rapid rise in income inequality.[96] The biology of chronic stress is a plausible pathway which helps us to understand why unequal societies are almost always unhealthy societies.

THE SECRET SHAME OF PARIS

PREDAWN ROUNDUP OF FAT FRENCHWOMEN

7

Obesity: wider income gaps,
wider waists

Food is the most primitive form of comfort
Sheila Graham

Obesity is increasing rapidly throughout the developed world. In some countries rates have doubled in just a few years. Obesity is measured by Body Mass Index (BMI)* to take height into account and avoid labelling people as overweight just because they are tall. The World Health Organization has set standards for using BMI to classify people as underweight (BMI < 18.5), normal weight (BMI 18.5–24.9), overweight (BMI 25–29.9) and obese (BMI > 30). In the USA, in the late 1970s, close to half the population were overweight and 15 per cent were obese; now three-quarters of the population are overweight, and close to a third are obese. In the UK in 1980, about 40 per cent of the population were overweight and less than 10 per cent were obese; now two-thirds of adults are overweight and more than a fifth are obese. [97-100] This is a major health crisis, because obesity is so bad for health – it increases the risk of hypertension, type II diabetes, cardiovascular disease, gallbladder disease and some cancers. Trends in childhood obesity are now so serious that they are widely expected to lead to shorter life expectancies for today's children. That would be the first reversal in life expectancy in many developed countries since governments started keeping track in the nineteenth century.[101]

Apart from the health consequences, obesity reduces emotional

*BMI = weight in kg/(height in m)^2

89

and social wellbeing: overweight and obese adults and children suffer terribly. A 17-year-old from Illinois, weighing 409 lb (29 stone) described her physical pain: 'my heart aches in my chest and I have arm pains and stuff and it gets scary'.[102] But just as hurtful are the memories she has of other children calling her names at school, her restricted social life and her feeling that her body is 'almost a prison to me'.

Britain's tabloid newspaper, the *Sun*, featured three obese children in the spring of 2007.[103-105] The youngest, a boy aged 8, weighed 218 lb (15.5 stone) and was being bullied at school – when he attended. His weight was so great that he often missed school due to his difficulties in walking there and back, and was exempt from wearing school uniform because none was available to fit him. His elder sister, aged 9, weighed 196 lb (14 stone) and was also being bullied and teased, by both children and adults. She said she found it 'hard to breathe sometimes', and did not like 'having to wear ugly clothes' and being unable to fit on the rides at amusement parks. Heaviest was the oldest boy who, at the age of 12, weighed 280 lbs (20 stone). He was desperately unhappy – expelled from two schools and suspended from a third, for lashing out at children who called him names.

THE 'OBESOGENIC' ENVIRONMENT

Many people believe that obesity is genetically determined, and genes do undoubtedly play a role in how susceptible different individuals are to becoming overweight. But the sudden rapid increase in obesity in many societies cannot be explained by genetic factors. The obesity epidemic is caused by changes in how we live. People often point to the changes in cost, ease of preparation and availability of energy-dense foods, to the spread of fast-food restaurants, the development of the microwave, and the decline in cooking skills. Others point to the decline in physical activity, both at work and in leisure time, increasing car use and the reduction in physical education programmes in schools. Modern life, it seems, conspires to make us fat. If there was no more to it than that, then we might expect to see more obesity among richer people, who are able to buy more food, more cars, etc., and high levels of obesity in all wealthy societies.

But this is not what happens. During the epidemiological transition, which we discussed in Chapters 1 and 6, in which chronic diseases replaced infectious diseases as the leading causes of death, obesity changed its social distribution. In the past the rich were fat and the poor were thin, but in developed countries these patterns are now reversed.[106] The World Health Organization set up a study in the 1980s to monitor trends in cardiovascular diseases, and the risk factors for these diseases, including obesity, in twenty-six countries. It found that, as rates of obesity have increased, their social gradient has steepened.[107] By the early 1990s obesity was more common among poorer women, compared to richer women, in all twenty-six countries, and among poorer men in all except five. As journalist Polly Toynbee declared in a newspaper article in 2004: 'Fat is a class issue.'[108] Pointing to the high rates of obesity in the USA and the low rates among the Scandinavian countries, which prove that we don't find high levels of obesity in all modern, rich societies, she suggested that income inequality might contribute to the obesity epidemic.

INCOME INEQUALITY AND OBESITY

Figure 7.1 shows that levels of obesity tend to be lower in countries where income differences are smaller. The data on obesity come from the International Obesity Task Force and show the proportion of the adult population, both men and women, who are obese – a Body Mass Index (BMI) of more than 30.[109]

The differences between countries are large. In the USA, just over 30 per cent of adults are obese; a level more than twelve times higher than Japan, where only 2.4 per cent of adults are obese. Because these figures are for BMI, not just weight, they're not due to differences in average height.

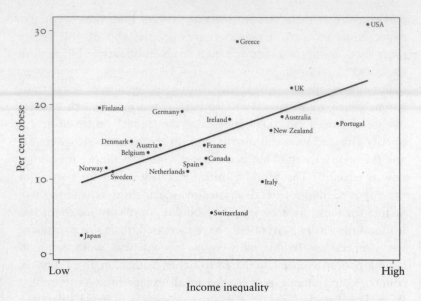

Figure 7.1 *More adults are obese in more unequal countries.*

The same pattern can be seen internationally for children (Figure 7.2). Our figures on the percentage of young people aged 13 and 15 who are overweight, reported in the 2007 UNICEF report on child wellbeing, came originally from the World Health Organization's Health Behaviour in School-age Children survey.[110] There are no data for Australia, New Zealand or Japan from this survey, but the relationship with inequality is still strong enough to be sure it is not due to chance. The differences between countries are smaller for overweight children than for adult obesity. In the country with the lowest level, the Netherlands, 7.6 per cent of children aged 13 and 15 are overweight, which is one-third the rate in the USA, where 25.1 per cent are overweight. (As these figures are based on children reporting their height and weight, rather than being measured, the true prevalence of overweight is probably higher in all countries, but that shouldn't make much difference to how they are related to inequality.)

Within the USA, there are no states with levels of adult obesity lower than 20 per cent. Colorado has the lowest obesity prevalence,

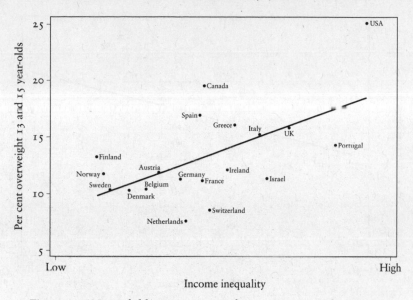

Figure 7.2 *More children are overweight in more unequal countries.*

at 21.5 per cent, compared to 34 per cent in Texas, which has the highest.* But the relationship with inequality is still strong enough for us to be confident it isn't due to chance. Other researchers have found similar relationships. One study found that higher state-level income inequality was associated with abdominal weight gain in men,[111] others have found that income inequality increases the risk of inactive lifestyles.[112] Overweight among the poor seems to be particularly strongly associated with income inequality.

For children in the USA, we obtained data from the National Survey of Children's Health (Figure 7.4). Just as for the international figures for children, these data are for overweight (rather than obese) children, aged 10–17 years. (The child's height and weight are reported by the parent, or the adult who knows the child best.) The

*The data on adult obesity within the USA were made available to us by Professor Majid Ezzati from Harvard University School of Public Health. Professor Ezzati bases his calculations of the prevalence of obesity in each state on actual measures of height and weight.

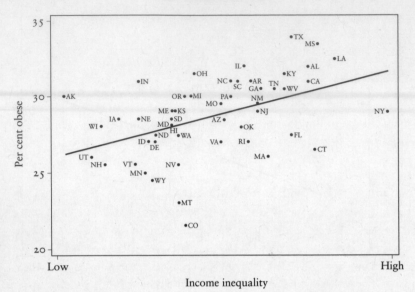

Figure 7.3 *More adults are obese in more unequal US states.*[113]

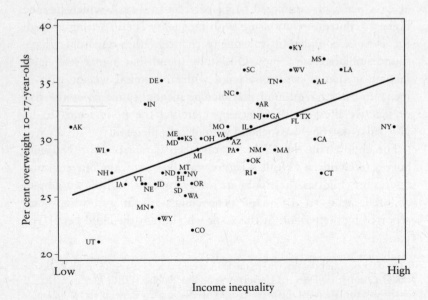

Figure 7.4 *More children are overweight in more unequal US states.*

relationship with inequality is even stronger for children than for adults.

EATING FOR COMFORT ...

The pathways linking income inequality to obesity are likely to include calorie intake and physical activity. Indeed, our own research has shown that per capita calorie intake is higher in more unequal countries. This explained part of the relationship between inequality and obesity, but less for women than for men.[114] Other researchers have shown that income inequality in US states is related to physical inactivity.[112] It seems that people in more unequal societies are eating more and exercising less. But in studies in Australia, the UK and Sweden the amount that people eat, and the amount of exercise they do, fails to fully account for social class differences in weight gain and obesity.[115-18]

Calorie intake and exercise are only part of the story. People with a long history of stress seem to respond to food in different ways from people who are not stressed. Their bodies respond by depositing fat particularly round the middle, in the abdomen, rather than lower down on hips and thighs.[119-20] As we saw in Chapter 6, chronic stress affects the action of the hormone cortisol, and researchers have found differences in cortisol and psychological vulnerability to stress tests among men and women with high levels of abdominal fat. People who accumulate fat around the middle are at particularly high risk of obesity-associated illnesses.

The body's stress reaction causes another problem. Not only does it make us put on weight in the worst places, it can also increase our food intake and change our food choices, a pattern known as stress-eating or eating for comfort. In experiments with rats, when the animals are stressed they eat more sugar and fat. People who are chronically stressed tend either to over-eat and gain weight, or under-eat and lose weight. In a study in Finland, people whose eating was driven by stress ate sausages, hamburgers, pizza and chocolate, and drank more alcohol than other people.[121] Scientists are starting to understand how comfort eating may be a way we cope with particular changes in our physiology when we are chronically stressed, changes that go with feelings of anxiety.[122]

The three obese children featured in the *Sun* newspaper, whom we described earlier, all seemed to have turned to comfort eating to deal with family break-ups. The nine-year-old girl said, 'Chocolate is the only thing I'm interested in. It's the only thing I live for . . . when I'm sad and worried I just eat.' Her older brother gained 210 pounds (15 stone) in five years, after his parents divorced.

A number of years ago, the *Wall Street Journal* ran a series, 'Deadly Diet', on the nutrition problems of America's inner cities.[123] Among the overweight people they interviewed was a 13-year-old girl living in a violent housing project (estate), who said that food and TV were a way of calming her nerves. An unemployed woman who knew that her diet and drinking were damaging her liver and arteries, still figured she 'might as well live high on the hog' while she could. A grandmother bringing up her grandchildren because of her daughter's addiction to crack cocaine, said:

Before I was so upset that my daughter was on this crack I couldn't eat. I turned to Pepsi – it was like a drug for me. I couldn't function without it. I used to wake up with a Pepsi in my hand. A three-liter bottle would just see me through the day.

Recent research suggests that food stimulates the brains of chronic over-eaters in just the same ways that drugs stimulate the brains of addicts.[124-6] Studies using brain scans have shown that obese people respond both to food and to feeling full differently from thin people.[127]

. . . EATING (OR NOT) FOR STATUS

But food choices and diets aren't just dictated by the way we feel – they're also patterned by social factors. We make food choices for complicated cultural reasons – sometimes we like foods we grew up eating, which represent home to us, sometimes we want foods that represent a lifestyle we're trying to achieve. We offer food to other people to show that we love them, or to show that we're sophisticated, or that we can afford to be generous. Food has probably always played this role; it's the necessary component of the feast, with all of its social meanings. But now, with the easy availability of cheap, energy-dense foods, whatever social benefits might come from frequent feasting, they are, so to speak, outweighed by the drawbacks.

In the *Wall Street Journal*'s 'Deadly Diet' series, a recent immigrant from Puerto Rico describes how her family used to live on an unchanging diet of rice, beans, vegetables, pork and dried fish. Since moving to Chicago, they have enjoyed fizzy drinks, pizza, hamburgers, sugared breakfast cereals, hotdogs and ice-cream. 'I can't afford to buy the children expensive shoes or dresses . . . but food is easier so I let them eat whatever they want.' Most of all, the family enjoy going to fast-food restaurants and eat out twice a month, although the children would like to go more often. 'We feel good when we go to those places . . . we feel like we're Americans, that we're here and we belong here.'

A 17-year-old in New Jersey described how being able to buy fast food proves your financial status, shows that you have money in your pocket and are not having to wait for the welfare cheque at the end of the month.

A 37-year-old man said he spent half his wages on fast food. On the day he was interviewed he had been to McDonalds three times and was planning to go to Kentucky Fried Chicken and a Chinese take-out shop before the day was out. But the fast-food restaurants had a meaning for him that went well beyond the cheap food. Despite working, he was homeless and they had become his sanctuary:

He has no home of his own and shuttles between his aunt's place in Brooklyn and a friend's apartment in a Harlem housing project [estate]. 'The atmosphere makes me feel comfortable and relaxed and you don't have to rush,' he says as he admires the hamburger restaurant's shiny floors and the picture of George Washington Carver [a famous nineteenth-century black American] on a wall. Lulled by the soft piped-in music, he nods off for a moment and then adds: 'ain't no hip-hop, ain't no profanity. The picture, the plants, the way people keep things neat here, it makes you feel like you're in civilization.'

A member of a Hispanic street gang eats all his meals at fast-food restaurants, boasting that he hasn't eaten a meal at home since he was 16:

Kids here don't want to eat their mother's food ... everyone is tired of their mother's food – rice and beans over and over. I wanted to live the life of a man. Fast food gets you status and respect.

FAT IS A FEMININE ISSUE?

Our own work, like the studies of other researchers, shows that the relation between income inequality and obesity is stronger for women than for men. In the World Health Organization's study in twenty-six countries the social gradient in obesity is seen more consistently, and tends to be steeper, for women than for men. In the 2003 Health Survey for England, the positive association between low socio-economic status and obesity is very clear for women but among men there is no association.[128]

It might be that these patterns result from obesity having a stronger negative effect on social mobility for women, than for men. Maybe obese young women suffer more discrimination in labour markets and the marriage market, than obese young men. Or maybe low social status is more of a risk factor for obesity in women than in men. Two studies within British birth 'cohorts' offer some clues. These studies are surveys of large samples of people born at the same time, and followed from birth. A study of people born in 1946 found that upwardly mobile men and women were less likely to be obese than those whose social class didn't change between childhood and adulthood.[129] In the 1970 cohort obese women, but not men, were more likely never to have had gainful employment and not to have a partner.[130]

In the USA and in Britain, female obesity in adolescence has been linked to lower earnings in adulthood.[131-2] Although not limited to women, a recent survey of more than 2,000 Human Resource professionals found that 93 per cent would favour a normal-weight job applicant over an equally qualified overweight candidate. Nearly

50 per cent of these professionals felt that overweight people were less productive; almost 33 per cent felt that obesity was a valid reason not to hire somebody; and 40 per cent felt that overweight people lacked self-discipline.[133]

Although being overweight clearly hampers social mobility, our own analysis of trends within women born in Britain in 1970 suggests that this doesn't explain the social gradient in obesity among women and, even in middle age, low social class is linked to weight gain.[117]

YOU CAN NEVER BE TOO RICH OR TOO THIN

Social class differences in the importance of body size and in the body image towards which women aspire also seem to contribute to the social gradient in obesity. In the past, women with voluptuous bodies were much admired, but in many modern, richer cultures, being thin signals high social class and attractiveness. British women in higher social classes are more likely to monitor their weight and to be dieting than women in lower social class groups, and are also more dissatisfied with their bodies.[134] Women who move down the social scale seem to place less emphasis on thinness and are more satisfied with their bodies. Changes in marital status also play a role: in a US study, women who married gained more weight than women who remained single or women who divorced or separated.[135] And not all women want to be thin – for example in inner-city African-American communities, thinness can be associated with an image of poverty, hunger and being on welfare, as well as AIDS and drug addiction. As one 19-year-old woman put it:

I've been a voluptuous female all my life. If I start losing a lot of weight, people will think I'm on drugs . . . in the ghetto, you just can't afford to look too thin.

Her words are a reminder of the ways in which social class is related to being overweight in the developing world, where only the affluent can afford to be fat. In wealthy countries, it looks as if women in higher social classes are more likely to have aspirations to thinness and be more able to achieve them.

But while women's body weight may be most affected by social factors, men are certainly not immune. A recent 12-year study of working age men in the USA found that if they became unemployed, they gained weight.[136] When their annual income dropped they gained, on average, 5.5 lbs.

THE THRIFTY PHENOTYPE

One additional idea that suggests a causal link between higher levels of income inequality in a society and higher body weights is known as the 'thrifty phenotype' hypothesis. Put simply, this theory suggests that when a pregnant woman is stressed, the development of her unborn child is modified to prepare it for life in a stressful environment. It isn't yet clear whether stress hormones themselves do the damage, or whether stressed foetuses are less well nourished, or both things happen, but these 'thrifty phenotype' babies have a lower birthweight and a lower metabolic rate. In other words, they are adapted for an environment where food is scarce – they are small and need less food. In conditions of scarcity during our evolutionary past this adaptation would have been beneficial, but in our modern world, where stress during pregnancy is unlikely to be due to food shortages and babies are born into a world of plenty, it's maladaptive. Babies with a thirfty phenotype in a world where food is plentiful are more prone to obesity, to diabetes and to cardiovascular disease. As this book shows, societies with higher levels of income inequality have higher levels of mistrust, illness, status insecurity, violence and other stressors, so the thrifty phenotype may well be contributing to the high prevalence of obesity in them.

THE EQUALITY DIET

It is clear that obesity and overweight are not problems confined to the poor. In the USA, about 12 per cent of the population are poor, but more than 75 per cent are overweight. In the UK, social class differences in women's obesity can be seen all the way up the social ladder. While obesity affects only 16 per cent of 'higher managerial and professional' women, just below them, 20 per cent of lower managerial and professional women are obese. It's hard to argue in the face of these facts that the obesity epidemic is due to poor nutritional knowledge among the uneducated. In a study of middle-aged British women,[137] 84 per cent knew they should be eating five fruits and vegetables each day, and another study showed that obese people are better than thinner people at guessing the calorie content of snack foods.[138]

Another piece of evidence that it's relative, not absolute, levels of income that matter for obesity comes from studies in which people are asked to describe subjectively their place in the social hierarchy. Researchers show subjects a diagram of a ladder and tell them that at the top are people with the highest status, and at the bottom people with the lowest status, and then ask them to place an 'X' on the ladder to mark their own standing. It has been shown that this measure of subjective social status is linked to an unhealthy pattern of fat distribution[139] and to obesity[140] – in other words, obesity was more strongly related to people's subjective sense of their status than to their actual education or income.

If we can observe that changes in societal income inequality are followed by changes in obesity, this would also be supportive evidence for a causal association. An example of a society that has experienced a rapid increase in inequality is post-reunification Germany. After the fall of the Berlin Wall, inequality increased in the former East Germany,[141] and there is evidence from studies following people over time that this social disruption led to increases in the body mass index of children, young adults and mothers.[142]

Health and social policies for obesity treatment and prevention tend to focus on the individual; these policies try to educate people about the risks associated with being overweight, and try to coach them into better habits. But these approaches overlook the reasons *why* people continue to live a sedentary lifestyle and eat an unhealthy diet, *how* these behaviours give comfort or status, *why* there is a social gradient in obesity, *how* depression and stress in pregnancy play a role. Because behaviour changes are easier for people who feel in control and in a good emotional state, lessening the burdens of inequality could make an important contribution towards resolving the epidemic of obesity.

8

Educational performance

Our progress as a nation can be no swifter than our progress in education. The human mind is our fundamental resource.

> John F. Kennedy, Special message to the Congress
> on Education, 20 February 1961

Across the developed world, and across the political spectrum, everybody agrees about the importance of education. It's good for society, which needs the contributions and economic productivity – not to mention the tax – of a skilled workforce, and it's good for individuals. People with more education earn more, are more satisfied with their work and leisure time, are less likely to be unemployed, more likely to be healthy, less likely to be criminals, more likely to volunteer their time and vote in elections.[143] In 2006, according to the US Department of Labor, if you had been to high school but didn't graduate with a diploma, you earned an average of $419 per week. That sum rose to $595 if you had the diploma, up to $1,039 if you'd gone on to college and got a bachelor's degree, and rose to over $1,200 for an advanced degree.[144]

THE HOME ADVANTAGE

Although good schools make a difference, the biggest influence on educational attainment, how well a child performs in school and later in higher education, is family background. In a report on the

"WITH JESSE CALDWELL'S FAMILY MOVING OUT OF TOWN, I'VE BEEN PROMOTED IN THE PLAYGROUND PECKING ORDER."

future of education in Britain, Melissa Benn and Fiona Millar describe how:

One of the biggest problems facing British schools is the gap between rich and poor, and the enormous disparity in children's home backgrounds and the social and cultural capital they bring to the educational table.[145, p. 23]

Children do better if their parents have higher incomes and more education themselves, and they do better if they come from homes where they have a place to study, where there are reference books and newspapers, and where education is valued.[146] Parental involvement in children's education is even more important.

So why, when all developed societies are committed to education and equality of opportunity (at least in theory), do disadvantaged children do less well at school and miss out on the myriad benefits of education, however good the school system? As we shall see, some societies come a lot closer to achieving equality of opportunity than others.

UNEQUAL ATTAINMENT

Figure 8.1 shows that international educational scores are closely related to income inequality and Figure 8.2 shows the same relationship for the USA. More unequal countries and more unequal states have worse educational attainment – and these relationships are strong enough for us to be sure that they are not due to chance. Comparable international data on educational achievement come from the Programme for International Student Assessment (PISA), which was set up to administer standardized tests to 15-year-olds in schools in different countries. The programme began in 43 countries in 2000, and assesses children every three years, typically testing between 4,500 and 10,000 children in each country each time; schools are randomly selected. PISA tests 15-year-olds because they are coming to the end of compulsory education in most countries. Each survey gives tests in reading, mathematical and scientific literacy. The goal is to test how well children can apply knowledge and skills.

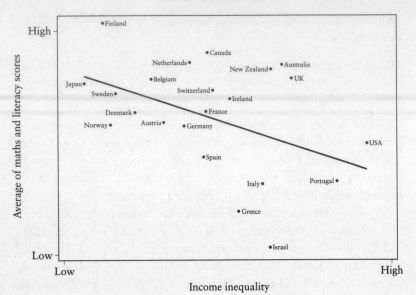

Figure 8.1 *Maths and literacy scores of 15-year-olds are lower in more unequal countries.*[148-9]

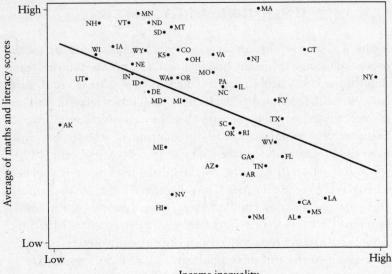

Figure 8.2 *Maths and literacy scores of eighth-graders are lower in more unequal US states.*

For consistency with the data available for the US, we combine national average scores for reading and maths only and plot them against income inequality (Figure 8.1). However, if scientific literacy scores are added in it makes little difference to the results. No data were available for the UK from PISA 2003, as too few schools agreed to take part in the survey to meet the PISA standards. The same strong international relationship with income inequality has been shown for adult literacy scores as well, using data from the International Adult Literacy Survey.[147]

To examine the same relationship among the fifty states of the USA, we combined maths and reading performance scores for eighth-graders (aged around 14 years old) from the US Department of Education, National Center for Education Statistics for 2003 (Figure 8.2). The scores are significantly lower in states with wider income differences.

As a further test, we looked at the proportion of children dropping out of high school in the USA. As Figure 8.3 shows, children are much more likely to drop out of school in more unequal states. The

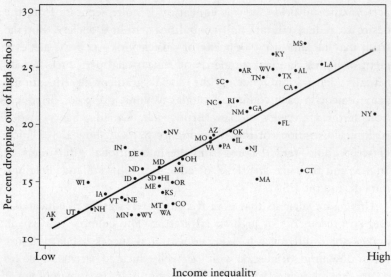

Figure 8.3 *More children drop out of high school in more unequal US states.*

states with the lowest drop-out rates are Alaska, Wyoming, Utah, Minnesota and New Hampshire, with drop-out rates around 12 per cent. In three states, Mississippi, Louisiana and Kentucky, more than a quarter of children drop out of high school with no educational qualifications.

You might think that this striking association is due to absolute poverty – that kids drop out of high school more frequently in poor states, so that they can start earning sooner and contribute to the family budget. And it is true that high school drop-out rates are higher in poor states, but poverty and inequality have independent effects. Poverty does not explain the inequality effect. No state has a poverty rate higher than 17 per cent but drop-out rates are above 20 per cent in sixteen states and dropping out is not confined to the poor.

STANDARDS OF PERFORMANCE

It is often assumed that the desire to raise national standards of performance in fields such as education is quite separate from the desire to reduce educational inequalities within a society. But the truth may be almost the opposite of this. It looks as if the achievement of higher national standards of educational performance may actually depend on reducing the social gradient in educational achievement in each country. Douglas Willms, professor of education at the University of New Brunswick, Canada, has provided striking illustrations of this.[150] In Figure 8.4 we show the relation between adult literacy scores from the International Adult Literacy Survey and their parents' level of education – in Finland, Belgium, the UK and the USA.

This figure suggests that even if your parents are well educated – and so presumably of high social status – the country you live in makes some difference to your educational success. But for those lower down the social scale with less well-educated parents, it makes a very much larger difference. An important point to note, looking at these four countries, is the steepness of the social gradient – steepest in the USA and the UK where inequality is high, flatter in Finland

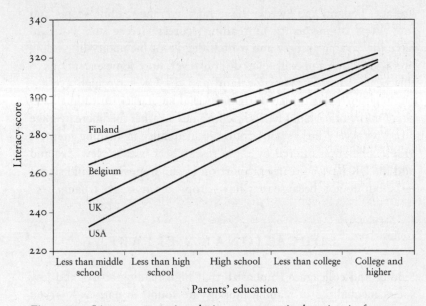

Figure 8.4 *Literacy scores in relation to parents' education in four countries (data source: International Adult Literacy Survey).*

and Belgium, which are more equal. It is also clear that an important influence on the average literacy scores – on national levels of achievement – in each of these countries is the steepness of the social gradient. The USA and UK will have low average scores, pulled down across the social gradient.

Willms has demonstrated that the pattern we've shown in Figure 8.4 holds more widely – internationally among twelve developed countries, as well as among Canadian provinces and the states of the USA.[151] As well as the tendency towards divergence – larger differences at the bottom of the social gradient than at the top – he says 'there is a strong inverse relationship between average proficiency levels and the slope of the socioeconomic gradients'.

Epidemiologist Arjumand Siddiqi and colleagues have also looked at social gradients in reading literacy in 15-year-olds, using data from PISA 2000.[152] They found that countries with a long history of welfare state provision did better and, like Willms, report that countries with higher average scores have smaller social differences in reading literacy. Finland and Sweden have high average reading scores and low levels of inequality in reading scores; Greece and Portugal have low average scores and a high degree of inequality in reading literacy. Siddiqi and colleagues do, however, note some exceptions to this general pattern. New Zealand and the UK have high average reading scores, but a high degree of social inequality in reading literacy. On the other hand Norway combines a rather mediocre average score with very little socio-economic inequality in reading literacy. One explanation offered by these researchers is that New Zealand and the UK have a greater proportion of children who should sit the tests, but do not, because they have dropped out, or are truants.

EDUCATIONAL WELFARE

Siddiqi and colleagues emphasize that high reading scores and low social inequalities in reading literacy are found in nations 'marked by stronger welfare provisions'. This is a point we will return to in Chapter 12, when we look at public spending on education in relation to income inequality. But how else might income inequality affect educational outcomes?

One important connection is likely to be through the impact of inequality on the quality of family life and relationships. Social inequalities in early childhood development are entrenched long before the start of formal education. We know a lot now about the importance of the early years for later development – learning begins at birth and the first few years of life are a critical period for brain development. This early learning can be enhanced or inhibited by the environment in which a child grows up. A nationwide study in the UK found that, by the age of three years, children from disadvantaged backgrounds were already educationally up to a year behind children from more privileged homes.[153]

Essential for early learning is a stimulating social environment. Babies and young children need to be in caring, responsive environments. They need to be talked to, loved and interacted with. They need opportunities to play, talk and explore their world, and they need to be encouraged within safe limits, rather than restricted in their activities or punished. All of these things are harder for parents and other care-givers to provide when they are poor, or stressed, or unsupported.

In Chapter 4 we described how the general quality of social relationships is lower in more unequal societies, and in Chapters 5 and 6 we showed how inequality is linked to poor physical and mental health and more substance abuse. It's not a great leap then to think how life in a more hierarchical, mistrustful society might affect intimate, domestic relationships and family life. Domestic conflict and violence, parental mental illness, poverty of time and resources will all combine to affect child development. The results of these stresses can perhaps be seen in an analysis by economists Robert Frank and Adam Levine, of Cornell University. They showed that in the United States, counties that had the largest increases in income inequality were the same counties that experienced the largest rises in divorce rates.[154] Children living in low-income families experience more family conflict and disruption and are more likely to witness or experience violence, as well as to be living in more crowded, noisy and substandard housing[155] – the quality of the home environment is directly related to income.[156] The way parents behave in response to relative poverty mediates its impact on children – there is evidence that some families are resilient to such problems, while others react with more punitive and unresponsive parenting, even to the extent of becoming neglectful or abusive.[157-8] It is important, once again, to note that difficulties in family relationships and parenting are not confined to the poor. Sociologist Annette Lareau describes how parenting differs between middle-class, working-class and poor families in America: there are key differences in the organization of daily life, the use of language, and the degree to which families are socially connected.[159] We have found that within the UK Millennium Cohort Study, a large survey of children born in 2000 and 2001, even mothers in the second from the top social class group are more likely to report feeling incompetent as a parent or having a poor relationship with their children, compared to those in the topmost group.

Societies can do a lot to ameliorate the stresses on families and to support early childhood development. From the very start of life, some societies do more than others to promote a secure attachment between mother and infant through the provision of paid maternity leave for mothers who work. Using data on the duration of paid maternity leave, provided by the Clearinghouse on International Developments in Child, Youth and Family Policies at Columbia University, we found that more equal countries provided longer periods of paid maternity leave.

Sweden provides parental leave (which can be divided between mothers and fathers) with 80 per cent wage replacement until the child is 18 months old; a further three months can be taken at a flat rate of pay, and then another three months of unpaid leave on top of that. Norway gives parents (again either mother or father) a year of leave at 80 per cent wage replacement, or forty-two weeks at 100 per cent. In contrast, the USA and Australia provide no statutory entitlement to paid leave – in Australia parents can have a year of unpaid leave, in the USA, twelve weeks.

As well as allowing parental leave, societies can improve the quality of early childhood through the provision of family allowances and tax benefits, social housing, health care, programmes to promote work/life balance, enforcing child support payments and, perhaps most importantly, through the provision of high-quality early childhood education. Early childhood education programmes can foster physical and cognitive development, as well as social and emotional development.[160-62] They can alter the long-term trajectories of children's lives, and cost-benefit analyses show that they are high-yield investments. In experiments, disadvantaged children who have received high-quality early childhood education are less likely to need remedial education, less likely to become involved in crime, and they earn more as adults.[160] All of this adds up to a substantial return on government investments in such programmes.

UNEQUAL LEARNING OPPORTUNITIES

So far we have described ways in which greater inequality may affect children's development through its impact on family life and relationships. But there is also evidence of more direct effects of inequality on children's cognitive abilities and learning.

In 2004, World Bank economists Karla Hoff and Priyanka Pandey reported the results of a remarkable experiment.[163] They took 321 high-caste and 321 low-caste 11 to 12-year-old boys from scattered rural villages in India, and set them the task of solving mazes. First, the boys did the puzzles without being aware of each other's caste. Under this condition the low-caste boys did just as well with the mazes as the high-caste boys, indeed slightly better.

Then, the experiment was repeated, but this time each boy was asked to confirm an announcement of his name, village, father's and grandfather's names, and caste. After this public announcement of caste, the boys did more mazes, and this time there was a large caste gap in how well they did – the performance of the low-caste boys dropped significantly (Figure 8.5).

This is striking evidence that performance and behaviour in an educational task can be profoundly affected by the way we feel we are seen and judged by others. When we expect to be viewed as inferior, our abilities seem to be diminished.

The same phenomenon has been demonstrated in experiments with white and black high-school students in America, most convincingly by social psychologists Claude Steele at Stanford University, and Joshua Aronson at New York University.[164] In one study they administered a standardized test used for college students' admission to graduate programmes. In one condition, the students were told that the test was a measure of ability; in a second condition, the students were told that the test was *not* a measure of ability. The white students performed equally under both conditions, but the black students performed much worse when they thought their ability was being judged. Steele and Aronson labelled this effect 'stereotype threat' and it's now been shown that it is a general effect, which applies to sex differences as well as racial and ethnic differences.[165]

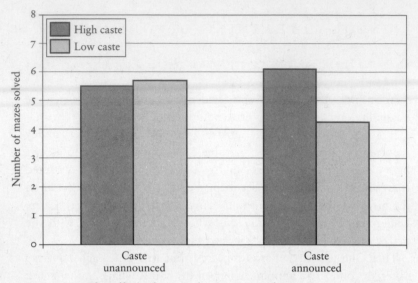

Figure 8.5 *The effect of caste identity on performance in Indian school boys.*[163]

Despite the work we mentioned on social anxiety and the effects of being judged negatively which we discussed in Chapter 3, it is perhaps surprising how easily stereotypes and stereotype threats are established, even in artificial conditions. Jane Elliott, an American schoolteacher, conducted an experiment with her students in 1968, in an effort to teach them about racial inequality and injustice.[166] She told them that scientists had shown that people with blue eyes were more intelligent and more likely to succeed than people with brown eyes, who were lazy and stupid. She divided her class into blue-eyed and brown-eyed groups, and gave the blue-eyed group extra privileges, praise and attention. The blue-eyed group quickly asserted its superiority over the brown-eyed children, treating them contemptuously, and their school performance improved. The brown-eyed group just as quickly adopted a submissive timidity, and their marks declined. After a few days, Elliott told the children she had got the information mixed up and that actually it was brown eyes that indicated superiority. The classroom situation rapidly reversed.

New developments in neurology provide biological explanations for how our learning is affected by our feelings.[167] We learn best in stimulating environments when we feel sure we can succeed. When we feel happy or confident our brains benefit from the release of dopamine, the reward chemical, which also helps with memory, attention and problem solving. We also benefit from serotonin which improves mood, and from adrenaline which helps us to perform at our best. When we feel threatened, helpless and stressed, our bodies are flooded by the hormone cortisol which inhibits our thinking and memory. So inequalities of the kind we have been describing in this chapter, in society and in our schools, have a direct and demonstrable effect on our brains, on our learning and educational achievement.

DIFFERENT STROKES FOR DIFFERENT FOLKS

Another way in which inequality directly affects educational achievement is through its impact on the aspirations, norms and values of people who find themselves lower down the social hierarchy. While education is viewed by the middle class and by teachers and policy makers as the way upwards and outwards for the poor and working class, these values are not always subscribed to by the poor and working class themselves.

In her 2006 book *Educational Failure and Working Class White Children in Britain*, anthropologist Gillian Evans describes the working-class culture of Bermondsey, in east London.[168] She shows how the kinds of activities expected of children in schools fit with the way middle-class parents expect their children to play and interact at home, but clash with the way in which working-class families care for, and interact with, their children. To a degree, working-class people resist the imposition of education and middle-class values, because becoming educated would require them to give up ways of being that they value. One woman tells Evans that being 'common' means 'knowin' 'ow to 'ave a good laugh 'cos you're not stuck up'. The things that the women she describes like to talk about are their families, their health, work and ways to get money, housework, relationships, shopping, sex and gossip. Talking about abstract ideas, books and culture, is seen as posh and pretentious. The children of these working-class mothers are constrained by minimal rules in their homes. Evans describes children who are allowed to eat and drink what they like, when they like; to smoke at home; to do homework or not, as they please. 'If they want to learn, they will, if they don't, they won't and that's that.' Of course these families want the best for their children, but that 'best' isn't always 'education, education, education'.

That poor and working-class children resist formal education and middle-class values does not, of course, mean that they have no aspirations or ambitions. In fact, when we first looked at data on children's aspirations from a UNICEF report on childhood well-being,[110] we were surprised at its relationship to income inequality (Figure 8.6). More children reported low aspirations in more equal countries; in unequal countries children were more likely to have high aspirations. Some of this may be accounted for by the fact that in more equal societies, less-skilled work may be less stigmatized,

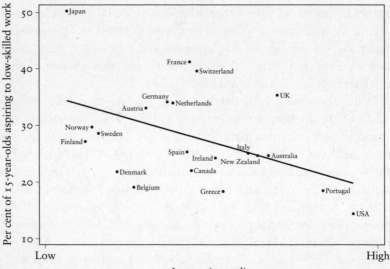

Figure 8.6 *Aspirations of 15-year-olds and inequality in rich countries.*

in comparison to more unequal societies where career choices are dominated by rather star-struck ideas of financial success and images of glamour and celebrity.

In more unequal countries, we found a larger gap between aspirations and actual opportunities and expectations. If we compare Figure 8.1 on maths and reading scores in different countries to Figure 8.6, it is clear that aspirations are higher in countries where educational achievement is lower. More children might be aspiring to higher-status jobs, but fewer of them will be qualified to get them. If inequality leads to unrealistic hopes it must also lead to disappointment.

Gillian Evans quotes a teacher at an inner-city primary school, who summed up the corrosive effect of inequality on children:

These kids don't know they're working class; they won't know that until they leave school and realize that the dreams they've nurtured through childhood can't come true.[168]

In the next two chapters we'll show how young women and young men in more unequal societies respond to their low social status, and in Chapter 12 we'll return to the theme of education and life chances when we examine the impact of inequality on social mobility.

"Is this birds and bees chat going to take long?
I'm late for my pre-natal class."

9

Teenage births: recycling deprivation

Just saying 'No' prevents teenage pregnancy the way 'Have a nice day' cures chronic depression.

Faye Wattleton, Conference speech, Seattle, 1988

In the summer of 2005, three sisters hit the headlines of Britain's tabloid newspapers – all three were teenage mothers. The youngest was the first of the girls to become pregnant and had her baby at the age of 12. 'We were in bed at my mum's house messing around and sex just sort of happened,' she said; 'I didn't tell anyone because I was too scared and didn't know what to do ... I wish it had happened to someone else.'[169] Soon after, the next older sister had a baby at age 14. 'It was just one of those things. I thought it would never happen to me,' she said. 'At first I wanted an abortion because I didn't want to be like [my sister], but I couldn't go through with it.' The oldest sister, the last of the girls to find out she was pregnant, gave birth aged 16; unlike her sisters she seemed to welcome motherhood. 'I left school ... as I wasn't really interested,' she admitted, 'all my friends were having babies and I wanted to be a mum, too'. At the time their stories became news, the girls were all living at home with their mother, sharing their bedrooms with their babies, the youngest two struggling with school, and all three trying to get by on social security benefits. With no qualifications and no support from the fathers of their babies, their futures were bleak. Media commentators and members of the public were quick to condemn the sisters and their mother, portraying them as feckless scroungers. 'Meet the kid sisters ... benefit bonanza' ... 'Girls' babies are the real victims,' exclaimed the newspapers.[170-71] Their mother blamed the lack of sex education in school.

WHY IT MATTERS

The press furore brings society's fears and concerns around teenage motherhood into sharp focus. Often described as 'babies having babies', teenage motherhood is seen as bad for the mother, bad for the baby and bad for society.

There is no doubt that babies born to teenage mothers are more likely to have low birthweight, to be born prematurely, to be at higher risk of dying in infancy and, as they grow up, to be at greater risk of educational failure, juvenile crime and becoming teenage parents themselves.[172-3] Girls who give birth as teenagers are more likely to be poor and uneducated. But are all the bad things associated with teenage birth really caused by the *age* of the mother? Or are they simply a result of the cultural world in which teenage mothers give birth?

This issue is hotly debated. On the one hand, some argue that teenage motherhood is *not* a health problem because young age is not in itself a cause of worse outcomes.[174] In fact, among poor African-Americans, cumulative exposure to poverty and stress across their lifetimes compromises their health to such an extent that their babies do better if these women have their children at a young age.[175-6] This idea is known as 'weathering' and suggests that, for poor and disadvantaged women, postponing pregnancy until later ages doesn't actually mean that they have healthier babies. Others have shown that the children of teenage mothers are more likely to end up excluded from mainstream society, with worse physical and emotional health and more deprivation. This is true even after taking account of other childhood circumstances such as social class, education, whether the parents were married or not, the parents' personalities, and so on.[177] But although we can sometimes separate out the influences of maternal age and economic circumstances in research studies, in real life they often seem inextricably intertwined and teenage motherhood is associated with an inter-generational cycle of deprivation.[178]

But how exactly are young women's individual experiences and choices – their personal choices about sleeping with their boyfriends, choices around contraception and abortion, choices about qualifications and careers, shaped by the society they live in? Like the issues discussed in earlier chapters, the teenage birth rate is strongly related to relative deprivation and to inequality.

BORN UNEQUAL

There are social class differences in both teenage *conceptions* and *births* but the differences are smaller for conceptions than for births, because middle-class young women are more likely to have abortions. Teenage birth rates are higher in communities that also have high divorce rates, low levels of trust and low social cohesion, high unemployment, poverty, and high crime rates.[173] It has been suggested by others that teenage motherhood is a choice that women make when they feel they have no other prospects for achieving the social credentials of adulthood, such as a stable intimate relationship or rewarding employment.[179] Sociologist Kristin Luker claims that it is 'the discouraged among the disadvantaged' who become teenage mothers.[180]

But it is important to remember that it isn't only poor young women who become teenage mothers: like all the problems we have looked at, inequality in teenage birth rates runs right across society. In Figure 9.1, we show the percentage of young British women who become teenage mothers in relation to household income. Each year almost 5 per cent of teenagers living in the poorest quarter of homes have a first baby, four times the rate in the richest quarter. But even in the second richest quarter of households the rate is double that of the richest quarter (2.4 per cent and 1.2 per cent). Similar patterns are seen in the United States. Although most of these births are to older teenagers, aged 18–19 years, the pattern is evident, and even stronger, for the 15–17-year-olds.

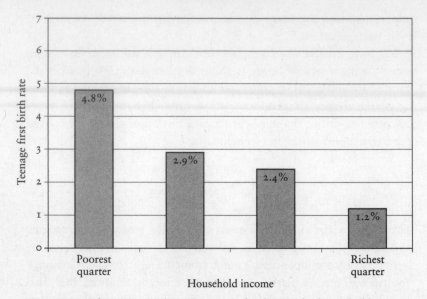

Figure 9.1 *There is a gradient in teenage birth rates by household income, from poorest to richest.*[181]

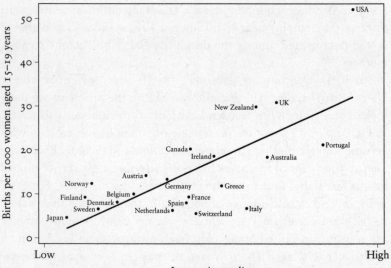

Figure 9.2 *Teenage birth rates are higher in more unequal countries.*[185]

Figure 9.2 shows that the international teenage birth rates provided by UNICEF[182] are related to income inequality and Figure 9.3 shows the same relationship for the fifty states of the USA, using teen pregnancy rates from the US National Vital Statistics System[183] and the Alan Guttmacher Institute.[184] There is a strong tendency for more unequal countries and more unequal states to have higher teenage birth rates – much too strong to be attributable to chance. The UNICEF report on teenage births showed that at least one and a quarter million teenagers become pregnant each year in the rich OECD countries and about three-quarters of a million go on to become teenage mothers.[182] The differences in teen birth rates between countries are striking. The USA and UK top the charts. At the top of the league in our usual group of rich countries, the USA has a teenage birth rate of 52.1 (per 1,000 women aged 15–19), more than four times the EU average and more than ten times higher than that of Japan, which has a rate of 4.6.

Rachel Gold and colleagues have studied income inequality and teenage births in the USA, and shown that teen birth rates are

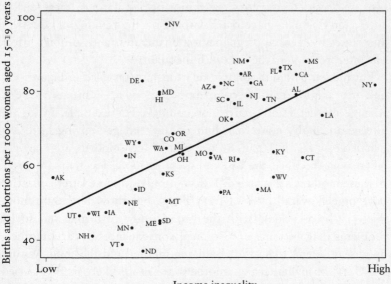

Fgure 9.3 *Teenage pregnancy rates are higher in more unequal US states.*

highest in the most unequal, as well as the most relatively deprived counties. She also reported that the effect of inequality was strongest for the youngest mothers, those aged 15–17 years.[186] For the US states, we show data for live births and abortions combined. There are substantial differences in pregnancy rates between US states. Mississippi has a rate close to twice that of Utah.

We might expect patterns of conceptions, abortions and births to be influenced by factors such as religion and ethnicity. We'd expect predominantly Catholic countries to have high rates of teenage births, because of low rates of abortion. But, while predominantly Catholic Portugal and Ireland have high rates that would indeed fit this alternative explanation, Italy and Spain have unexpectedly low rates, although they are also predominantly Catholic. Within countries, different ethnic groups can have different cultures and values around sexuality, contraception, abortion, early marriage and women's roles in society. In the USA, for example, Hispanic and African-American girls are almost twice as likely to be teenage mothers as white girls, and in the UK similarly, comparatively high rates are seen in the Bangladeshi and Caribbean communities.[182] But, because these communities are minority populations, these differences don't actually have much impact on the ranking of countries and states by teenage pregnancy or birth rates, and so don't affect our interpretation of the link with inequality.

But hidden within the simple relationships revealed in Figures 9.2 and 9.3 are the real-life complexities of what it means to be a teenage mother in any particular country. For example, in Japan, Greece and Italy, more than half of the teenagers giving birth are married – in fact in Japan, 86 per cent of teen mothers are married, whereas in the USA, the UK and New Zealand, less than a quarter of these mothers are married.[182] So not only do these latter countries have higher overall rates of teen births, but those births are more likely to be associated with the broad range of health and social problems that we think of as typical consequences of early motherhood – problems that affect both the mother and the child. Within the USA, Hispanic teenage mothers are more likely to be married than those from other ethnic groups, but they are also more likely to be poor;[187–8] the same is true for Bangladeshis in the UK.

So what do we know about who becomes a teenage mother that can help us understand this particular effect of inequality?

THE FAST LANE TO ADULTHOOD

Interestingly, there is not much of a connection between *teenage* birth rates and birth rates for women of *all ages* in rich countries. The most unequal countries, the US, UK, New Zealand and Portugal, have much higher teenage birth rates relative to older women's birth rates than the more equal countries, such as Japan, Sweden, Norway and Finland, which have teenage birth rates that are lower relative to the rates of birth of older women.[182] So whatever drives teenage birth rates up in more unequal countries is unconnected with the factors driving overall fertility. Unequal societies affect teenage childbearing in particular.

A report from the Rowntree Foundation called *Young People's Changing Routes to Independence*, which compares how children born in 1958 and 1970 grew up, describes a 'widening gap between those on the fast and the slow lanes to adulthood'.[189] In the slow lane, young people born into families in the higher socio-economic classes spend a long time in education and career training, putting off marriage and childbearing until they are established as successful adults. For young people on the fast track, truncated education often leads them into a disjointed pattern of unemployment, low-paid work and training schemes, rather than an ordered, upward career trajectory.

As sociologists Hilary Graham and Elizabeth McDermott point out, teenage motherhood is a pathway through which women become excluded from the activities and connections of the wider society, and a way in which generations become trapped by inequality.[190] But as well as the constraints that relative poverty imposes on life chances for young people, there seem to be additional reasons why teenage motherhood is sensitive to degrees of inequality in society.

EARLY MATURITY AND
ABSENT FATHERS

The first of these additional reasons was touched on in Chapter 8, where we discussed the impact of inequality on family relationships and stress in early life. Experiences in early childhood may be just as relevant to teenage motherhood as the educational and economic opportunities available to adolescents. In 1991, psychologist Jay Belsky at the University of London and his colleagues proposed a theory, based on evolutionary psychology, in which experiences in early childhood would lead individuals towards either a *quantity* or a *quality* reproductive strategy, depending on how stressful their early experiences had been.[191] They suggested that people who learned, while growing up, 'to perceive others as untrustworthy, relationships as opportunistic and self-serving, and resources as scarce and/or unpredictable' would reach biological maturity earlier, be sexually active earlier, be more likely to form short-term relationships and make less investment in parenting. In contrast, people who grow up learning 'to perceive others as trustworthy, relationships as enduring and mutually rewarding and resources more or less constantly available' would mature later, defer sexual activity, be better at forming long-term relationships and invest more heavily in their children's development.

In the world in which humans evolved, these different strategies make sense. If you can't rely on your mate or other people, and you can't rely on resources, then it may once have made sense to get started early and have lots of children – at least some will survive. But if you can trust your partner and family to be committed to you and to provide for you, it makes sense to have fewer children and to devote more attention and resources to each one.

Rachel Gold and colleagues found that the relationship between inequality and teenage birth rates in the USA might be acting through the impact of inequality on social capital, which we discussed in Chapter 4.[192] Among US states, that is, those with lower levels of social cohesion, civic engagement and mutual trust – exactly the conditions which might favour a quantity strategy – teenage birth rates are higher.

Several studies have also shown that early conflict and the absence of a father *do* predict earlier maturation – girls in such a situation become physically mature and start their periods earlier than girls who grow up without those sources of stress.[193, 194] And reaching puberty earlier increases the likelihood of girls becoming sexually active at an early age and of teenage motherhood.[195]

Father absence may be particularly important for teenage pregnancy. In a study of two large samples in the USA and New Zealand, psychologist Bruce Ellis and his colleagues followed girls from early childhood through to adulthood.[196] In both countries, the longer a father was absent from the family, the more likely it was that his daughter would have sex at a young age and become a teenage mother – and this strong effect could not be explained away by behavioural problems of the girls, by family stress, parenting style, socio-economic status, or by differences in the neighbourhoods in which the girls grew up. So there may be deep-seated adaptive processes which lead from more stressful and unequal societies – perhaps particularly from low social status – to higher teenage birth rates. Unfortunately, while we can obtain international data on single-parent households, being a single parent means very different things in different countries, and there are no international data that tell us how many fathers are absent from their children's lives.

WHAT ABOUT THE DADS?

Throughout this chapter, we've been discussing the problem of teenage parenting exclusively in terms of teenage mothers, but what about the fathers? Let's return to the story of the three sisters. The father of the 12-year-old girl's baby left her shortly after his son was born. The boy named by the middle sister as the father of her little girl denied having sex with her and demanded a paternity test. And the 38-year-old father of the oldest sister's baby already had at least four other children.

Sociologists Graham and McDermott discuss what has been learned from studies where researchers talk at length to young women about their experiences. What they show is that these sisters' experiences with their babies' fathers are typical.[190] Motherhood is a way in which young women in deprived circumstances join adult social networks – networks which usually include their own mothers and other relatives, and these supportive networks help them transcend the social stigma of being a teenage mother. According to Graham and McDermott, young women prioritize their relationships with the babies, over their often difficult relationships with the babies' fathers, because they feel this relationship is a 'more certain source of intimacy than the heterosexual relationships they had . . . experienced'.

Young men living in areas of high unemployment and low wages often can't offer much in the way of stability or support. In communities with high levels of teenage motherhood, young men are themselves trying to cope with the many difficulties that inequality inflicts on their lives, and young fatherhood adds to those stresses.

10

Violence: gaining respect

> Where justice is denied, where poverty is enforced, where
> ignorance prevails and where any one class is made to
> feel that society is in an organized conspiracy to oppress,
> rob and degrade them, neither persons nor property will
> be safe.
>
> Frederick Douglas, Speech on the 24th anniversary
> of emancipation, Washington, DC, 1886

As we began to write this chapter, violence was in the headlines on
both sides of the Atlantic. In the USA, an 18-year-old man with a
shotgun entered a shopping mall in Salt Lake City, Utah, killing five
people and wounding four others, apparently at random, before
being shot dead by police. In the UK, there was a wave of killings
in South London, including the murder of three teenage boys in
less than a fortnight. But perhaps the story that best illustrates what
this chapter is about occurred in March 2006, in a quiet suburb
of Cincinnati, Ohio. Charles Martin, a 66-year-old, telephoned the
emergency services.[197] 'I just killed a kid,' he told the operator, 'I
shot him with a goddamn 410 shotgun twice.' Mr Martin had shot
his 15-year-old neighbour. The boy's crime? He had run across Mr
Martin's lawn. 'Kid's just been giving me a bunch of shit, making the
other kids harass me and my place.'

Violence is a real worry in many people's lives. In the most recent
British Crime Surveys, 35 per cent of people said they were very
worried or fairly worried about being a victim of mugging, 33 per
cent worried about physical attack, 24 per cent worried about rape,

"And finally, would you say your fear
of crime had increased?"

and 13 per cent worried about racially motivated violence. More than a quarter of the people who responded said they were worried about being insulted or pestered in public.[198] Surveys in America and Australia report similar findings – in fact fear of crime and violence may be as big a problem as the actual level of violence. Very few people are victims of violent crime, but fear of violence affects the quality of life of many more. Fear of violence disproportionately affects the vulnerable – the poor, women and minority groups.[199] In many places, women feel nervous going out at night or coming home late; old people double-lock their doors and won't open them to strangers. These are important infringements of basic human freedoms.

People's fears of crime, violence and anti-social behaviour don't always match up with rates and trends in crime and violence. A recent down-swing in homicide rates in America (which has now ended), was not matched by a reduction in people's fear of violence. We will return to recent trends later. First, let's turn our attention to differences in rates of actual violence between different societies and look at some of the similarities and the differences between them.

In some ways patterns of violence are remarkably consistent across time and space. In different places and at different times, violent acts are overwhelmingly perpetrated by men, and most of those men are in their teens or early twenties. In her book, *The Ant and the Peacock*, philosopher and evolutionary psychologist Helena Cronin shows how closely correlated the age and sex characteristics of murderers are in different places.[200] We reproduce her graph showing murder rates, comparing Chicago with England and Wales (Figure 10.1). The age of the perpetrator is shown along the bottom; up the side is the murder rate, and there are separate lines for men and women. It is immediately apparent that murder rates peak in the late teens and early twenties for men, and that rates for women are much lower at all ages. The age and sex distribution is astonishingly similar both in Chicago and in England and Wales. However, what is less obvious is that the scales on the left- and right-hand sides of the graph are very different. On the left-hand side of the graph, the scale shows homicide rates per million people in England and

Figure 10.1 *Homicides by age and sex of perpetrator. England and Wales compared with Chicago.*[200]

Wales, going from zero to 30. On the right-hand side, the scale shows homicide rates in Chicago, and here the scale runs from zero to 900 murders per million. Despite the striking similarities in the patterns of age and sex distribution, there is something fundamentally different in these places; the city of Chicago had a murder rate 30 times higher than the rate in England and Wales. On top of the biological similarities there are huge environmental differences.

Violent crimes are almost unknown in some societies. In the USA, a child is killed by a gun every three hours. Despite having a much lower rate than the USA, the UK is a violent society, compared to many other countries: over a million violent crimes were recorded in 2005–2006. And within any society, while it is generally young men who are violent, most young men are not. Just as it is the discouraged and disadvantaged among young women who become teenage mothers, it is poor young men from disadvantaged neighbourhoods who are most likely to be both victims and perpetrators of violence. Why?

'IF YOU AIN'T GOT PRIDE, YOU GOT NOTHING.' [201, p. 29]

James Gilligan is a psychiatrist at Harvard Medical School, where he directs the Center for the Study of Violence, and has worked on violence prevention for more than thirty years. He was in charge of mental health services for the Massachusetts prison system for many years, and for most of his years as a clinical psychiatrist he worked with the most violent of offenders in prisons and prison mental hospitals. In his books, *Violence* [202] and *Preventing Violence*, [201] he argues that acts of violence are 'attempts to ward off or eliminate the feeling of shame and humiliation – a feeling that is painful, and can even be intolerable and overwhelming – and replace it with its opposite, the feeling of pride'. Time after time, when talking to men who had committed violent offences, he discovered that the triggers to violence had involved threats – or perceived threats – to pride, acts that instigated feelings of humiliation or shame. Sometimes the incidents that led to violence seemed incredibly trivial, but they all evoked shame. A young neighbour walking disrespectfully across your immaculate lawn . . . the popular kids in the school harassing you and calling you a faggot . . . being fired from your job . . . your woman leaving you for another man . . . someone looking at you 'funny' . . .

Gilligan goes so far as to say that he has 'yet to see a serious act of violence that was not provoked by the experience of feeling shamed and humiliated . . . and that did not represent the attempt to . . . undo this "loss of face"'.[202, p. 110] And we can all recognize these feelings, even if we would never go so far as to act on them. We recognize the stomach-clenching feelings of shame and embarrassment, the mortification that we feel burning us up when we make ourselves look foolish in the eyes of others. We know how important it is to feel liked, respected, and valued.[203] But if all of us feel these things, why is it predominantly among young men that those feelings escalate into violent acts?

Here the work of evolutionary psychologists Margo Wilson and Martin Daly helps to make sense of these patterns of violence. In their 1988 book *Homicide*[204] and a wealth of books, chapters and articles since, they use statistical, anthropological and historical data to show how young men have strong incentives to achieve and maintain as high a social status as they can – because their success in sexual competition depends on status.[77, 205-8] While looks and physical attractiveness are more important for women, it is status that matters most for sexual success among men. Psychologist David Buss found that women value the financial status of prospective partners roughly twice as much as men do.[209] So while women try to enhance their sexual attractiveness with clothes and make-up, men compete for status. This explains not only why feeling put down, disrespected and humiliated are the most common trigger for violence; it also explains why most violence is between men – men have more to win or lose from having (or failing to gain) status. Reckless, even violent behaviour comes from young men at the bottom of society, deprived of all the markers of status, who must struggle to maintain face and what little status they have, often reacting explosively when it is threatened.

But while it seems clear that the propensity for violence among young men lies partially in evolved psychological adaptations related to sexual competition, most men are not violent. So what factors explain why some societies seem better than others at preventing or controlling these impulses to violence?

INEQUALITY IS 'STRUCTURAL' VIOLENCE

The simple answer is that increased inequality ups the stakes in the competition for status: status matters even more. The impact of inequality on violence is even better established and accepted than the other effects of inequality that we discuss in this book.[203] In this chapter we show relationships between violence and inequality for the same countries and the same time period as we use in other chapters. Many similar graphs have been published by other researchers, for other time periods or sets of countries, including one covering more than fifty countries between 1970 and 1994 from researchers at the World Bank.[207, 210] A large body of evidence shows a clear relationship between greater inequality and higher homicide rates. As early as 1993, criminologists Hsieh and Pugh wrote a review which included thirty-five analyses of income inequality and violent crime.[211] All but one found a positive link between the two – as inequality increased so did violent crime. Homicides and assaults were most closely associated with income inequality, and robbery and rape less so. We have found the same relationships when looking at more recently published studies.[10] Homicides are more common in the more unequal areas in cities ranging from Manhattan to Rio de Janeiro, and in the more unequal American states and cities and Canadian provinces.

Figure 10.2 shows that international homicide rates from the United Nations *Surveys on Crime Trends and the Operations of Criminal Justice Systems*[212] are related to income inequality, and Figure 10.3 shows the same relationship for the USA, using homicide rates from the Federal Bureau of Investigation.[213] The differences between some countries in the first graph are very large. The USA is

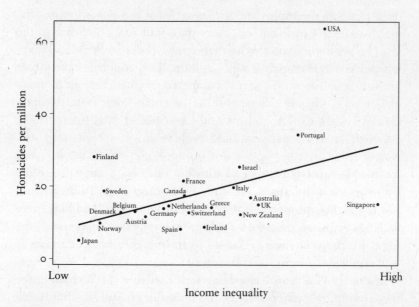

Figure 10.2 *Homicides are more common in more unequal countries.*

135

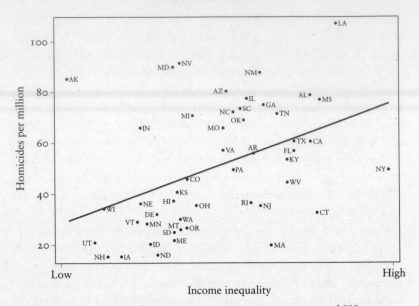

Figure 10.3 *Homicides are more common in more unequal US states.*

once again at the top of the league table of the rich countries. Its murder rate is 64 per million, more than four times higher than the UK (15 per million) and more than twelve times higher than Japan, which has a rate of only 5.2 per million. Two countries take rather unusual positions in this graph, compared to where they sit in many of our other chapters: Singapore has a much lower homicide rate than we might expect, and Finland has a higher rate. Interestingly, although international relationships between gun ownership and violent crime are complicated (for instance, gun ownership is linked to murders involving female victims but not male victims),[214] in the United Nations International Study on Firearm Regulation, Finland had the highest proportion of households with guns, and Singapore had the lowest rate of gun ownership.[215] Despite these exceptions, the trend for more unequal countries to have higher homicide rates is well established.

In the USA, although no data were available for Wyoming, the relationship between inequality and homicides is still significant and the differences between states are almost as great as the differences between countries. Louisiana has a murder rate of 107 per million, more than seven times higher than that of New Hampshire and Iowa, which are bottom of the league table with murder rates of 15 per million. The homicide rate in Alaska is much higher than we would expect, given its relatively low inequality, and rates in New York, Connecticut and Massachusetts are lower. In the United States, two out of every three murders are committed with guns, and homicide rates are higher in states where more people own guns.[216] Among the states on our graph, Alaska has the highest rate of gun ownership of all, and New York, Connecticut and Massachusetts are among the lowest.[217] If we allow for gun ownership, we find a slightly stronger relationship between inequality and homicides.

HAVENS IN A HEARTLESS WORLD

We have already seen some features of more unequal societies that help to tie violence to inequality – family life counts, schools and neighbourhoods are important, and status competition matters.

In Chapter 8 we mentioned a study which found that divorce rates are higher in more unequal American counties. In his book, *Life Without Father*, sociologist David Popenoe describes how 60 per cent of America's rapists, 72 per cent of juvenile murderers and 70 per cent of long-term prisoners grew up in fatherless homes.[218] The effect of fatherlessness on delinquency and violence is only partly explained by these families being poorer. Why do fathers matter so much?

One researcher has described the behaviour of boys and young men who grow up without fathers as 'hypermasculine', with boys engaging in 'rigidly overcompensatory masculine behaviors'[219, pp. 1–2] – crimes against property and people, aggression and exploitation and short-term sexual conquests. This could be seen as the male version of the quantity versus quality strategy in human relationships that we described in relation to teenage mothers in Chapter 9. The absence of a father may predispose some boys to a different reproductive strategy: shifting the balance away from long-term relationships and putting more emphasis on status competition.

Fathers can, of course, act as positive role models for their sons. Fathers can teach boys, just by being present in the family, the positive aspects of manhood – how to relate to the opposite sex, how to be a responsible adult, how to be independent and assertive, yet included with, and connected to, other people. Particularly important is the way in which fathers can provide authority and discipline for teenage boys; without that security, young men are more influenced by their peers and more likely to engage in the kinds of anti-social behaviour so often seen when groups of young men get together. But fathers can also be negative role models. One study found that, although children had more behavioural problems the *less* time they had lived with their fathers, this was not true when the fathers themselves had behavioural problems.[220] If the fathers engaged in anti-social behaviour, then their children were at higher risk when they spent *more* time living with them.

Perhaps most importantly, fathers love their children in a way that studies show step-parents do not. This is not, of course, to say that most step-fathers and other men don't lovingly raise other men's children, but on average children living with their biological fathers are less likely to be abused, less likely to be delinquent, less likely to drop out of school, less likely to be emotionally neglected. Psychiatrist Gilligan says of the violent men he worked with[201, p. 36]:

They had been subjected to a degree of child abuse that was off the scale of anything I had previously thought of describing with that term. Many had been beaten nearly to death, raped repeatedly or prostituted, or neglected to a life-threatening degree by parents too disabled to care for their child. And of those who had not experienced these extremes of physical abuse or neglect, my colleagues and I found that they had experienced a degree of emotional abuse that had been just as damaging ... in which they served as the scapegoat for whatever feelings of shame and humiliation their parents had suffered and then attempted to rid themselves of by transferring them onto their child, by subjecting him to systematic and chronic shaming and humiliation, taunting and ridicule.

The increased family breakdown and family stress in unequal societies leads to inter-generational cycles of violence, just as much as inter-generational cycles of teenage motherhood.

Of course it isn't just the family environment that can breed shame, humiliation and violence. Children experience things in their schools and in their neighbourhoods that influence the probability that they will turn to violence when their status is threatened. The American high-school massacres have shown us the significance of bullying as a trigger to violence.[221-2]

In UNICEF's 2007 report on child wellbeing in rich countries, there are measures of how often young people in different countries were involved in physical fighting, had been the victim of bullying, or found their peers were not 'kind and helpful'.[110] We combined these three measures into an index of children's experiences of conflict and found that it was significantly correlated with income inequality, as shown in Figure 10.4. In more unequal societies children experience more bullying, fights and conflict. And there is no better predictor of later violence than childhood violence.

Environmental influences on rates of violence have been

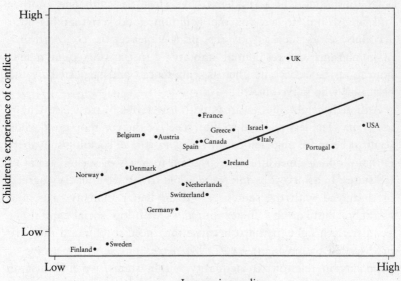

Figure 10.4 *There is more conflict between children in more unequal countries (based on percentages reporting fighting, bullying and finding peers not kind and helpful).*

recognized for a long time. In the 1940s, sociologists of the Chicago School described how some neighbourhoods had persistent reputations for violence over the years – different populations moved in and out but the same poor neighbourhoods remained dangerous, whoever was living in them.[223] In Chicago, neighbourhoods are often identified with a particular ethnic group. So a neighbourhood which might once have been an enclave of Irish immigrants and their descendants later becomes a Polish community, and later still a Latino neighbourhood. What the Chicago school sociologists drew attention to was the persistent effect of deprivation and poverty in poor neighbourhoods – on whoever lived there. In neighbourhoods where people can't trust one another, where there are high levels of fear and groups of youths hanging around on street corners, neighbours won't intervene for the common good – they feel helpless in the face of public disturbance, drug dealing, prostitution, graffiti and litter. Sociologist Robert Sampson and colleagues at Harvard University have shown that violent crime rates are lower in cohesive neighbourhoods where residents have close ties with one another and are willing to act for the common good, even taking into account factors such as poverty, prior violence, the concentration of immigrants and residential stability.[224] In the USA poor neighbourhoods have become ghettos, ring-fenced and neglected by the better-off who move out.[225]

Although neighbours in areas with low levels of trust (see Chapter 4) may feel less inclined to intervene for the common good, they seem to be more pugnacious. In *Bowling Alone*, sociologist Robert Putnam linked a measure of aggression to levels of social capital in US states. In a survey, people were asked to say whether they agreed or disagreed with the sentence: 'I'd do better than average in a fist fight.' Putnam says citizens in states with low social capital are 'readier for a fight (perhaps because they need to be), and they are predisposed to mayhem'.[25, p. 310] When we analyse this measure of pugnacity in relation to inequality within states, we find just as strong a relation as Putnam showed with social capital (Figure 10.5).

So violence is most often a response to disrespect, humiliation and loss of face, and is usually a male response to these triggers. Even within the most violent of societies, most people don't react violently

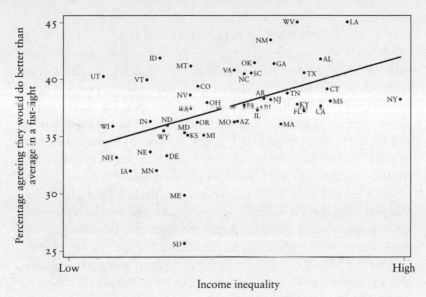

Figure 10.5 *In less equal states more people think they would do better than average in a fist fight.*

to these triggers because they have ways of achieving and maintaining their self-respect and sense of status in other ways. They might have more of the trappings of status – a good education, nice houses and cars, good jobs, new clothes. They may have family, friends and colleagues who esteem them, or qualifications they are proud of, or skills that are valued and valuable, or education that gives them status and hope for the future. As a result, although everybody experiences disrespect and humiliation at times, they don't all become violent; we all experience loss of face but we don't turn round and shoot somebody. In more unequal societies more people lack these protections and buffers. Shame and humiliation become more sensitive issues in more hierarchical societies: status becomes more important, status competition increases and more people are deprived of access to markers of status and social success. And if your source of pride is your immaculate lawn, you're going to be more than a bit annoyed when that pride gets trampled on.

PEAKS AND TROUGHS

Homicide rates in America, after rising for decades, peaked in the early 1990s, then fell to their lowest level in the early 2000s. In 2005, they started to rise again.[226] Similarly, after peaking in the early 1990s, teenage pregnancy and birth rates began to fall in America, and the decline was particularly steep for African-Americans.[227] But in 2006, the teenage birth rate also started to rise again, and the biggest reversal was for African-American women.[228]

Some people have tried to explain the decline in violence by pointing to changes in policing or drug use or access to guns, or even the 'missing' cohort of young men who were *not* born because of increased access to abortion. Explanations for the fall in teenage birth rates focused on changes in the number of teenagers who are sexually active and increasing contraceptive use. But what influences whether or not young people use drugs, buy guns, have sex or use contraception? Why are homicides and teenage births now rising again? And how do these trends match up with changes in inequality? Why have homicides and teenage births moved in parallel?

To examine this in more detail, we need data on recent short-term fluctuations in overall income inequality in the USA. The best data come from a collaborative team of researchers from the USA, China and the UK, who have produced a series of annual estimates.[229] These show inequality rising through the 1980s to a peak in the early 1990s. The following decade saw an overall decline in inequality, with an upturn since 2000. So there is a reasonable match between recent trends in homicides, teenage births and inequality – rising through the early 1990s and declining for a decade or so, with a very recent upturn.

Although violence and teenage births are complex issues and rates in each can respond to lots of other influences, the downward trends through the 1990s were consistent with improvements in the relative incomes of people at the very bottom of the income distribution. The distribution of income can be more stretched out over some parts of its range than others. A society may get more unequal because the poor are getting left further behind the middle, or because the rich are pulling further ahead. And who suffers from low social status may also vary from one society to another. Among societies with the same overall level of inequality, in one it may be the elderly who are most deprived relative to the rest of society, in another it may be ethnic minority groups.

From the early 1990s in America there was a particularly dramatic decline in relative poverty and unemployment for young people at the bottom of the social hierarchy. Although the rich continued to pull further away from the bulk of the population, from the early 1990s the *relative* position of the very poorest Americans began to improve.[230-31] As violence and teenage births are so closely connected to relative deprivation and concentrated in the poorest areas, it is what happens at the very bottom that matters most – hence the trends in violence and teenage births.[232]

These trends, during the 1990s, contrast with what had been happening previously. The decades leading up to the 1990s saw a long sustained deterioration in opportunities and status for young people at the bottom of both American and British society. In the USA, from about 1970 through the early 1990s, the earning position of young men declined, and employment prospects for young people who dropped out of high school or who completed high school but didn't go on to college worsened,[233] and violence and teenage births increased. In a recent study, demographer Cynthia Colen and her colleagues showed that falling levels of unemployment during the 1990s explained 85 per cent of the decline in rates of first births to 18–19-year-old African-Americans.[234] This was the group experiencing the biggest drop in teen births. Welfare reform and changes in the availability of abortion, in contrast, appeared to have had little impact.

In the UK, the impact of the economic recession and widening income differences during the 1980s can also be traced in the homicide rate. As health geographer Danny Dorling pointed out, with respect to these trends:[235, pp. 36-7]

There is no natural level of murder ... For murder rates to rise in particular places ... people have to be made to feel more worthless. Then there are more fights, more brawls, more scuffles, more bottles and more knifes and more young men die ... These are the same young men who saw many of their counterparts, brought up in better circumstances and in different parts of Britain, gain good work, or university education, or both, and become richer than any similarly sized cohort of such young ages in British history.

In summary, we can see that the association between inequality and violence is strong and consistent; it's been demonstrated in many different time periods and settings. Recent evidence of the close correlation between ups and downs in inequality and violence show that if inequality is lessened, levels of violence also decline. And the evolutionary importance of shame and humiliation provides a plausible explanation of why more unequal societies suffer more violence.

11

Imprisonment and punishment

The degree of civilization in a society can be judged by entering its prisons.

Fyodor Dostoevsky, *The House of the Dead*

In the USA, prison populations have been increasing steadily since the early 1970s. In 1978 there were over 450,000 people in jail, by 2005 there were over 2 million: the numbers had quadrupled. In the UK, the numbers have doubled since 1990, climbing from around 46,000 to 80,000 in 2007. In fact, in February 2007, the UK's jails were so full that the Home Secretary wrote to judges, asking them to send only the most serious criminals to prison.

This contrasts sharply with what has been happening in some other rich countries. Through the 1990s, the prison population was stable in Sweden and declined in Finland; it rose by only 8 per cent in Denmark, 9 per cent in Japan.[236] More recently, rates have been falling in Ireland, Austria, France and Germany.[237]

CRIME OR PUNISHMENT?

The number of people locked up in prison is influenced by three things: the rate at which crimes are actually committed, the tendency to send convicted criminals to prison for particular crimes, and the lengths of prison sentences. Changes in any of these three can lead to changes in the proportion of the population in prison at any point in

time. We've already described the tendency for violent crimes to be more common in more unequal societies in Chapter 10. What has been happening to crime rates in the USA and UK as rates of imprisonment have skyrocketed?

Criminologists Alfred Blumstein and Allen Beck have examined the growth in the US prison population.[238] Only 12 per cent of the growth in state prisoners between 1980 and 1996 could be put down to increases in criminal offending (dominated by a rise in drug-related crime). The other 88 per cent of increased imprisonment was due to the increasing likelihood that convicted criminals were sent to prison rather than being given non-custodial sentences, and to the increased length of prison sentences. In federal prisons, longer prison sentences are the main reason for the rise in the number of prisoners. 'Three-strikes' laws, minimum mandatory sentences and 'truth-in-sentencing' laws (i.e., no remission) mean that some convicted criminals are receiving long sentences for minor crimes. In California in 2004, there were 360 people serving life sentences for shoplifting.[239]

In the UK, prison numbers have also grown because of longer sentences and the increased use of custodial sentences for offences that a few years ago would have been punished with a fine or community sentence.[240] About forty prison sentences for shoplifting are handed out every day in the UK. Crime rates in the UK were falling as inexorably as imprisonment rates were rising.

The prison system in the Netherlands has been described by criminologist David Downes, professor emeritus of social administration at the London School of Economics.[241] He describes how two-thirds of the difference between the low rate of imprisonment in the Netherlands and the much higher rate in the UK is due to the different use of custodial sentences and the length of those sentences, rather than differences in rates of crime.

Comparing different countries, Marc Mauer of the Sentencing Project[242] shows that in the USA, people are sent to prison more often, and for longer, for property and drug crimes than they are in Canada, West Germany and England and Wales. For example, in the USA burglars received average sentences of sixteen months, whereas in Canada the average sentence was five months. And variations in crime rates didn't explain more than a small amount of the variation in rates of imprisonment when researchers looked at Australia, New Zealand and a number of European countries. If crime rates can't explain different rates of imprisonment, can inequality do better?

IMPRISONMENT AND INEQUALITY

We used statistics on the proportion of the population imprisoned in different countries from the United Nations *Survey on Crime Trends and the Operations of Criminal Justice Systems*.[212] Figure 11.1 shows (on a log scale) that more unequal countries have higher rates of imprisonment than more equal countries.

In the USA there are 576 people in prison per 100,000, which is more than four and a half times higher than the UK, at 124 per 100,000, and more than fourteen times higher than Japan, which has a rate of 40 per 100,000. Even if the USA and Singapore are

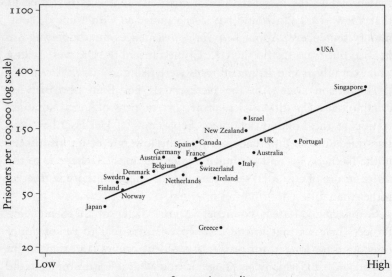

Figure 11.1 *More people are imprisoned in more unequal countries.*[149]

148

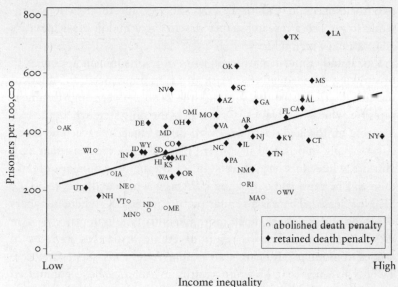

Figure 11.2 *More people are imprisoned in more unequal US states.*[149]

excluded as outliers, the relationship is robust among the remaining countries.

For the fifty states of the USA, figures for imprisonment in 1997–8 come from the US Department of Justice, Bureau of Justice Statistics.[243] As Figure 11.2 shows, there is again a strong relationship between imprisonment and inequality, and big differences between states – Louisiana imprisons people at more than six times the rate of Minnesota.

The other thing to notice on this graph is that states are shown using two different symbols. The circles represent states that have abolished the death penalty; diamonds are states which have retained it.

As we pointed out in Chapter 2, these relationships with in-equality occur for problems which have steep social gradients within societies. There is a strong social gradient in imprisonment, with people of lower class, income and education much more likely to be sent to prison than people higher up the social scale. The rarity of middle-class people being imprisoned is highlighted by the fact that two sociologists at California State Polytechnic thought it worthwhile to publish a research paper describing a middle-class inmate's adaptation to prison life.[244]

Racial and ethnic disparities in rates of imprisonment are one way of showing the inequalities in risk of being imprisoned. In America, the racial gap can be measured as the ratio between imprisonment rates for whites and blacks.[245] Hawaii is the only state where the risk of being imprisoned doesn't seem to differ much by race. There, the risk of being imprisoned if you are black is 1.34 times as high as if you are white. In every other state of the union ratios are greater than 2. The ratio is 6.04 for the USA as a whole and rises to 13.15 for New Jersey. There is a similar picture in the UK, where members of ethnic minorities are much more likely to end up in prison.[246] Are these ethnic inequalities a result of ethnic disparities in rates of crimes committed? Research on young Americans suggests not.[247] Twenty-five per cent of white youths in America have committed one violent offence by age 17, compared to 36 per cent of African-Americans, ethnic rates of property crime are the same, and African-American youth commit fewer drug crimes. But African-American youth are overwhelmingly more likely to be arrested, to be detained, to be charged, to be charged as if an adult and to be imprisoned. The same pattern is true for African-American and Hispanic adults, who are treated more harshly than whites at every stage of judicial proceedings.[248] Facing the same charges, white defendants are far more likely to have the charges against them reduced, or to be offered 'diversion' – a deferment or suspension of prosecution if the offender agrees to certain conditions, such as completing a drug rehabilitation programme.

DEGREES OF CIVILIZATION

Prison data show us that more unequal societies are more punitive. There are other indicators of this in the ways that offenders are treated in different penal systems. First, as Figure 11.2 shows, more unequal US states are more likely to retain the death penalty. Second, how prisoners are treated seems to differ.

Discussing the Netherlands, David Downes describes how a group of criminal lawyers, criminologists and psychiatrists came together to influence the prison system. They believed that:

the offender must be treated as a thinking and feeling fellow human being, capable of responding to insights offered in the course of a dialogue ... with therapeutic agents.[241, p. 147]

This philosophy has, he says, resulted in a prison system that emphasizes treatment and rehabilitation. It allows home leave and interruptions to sentences, as well as extensive use of parole and pardons. Prisoners are housed in single cells, relations among prisoners and between prisoners and staff are good, and programmes for education, training and recreation are considered a model of best practice. Although the system has toughened up somewhat since the 1980s in response to rising crime (mostly a consequence of rising rates of drug trafficking and the use of the Netherlands as a base for international organized crime), it remains characteristically humane and decent.

Japan is another country with a very low rate of imprisonment. Prison environments there have been described as 'havens of tranquillity'.[249] The Japanese judicial system exercises remarkable flexibility in prosecution and criminal proceedings. Offenders who confess to their crimes and express regret and a desire to reform are generally trusted to do so, by police, judges and the public at large. One criminologist writes that:

the vast majority [of those prosecuted] ... confess, display repentance, negotiate for their victims' pardon and submit to the mercy of the authorities. In return they are treated with extraordinary leniency.[250, p. 495]

Many custodial sentences are suspended, even for serious crimes that in other countries would lead to long mandatory sentences. Apparently, most prison inmates agree that their sentences are appropriate. Prisoners are housed in sleeping rooms holding up to eight people, and meals are taken in these small group settings. Prisoners work a forty-hour week and have access to training and recreational activities. Discipline is strict, with exact rules of conduct, but this seems to serve to maintain a calm atmosphere rather than provoke an aggressive reaction. Prison staff are expected to act as moral educators and lay counsellors as well as guards.

The picture is far starker in the prison systems of the USA. The harshness of the US prison systems at federal, state and county levels has led to repeated condemnations by such bodies as Amnesty International,[251-2] Human Rights Watch[253-4] and the United Nations Committee against Torture.[255] Their concerns relate to such practices as the incarceration of children in adult prisons, the treatment of the mentally ill and learning disabled, the prevalence of sexual assaults within prisons, the shackling of women inmates during childbirth, the use of electro-shock devices to control prisoners, the use of prolonged solitary confinement and the brutality and ill-treatment sometimes perpetrated by police and prison guards, particularly against ethnic minorities, migrants and homosexuals.

Eminent American criminologist John Irwin has spent time studying high-security prisons, county jails and Solano State Prison in California, a medium-security facility housing around 6,000 prisoners, where prisoners are crowded together, with very limited access to recreation facilities or education, training or substance abuse programmes.[256] He describes serious psychological harm done to prisoners, and their difficulties in coping with the world outside when released, across all security levels and types of institutions.

In some prisons, inmates are denied recreational activities, including television and sport activities. In others, prisoners have to pay for health care, as well as room and board. Some have brought back 'prison stripe' uniforms and chain gangs. 'America's toughest sheriff', Joe Arpaio, has become famous for his 'tent city' county jail in the Arizona desert, where prisoners live under canvas, despite temperatures that can rise to 130°F, and are fed on meals costing less than 10p (20 cents) per head.[257-8]

America's development of the 'supermax' prison,[201] facilities designed to create a permanent state of social isolation, has been condemned by the United Nations Committee on Torture.[255] Sometimes free-standing, but sometimes constructed as 'prisons-within-prisons', these are facilities where prisoners are kept in solitary confinement for twenty-three hours out of every day. Inmates leave their cells only for solitary exercise or showers. Medical anthropologist Lorna

Rhodes, who has worked in a supermax, describes prisoners' lives as characterized by 'lack of movement, stimulation and social contact'.[259] Prisoners kept in such conditions often are (or become) mentally ill and are unprepared for eventual release: they have no meaningful work, get no training or education. Estimates vary, but as many as 40,000 people may be imprisoned under these conditions, and new supermax prisons continue to be built.

There is, of course, considerable variation in prison regimes within the USA. A recent report by the Committee on Safety and Abuse in America's prisons gives a comprehensive picture of the problems of the system, and describes some of the more humane systems and practices.[260] A health care initiative in Massachusetts provides continuity of care for prisoners within prison and in the community after their release. Maryland has an exemplary programme for screening inmates for mental illness. Vermont ensures that prisoners have access to low-cost telephone calls to maintain their contacts with the outside world. And in Minnesota there is a high-security prison that emphasizes human contact, natural light and sensory stimulation, regular exercise and the need to treat inmates with dignity and respect. If you look back at Figure 11.2, you can see that most of these examples come from among the more equal US states.

Not only do the higher rates of imprisonment in more unequal societies seem to reflect more punitive sentencing rather than crime rates, but both the harshness of the prison systems and use of capital punishment point in the same direction.

DOES PRISON WORK?

Perhaps a high rate of imprisonment, and a harsh system for dealing with criminals would seem worthwhile if prison worked to deter crime and protect the public.* Instead, the consensus among experts worldwide seems to be that it doesn't work very well.[261-4] Prison

---

*John Irwin writes that while imprisonment is generally believed to have four 'official' purposes – retribution for crimes committed, deterrence, incapacitation of dangerous criminals and the rehabilitation of criminals, in fact three other purposes have shaped America's rates and conditions of imprisonment. These 'unofficial'

psychiatrist James Gilligan says that the *most effective way to turn a non-violent person into a violent one is to send him to prison*.[201, p. 117] In fact, imprisonment doesn't seem to work as well now as it used to in the US: parole violation and repeat offending are an increasing factor in the growth of imprisonment rates. Between 1980 and 1996, prison admissions for parole violations rose from 18 per cent to 35 per cent.[238] Long sentences seem to be less of a deterrent than higher conviction rates, and the longer someone is incarcerated, the harder it is for them to adapt to life outside. Gilligan says that:

the criminal justice and penal systems have been operating under a huge mistake, namely, the belief that punishment will deter, prevent or inhibit violence, when in fact it is the most powerful stimulant of violence that we have yet discovered.[201, p. 116]

Some efforts to use punishment systems to deter crime are not just ineffective, they actually increase crime. In the UK, the introduction of Anti-Social Behaviour Orders (ASBOs) for delinquent youths has been controversial, partly because they can criminalize behaviour that is otherwise lawful, but also because the acquisition of an ASBO has come to be seen as a rite of passage and badge of honour among some young people.[265-6]

Although there seems to be a growing consensus among experts that prison doesn't work, it is difficult to find good, comparable data on re-offending rates in different countries. If a country imprisons a smaller proportion of its citizens, these are more likely to be hardened criminals than those imprisoned under a harsher regime. So we might expect countries with lower overall rates of imprisonment to have higher rates of re-offending. In fact, there appears to be a trend towards higher rates of re-offending in more punitive systems (in the USA and UK, re-offending rates are generally reported to be between 60 and 65 per cent) and lower rates in

---

purposes are *class control* – the need to protect honest middle-class citizens from the dangerous criminal underclass; *scapegoating* – diverting attention away from more serious social problems (and here he singles out growing inequalities in wealth and income); and using the threat of the dangerous class for *political gain*.[256]

less harsh environments (Sweden and Japan are reported to have recidivism rates between 35 and 40 per cent).

HARDENING ATTITUDES

We've seen that imprisonment rates are not determined by crime rates so much as by differences in official attitudes towards punishment versus rehabilitation and reform. In societies with greater inequality, where the social distances between people are greater, where attitudes of 'us and them' are more entrenched and where lack of trust and fear of crime are rife, public and policy makers alike are more willing to imprison people and adopt punitive attitudes towards the 'criminal elements' of society. More unequal societies are harsher, tougher places. And as prison is not particularly effective for either deterrence or rehabilitation, then a society must only be willing to maintain a high rate (and high cost) of imprisonment for reasons unrelated to effectiveness.

Societies that imprison more people also spend less of their wealth on welfare for their citizens. This is true of the US states and also of OECD countries.[267-8] Criminologists David Downes and Kirstine Hansen report that this phenomenon of 'penal expansion and welfare contraction' has become more pronounced over the past couple of decades. In his book *Crime and Punishment in America*, published in 1998, sociologist Elliott Currie points out that, since 1984, the state of California built only one new college but twenty-one new prisons.[264] In more unequal societies, money is diverted away from positive spending on welfare, education, etc., into the criminal and judicial systems. Among our group of rich countries, there is a significant correlation between income inequality and the number of police and internal security officers per 100,000 people.[212] Sweden employs 181 police per 100,000 people, while Portugal has 450.

Our impression is that, in more equal countries and societies, legal and judicial systems, prosecution procedures and sentencing, as well as penal systems, are developed in consultation with experts – criminologists, lawyers, prison psychiatrists and psychologists, etc., and so reflect both theoretical and evidence-based considerations of what works to deter crime and rehabilitate offenders. In contrast, more unequal countries and states seem to have developed legal frameworks and penal systems in response to media and political pressure, a desire to get tough on crime and be seen to be doing so, rather than on a considered reflection on what works and what doesn't. John Silverman, writing for the UK's Economic and Social Research Council, says that prisons are effective only 'as a means of answering a sustained media battering with an apparent show of force'.[269] In conclusion, Downes and Hanson deserve to be quoted in full:[268, pp. 4-5]

A growing fear of crime and loss of confidence in the criminal justice system among the population, ... made the general public more favourable towards harsh criminal justice policies. Thus, in certain countries, in particular the United States and to a lesser extent the United Kingdom – public demand for tougher and longer sentences has been met by public policy and election campaigns which have been fought and won on the grounds of the punitiveness of penal policy. In other countries, such as Sweden and Finland, where the government provides greater 'insulation against emotions generated by moral panic and long-term cycles of tolerance and intolerance' (Tonry, 1999),[270] citizens have been less likely to call for, and to support, harsher penal policies and the government has resisted the urge to implement such plans.

12

Social mobility: unequal opportunities

All the people like us are We, and every one else is
They.   Rudyard Kipling, *We and They*

In some historical and modern societies, social mobility has been virtually impossible. Where social status is determined by religious or legal systems, such as the Hindu caste system, the feudal systems of medieval Europe, or slavery, there is little or no opportunity for people to move up or down the social ladder. But in modern market democracies, people can move up or down within their lifetime (*intra-generational* mobility) or offspring can move up and down relative to their parents (*inter-generational* mobility). The possibility of social mobility is what we mean when we talk about equality of opportunity: the idea that anybody, by their own merits and hard work, can achieve a better social or economic position for themselves and their family. Unlike greater equality itself, equality of opportunity is valued across the political spectrum, at least in theory. Even if they do nothing to actively promote social mobility, very few politicians would take a public stance against equal opportunity. So how mobile are our rich market democracies?

It's not easy to measure social mobility in societies. Doing so requires longitudinal data – studies that track people over time to see where they started from and where they end up. One convenient way is to take *income mobility* as a measure of social mobility: to see how much people's incomes change over their lifetimes, or how much they earn in comparison to their parents. To measure

inter-generational mobility these longitudinal studies need to cover periods of as much as thirty years, in order for the offspring to establish their position in the income hierarchy. When we have income data for parents and offspring, social mobility can be measured as the correlation between the two. If the correlation between parent's income and child's income is high, that means that rich parents tend to have children who are also rich, and poor parents tend to have children who stay poor. When the correlation is low, children's income is less influenced by whether their parents were rich or poor. (These comparisons are not affected by the fact that average incomes are now higher than they used to be.)

LIKE FATHER, LIKE SON?

Comparable international data on inter-generational social mobility are available for only a few of our rich countries. We take our figures from a study by economist Jo Blanden and colleagues at the London School of Economics.[271] Using large, representative longitudinal studies for eight countries, these researchers were able to calculate social mobility as the correlation between fathers' incomes when their sons were born and sons' incomes at age thirty. Despite having data for only eight countries, the relationship between inter-generational social mobility and income inequality is very strong. Figure 12.1 shows that countries with bigger income differences tend to have much lower social mobility. In fact, far from enabling the ideology of the American Dream, the USA has the lowest mobility rate among these eight countries. The UK also has low social mobility, West Germany comes in the middle, and Canada and the Scandinavian countries have much higher mobility.

With data for so few countries we need to be cautious, particularly as there are no data of this sort that allow us to estimate social mobility for each state and test the relationship with inequality independently in the USA. But other observations, looking at changes in social mobility over time, public spending on education, changes in geographical segregation, the work of sociologists on matters of taste and psychologists on displaced aggression, and so-called group

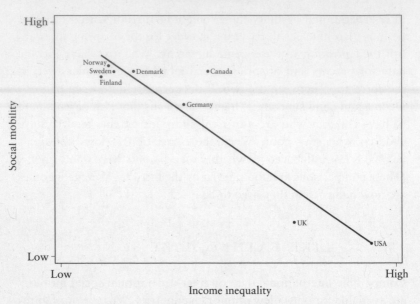

Figure 12.1 *Social mobility is lower in more unequal countries.*[149]

density effects on health, lend plausibility to the picture we see in Figure 12.1.

The first of these observations is that, after slowly increasing from 1950 to 1980, social mobility in the USA declined rapidly, as income differences widened dramatically in the later part of the century.

Figure 12.2 uses data from *The State of Working America 2006/7* report. The height of each column shows the power of fathers' income to determine the income of their sons, so *shorter* bars indicate more social mobility: fathers' incomes are less predictive of sons' incomes. Higher bars indicate less mobility: rich fathers are more likely to have rich sons and poor fathers to have poor sons.

.Data from the 1980s and 1990s show that about 36 per cent of children whose parents were in the bottom fifth of the wealth distribution end up in that same bottom fifth themselves as adults, and among children whose parents were in the top fifth for wealth, 36 per cent of them can be found in the same top fifth.[272] Those at the top can maintain their wealth and status, those at the bottom

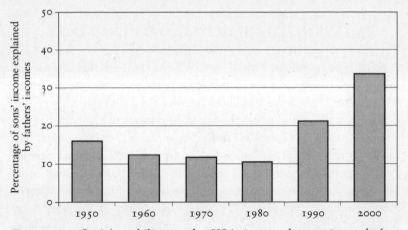

Figure 12.2 *Social mobility in the USA increased to 1980 and then decreased.*[272]

find it difficult to climb up the income ladder, but there is more flexibility in the middle. Inter-generational social mobility has also been falling in Britain over the time period that income differences have widened.[271]

A second observation that supports our belief that greater income inequality reduces social mobility comes from data on spending on education. Education is generally thought of as the main engine of social mobility in modern democracies – people with more education earn more and have higher social status. We saw in Chapter 8 how inequality affects educational achievements and aspirations, but it's worth noting that, among the eight countries for which we have information about social mobility, public expenditure on education (elementary/primary and high/secondary schools) is strongly linked to the degree of income equality. In Norway, the most equal of the eight, almost all (97.8 per cent) spending on school education is public expenditure.[273] In contrast, in the USA, the least equal of this group of countries, only about two-thirds (68.2 per cent) of the spending on school education is public money. This is likely to have a substantial impact on social differences in access to higher education.

MOVING UPWARDS, MOVING OUT

A third type of evidence that may confirm the correlation between income inequality and social mobility is the way in which greater social distances become translated into greater geographical segregation between rich and poor in more unequal societies.

As inequality has increased since the 1970s in the USA, so too has the geographical segregation of rich and poor.[274] Political economist Paul Jargowsky has analysed data from the 1970, 1980 and 1990 US Census and shown that the residential *concentration of poverty* increased over that period.[275-6] Neighbourhood concentration of poverty is a measure that tells us what proportion of poor people in a city live in high-poverty areas. Jargowsky estimates that in 1970 about one in four poor blacks lived in high-poverty neighbourhoods, but by 1990 that proportion had risen to one in three. Among whites, poverty concentration doubled during the two decades, while income differences were widening. When poverty concentration is high, poor people are not only coping with their own poverty but also the consequences of the poverty of their neighbours. Between the 1990 and the 2000 census, Jargowsky reports a decline in poverty concentration, particularly for black Americans in the inner cities, which goes along with the improvements in the relative position of the very poorest Americans which we described at the end of Chapter 10.[277] Even as poverty concentration has declined in the inner city, though, it has grown in the inner ring of suburbs and, with the recent economic downturn in America, Jargowsky warns that the gains of the 1990s may have already been reversed.

A similar pattern of segregation by poverty and wealth during a period of increasing income differences has been taking place in the UK.[278] The rich are willing to pay to live separately from the poor,[279] and residential segregation along economic lines increased throughout the 1980s and 1990s.[280] The image of the 'sink estate' provokes just as clear a picture of a deprived underclass as does the image of the ghetto and the barrio in the USA.

Researchers on both sides of the Atlantic are clear that increased income inequality is responsible for increasing the segregation of rich and poor.[281-3] The concentration of poor people in poor areas increases all kinds of stress, deprivation and difficulty – from increased commuting times for those who have to leave deprived communities to find work elsewhere, to increased risk of traffic accidents, worse schools, poor levels of services, exposure to gang violence, pollution and so on. Sociologist William Julius Wilson, in his classic study of inner-city poverty, refers to poor people in poor neighbourhoods as the 'truly disadvantaged'.[225] Two studies from the USA have shown that residential economic segregation increases people's risk of dying, and one showed that more unequal cities were also more economically segregated.[284-5] These processes will of course feed back into further reductions in social mobility.

MATTERS OF TASTE – AND CULTURE

So social mobility is lower and geographical segregation greater in more unequal societies. It is as if greater inequality makes the social structure of society more rigid and movement up and down the social ladder more difficult.

The work of French sociologist Pierre Bourdieu also helps us to understand how social mobility becomes more limited within more hierarchical societies.[286] He describes how material differences between people, the amount of money and resources they have, become overlaid with cultural markers of social difference, which become matters of snobbery and prejudice. We all use matters of taste as marks of distinction and social class – we judge people by their accent, clothing, language, choice of reading matter, the television programmes they watch, the food they eat, the sports they play, the music they prefer, and their appreciation – or lack of it – of art.

Middle-class and upper-class people have the right accents, know how to behave in 'polite society', know that education can enhance their advantages. They pass all of this on to their children, so that they in turn will succeed in school and work, make good marriages, find high-paying jobs, etc. This is how elites become established and maintain their elite status.

People can use markers of distinction and class, their 'good taste', to maintain their position, but throughout the social hierarchy people also use discrimination and downward prejudice to prevent those below them from improving their status. Despite the modern ideology of equality of opportunity, these matters of taste and class still keep people in their place – stopping them from believing they can better their position and sapping their confidence if they try. The experiments on stereotype threat described in Chapter 8 show how strong the effects on performance can be. Bourdieu calls the actions by which the elite maintain their distinction *symbolic violence*; we might just as easily call them discrimination and snobbery. Although racial prejudice is widely condemned, class prejudice is, despite the similarities, rarely mentioned.

These social systems of taste, which define what is highbrow and cultured, and what is lowbrow or popular, constantly shift in content but are always with us. The examples that Bourdieu collected in the 1960s seem very dated now, but illustrate the point. He found that different social class groups preferred different types of music; the lower social class groups preferred the catchy tune of the 'Blue Danube', while the upper classes expressed a preference for the more 'difficult' 'Well-Tempered Clavier'. The upper classes preferred abstract art and experimental novels, while the lower classes liked representational pictures and a good plot. But if everybody starts to enjoy Bach and Picasso and James Joyce, then upper-class taste will shift to appreciate something new – elitism is maintained by shifting the boundaries. What Bourdieu is describing is an 'economy of cultural goods', and inequalities in that economy affect people almost as profoundly as inequalities in income.

In her book, *Watching the English*, anthropologist Kate Fox describes the social class markers of the English – in conversation, homes, cars, clothes, food and more.[287] Joseph Epstein does the same for the USA in *Snobbery: The American Version*.[288] Both books are amusing, as well as erudite, and it's difficult not to laugh at our own pretensions and the poor taste of others.

In the UK, for example, you can tell if someone is working class, middle class or upper class by whether they call their evening meal 'tea', 'dinner' or 'supper'. By whether they call their mother 'mam', 'mum' or 'mummy', by whether they go out to a 'do', a 'function' or a 'party', and so on.

Snobbery, says Epstein, is 'sitting in your BMW 740i and feeling quietly, assuredly better than the poor vulgarian ... who pulls up next to you at the stoplight in his garish Cadillac. It is the calm pleasure with which you greet the news that the son of the woman you have just been introduced to is majoring in photojournalism at Arizona State University while your own daughter is studying art history at Harvard ...' But snobbishness and taste turn out to be a zero-sum game. Epstein goes on to point out that another day, at another stoplight, a Bentley will pull up next to your pathetic BMW, and you may be introduced to a woman whose son is studying classics at Oxford.

The ways in which class and taste and snobbery work to constrain people's opportunities and wellbeing are, in reality, painful and pervasive. They are forms of discrimination and social exclusion. In their 1972 book, *The Hidden Injuries of Class*, sociologists Richard Sennett and Jonathan Cobb described the psychological damage done to working-class men in Boston, who had come to view their failures to get on in the world as a result of their own inadequacies, resulting in feelings of hostility, resentment and shame.[289] More recently, sociologist Simon Charlesworth, in an interview with a working-class man in Rotherham, in the English Midlands, is told how ashamed the man feels encountering a middle-class woman.[290] Even without anything being said between them, he is immediately filled with a sense of his inferiority, becomes self-conscious and eventually hostile and angry:

I went in to the social [Social Security Office] the other day ... there were chairs and a space next to this stuck-up cow, you know, slim, attractive, middle class, and I didn't want to sit with her, you feel you shouldn't ... I became all conscious, of my weight, I felt overweight, I start sweating, I start bungling, shuffling, I just thought 'no, I'm not going to sit there, I don't want to put her out', I don't want to feel that she's put out, you don't want to bother them ... you know you insult them ... the way they look at you like they're disgusted ... they look at you like you're invading their area ... you know, straight away ... you feel 'I shouldn't be there'

... it makes you not want to go out. What it is, it's a form of violence ... right, it's like a barrier saying 'listen low-life, don't even [*voice rises with pain and anger*] come near me! ... 'What the fuck are you doing in my space ... We pay to get away from scum like you ... It fucking stresses you, you get exhausted ... It's everywhere ... I mean, I clocked her [*looked at her*] like they clock us, right, ... and I thought 'fuck me, I ain't even sitting there'. She would be uncomfortable, and it'll embarrass me, you know, [*voice rises in anger/pain.*] ... Just sitting there, you know what I'm trying to say? ... It's like a common understanding, you know how they feel, *you feel* it, I'm telling you ... They are fuck all, they've got nothing, but it's that air about them you know, they've got the right body, the clothes and everything, the confidence, the attitude, know what I mean.... We [*sadly, voice drops*] ain't got it, we can't have it. We walk in like we've been beaten, dragging our feet when we're walking in ... you feel like you want to hide ...

THE BICYCLING REACTION

Bigger differences in material wealth make status differences more important, and in more unequal societies the weight of downward prejudice is bound to be heavier; there is more social distance between the 'haves' at the very top and the 'have-nots' at the bottom. In effect, greater inequality increases downward social prejudices. We maintain social status by showing superiority to those below. Those deprived of status try to regain it by taking it out on more vulnerable people below them. Two lines of doggerel capture these processes. The English say 'The captain kicks the cabin boy and the cabin boy kicks the cat', describing the downward flow of aggression and resentment, while a line from an American rhyme famously describes Boston as the place, 'where the Lowells talk only to Cabots, and the Cabots talk only to God', invoking the snobbery and social climbing of people looking up to those above them.

When people react to a provocation from someone with higher status by redirecting their aggression on to someone of lower status, psychologists label it *displaced aggression*.[291] Examples include: the man who is berated by his boss and comes home and shouts at his wife and children; the higher degree of aggression in workplaces where supervisors treat workers unfairly;[292] the ways in which people in deprived communities react to an influx of foreign immigrants;[293-4] and the ways in which prisoners who are bullied turn on others below them – particularly sex offenders – in the prison hierarchy.[295]

In his book, *The Hot House*, which describes life inside a high-security prison in the US, Pete Earley tells a story about a man in prison with a life sentence for murder.[296, pp. 74-5] Bowles had been incarcerated for the first time at the age of 15 when he was sent to a juvenile reformatory. The day he arrived, an older, bigger boy came up to him:

'Hey, what size shoes do you wear?' the boy asked.

'Don't know' said Bowles

'Let me see one of 'em will ya?' the boy asked politely.

Bowles sat down on the floor and removed a shoe. The older boy took off one of his own shoes and put on Bowles's.

'How 'bout letting me see the other one?'

'I took off my other shoe and handed it to him,' Bowles remembered, 'and he puts it on and ties it and then walks over to this table and every boy in the place starts laughing at me.

That's when I realized I am the butt of the joke.'

Bowles grabbed a pool cue and attacked the boy, for which he received a week of hard labour. When a new boy arrived at the reformatory the following week, 'he too was confronted by a boy who demanded his shoes. Only this time it was Bowles who was taking advantage of the new kid. "It was my turn to dish it out," he recalled. "I had earned that right."'

In the same book, Earley tells almost exactly the same story again, only this time he describes a man's reaction to being sexually assaulted and sodomized on his first night in a county jail at the age of 16. Six years later, arrested in another town, he is put in a jail cell with a 'kid, probably seventeen or so, and you know what I did? I fucked him.'[296, pp. 430-31]

Displaced aggression among non-human primates has been labelled 'the bicycling reaction'. Primatologist Volker Summer explains that the image being conjured up is of someone on a racing bicycle, bowing to their superiors, while kicking down on those beneath. He was describing how animals living in strict social hierarchies appease dominant animals and attack inferior ones. Psychologists Jim Sidanius and Felicia Pratto have suggested that human group conflict and oppression, such as racism and sexism, stem from the way in which inequality gives rise to individual and institutional discrimination and the degree to which people are complicit or resistant to some social groups being dominant over others.[297] In more unequal societies, more people are oriented towards dominance; in more egalitarian societies, more people are oriented towards inclusiveness and empathy.

Our final piece of evidence that income inequality causes lower social mobility comes from research which helps to explain why stigmatized groups of people living in more unequal societies can feel more comfortable when separated from the people who look down on them. In a powerful illustration of how discrimination and prejudice damage people's wellbeing, research shows that the health of ethnic minority groups who live in areas with more people like themselves is sometimes better than that of their more affluent counterparts who live in areas with more of the dominant ethnic group.[298] This is called a 'group density' effect, and was first shown in relation to mental illness. Studies in London, for example, have shown a higher incidence of schizophrenia among ethnic minorities living in neighbourhoods with fewer people like themselves,[299] and the same has been shown for suicide[300] and self-harm.[301] More recently, studies in the United States have demonstrated the same effects for heart disease[302-3] and low birthweight.[304-8] Generally, living in a poorer area is associated with worse health. Members of ethnic minorities who live in areas where there are few like themselves tend to be more affluent, and to live in better neighbourhoods, than those who live in areas with a higher concentration. So to find that these more ethnically isolated individuals are sometimes less healthy is surprising. The probable explanation is that, through the eyes of the majority community, they become more aware of belonging to a low-status minority group and perhaps encounter more frequent prejudice and discrimination and have less support. That the psychological effects of stigma are sometimes strong enough to override the health benefits of material advantage tells us a lot about the power of inequality and brings us back to the importance of social status, social support and friendship, and the influence of social anxiety and stigma discussed in Chapter 3.

Bigger income differences seem to solidify the social structure and decrease the chances of upward mobility. Where there are greater inequalities of outcome, equal opportunity is a significantly more distant prospect.

PART THREE

A Better Society

"IT GOES IN CYCLES, JUNIOR. SOMETIMES, THE RICH GET RICHER AND THE POOR GET POORER. SOMETIMES, THE RICH GET RICHER AND THE POOR STAY THE SAME."

13

Dysfunctional societies

No man is an Island, entire of itself; every man is a piece of
the continent, a part of the main.

John Donne, *Meditation XVII*

The last nine chapters have shown, among the rich developed
countries and among the fifty states of the United States, that
most of the important health and social problems of the rich world
are more common in more unequal societies. In both settings the
relationships are too strong to be dismissed as chance findings. The
importance of these relationships can scarcely be overestimated.
First, the differences between more and less equal societies are large
– problems are anything from three times to ten times as common in
the more unequal societies. Second, these differences are not differences between high- and low-risk groups within populations which
might apply only to a small proportion of the population, or just to
the poor. Rather, they are differences between the prevalence of
different problems which apply to whole populations.

DYSFUNCTIONAL SOCIETIES

One of the points which emerge from Chapters 4–12 is a tendency
for some countries to do well on just about everything and others to
do badly. You can predict a country's performance on one outcome
from a knowledge of others. If – for instance – a country does badly
on health, you can predict with some confidence that it will also

imprison a larger proportion of its population, have more teenage pregnancies, lower literacy scores, more obesity, worse mental health, and so on. Inequality seems to make countries socially dysfunctional across a wide range of outcomes.

Internationally, at the healthy end of the distribution we always seem to find the Scandinavian countries and Japan. At the opposite end, suffering high rates of most of the health and social problems, are usually the USA, Portugal and the UK. The same is true among the fifty states of the USA. Among those that tend to perform well across the board are New Hampshire, Minnesota, North Dakota and Vermont, and among those which do least well are Mississippi, Louisiana and Alabama.

Figure 13.1 summarizes our findings. It is an exact copy of Figure 2.2. It shows again the relationship between inequality and our combined Index of Health and Social Problems. This graph also shows that the relationship is not dependent on any particular group of countries – for instance those at either end of the distribution.

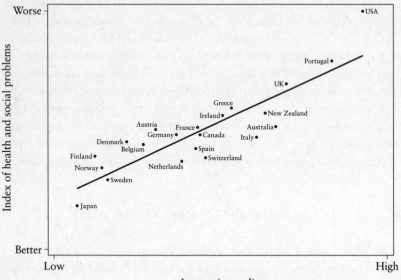

Figure 13.1 *Health and social problems are more common in more unequal countries.*

Instead it is robust across the range of inequality found in the developed market democracies. Even though we sometimes find less strong relationships among our analyses of the fifty US states, in the international analyses the USA as a whole is just where its inequality would lead us to expect.

Though some countries' figures are presumably more accurate than others, it is clearly important that we do not cherry-pick the data. That is why we have used the same set of inequality data, published by the United Nations, throughout. In the analyses of the American states we have used the US census data as published. However, even if someone had a strong objection to the figures for one or other society, it would clearly not change the overall picture presented in Figure 13.1. The same applies to the figures we use for all the health and social problems. Each set is as provided at source – we take them as published with no ifs or buts.

The only social problem we have encountered which tends to be more common in more equal countries (but not significantly among more equal states in the USA) is, perhaps surprisingly, suicide. The reasons for this are twofold. First, in some countries suicide is not more common lower down the social scale. In Britain a well-defined social gradient has only emerged in recent decades. Second, suicide is often inversely related to homicide. There seems to be something in the psychological cliché that anger sometimes goes in and sometimes goes out: do you blame yourself or others for things that go wrong? In Chapter 3 we noted the rise in the tendency to blame the outside world – defensive narcissism – and the contrasts between the US and Japan. It is notable that in a paper on health in Harlem in New York, suicide was the only cause of death which was less common there than in the rest of the USA.[80]

EVERYONE BENEFITS

A common response to research findings in the social sciences is for people to say they are obvious, and then perhaps to add a little scornfully, that there was no need to do all that expensive work to tell us what we already knew. Very often, however, that sense of knowing only seeps in with the benefit of hindsight, after research results have been made known. Try asking people to predict the results in advance and it is clear that all sorts of different things can seem perfectly plausible. Having looked at the evidence in the preceding chapters of how inequality is related to the prevalence of so many problems, we hope that most readers will feel the picture makes immediate intuitive sense. Indeed, it may seem obvious that problems associated with relative deprivation should be more common in more unequal societies. However, if you ask people why greater equality reduces these problems, much the most common guess is that it must be because more equal societies have fewer poor people. The assumption is that greater equality helps those at the bottom. As well as being only a minor part of the proper explanation, it is an assumption which reflects our failure to recognize very important processes affecting our lives and the societies we are part of. The truth is that the vast majority of the population is harmed by greater inequality.

One of the clues, and one which we initially found surprising, is just how big the differences between societies are in the rates of the various problems discussed in Chapters 4–12. Across *whole* populations, rates of mental illness are five times higher in the most unequal compared to the least unequal societies. Similarly, in more unequal societies people are five times as likely to be imprisoned, six times as likely to be clinically obese, and murder rates may be many times higher. The reason why these differences are so big is, quite simply, because the effects of inequality are not confined just to the least well-off: instead they affect the vast majority of the population. To take an example, the reason why life expectancy is 4.5 years shorter for the average American than it is for the average Japanese, is not primarily because the poorest 10 per cent of Americans suffer a life expectancy deficit ten times as large (i.e., forty-five years) while the rest of the population does as well as the Japanese. As epidemiologist Michael Marmot frequently points out, you could take away all the health problems of the poor and still leave most of the problem of health inequalities untouched. Or, to look at it another way, even if you take the death rates just of white Americans, they still do worse – as we shall see in a moment – than the populations of most other developed countries.

Comparisons of health in different groups of the population in more and less equal societies show that the benefits of greater equality are very widespread. Most recently, a study in the *Journal of the American Medical Association* compared health among middle-aged men in the USA and England (not the whole UK).[315] To increase comparability the study was confined to the non-Hispanic white populations in both countries. People were divided into both income and educational categories. In Figure 13.2 rates of diabetes, hypertension, cancer, lung disease and heart disease are shown in each of three educational categories – high, medium and low. The American rates are the darker bars in the background and those for England are the lighter ones in front. There is a consistent tendency for rates of these conditions to be higher in the US than in England, not just among the less well-educated, but across all educational levels. The same was also true of death rates and various biological markers such as blood pressure, cholesterol and stress measures.

Though this is only just apparent, the authors of the study say that the social class differences in health tend to be steeper in the USA than in England regardless of whether people are classified by income or education.[316]

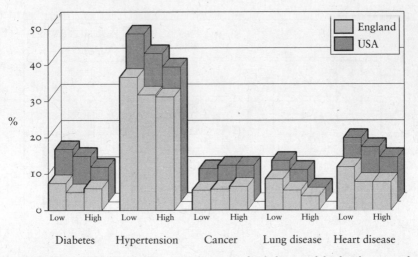

Figure 13.2 *Rates of illness are lower at both low and high educational levels in England compared to the USA.*[315]

In that comparison, England was the more equal and the healthier of the two countries. But there have also been similar comparisons of death rates in Sweden with those in England and Wales. To allow accurate comparisons, Swedish researchers classified a large number of Swedish deaths according to the British occupational class classification. The classification runs from unskilled manual occupations in class V at the bottom, to professional occupations in class I at the top. Figure 13.3 shows the differences they found in death rates for working-age men.[317] Sweden, as the more equal of the two countries, had lower death rates in all occupational classes; so much so that their highest death rates – in the lowest classes – are lower than the highest class in England and Wales.

Another similar study compared infant mortality rates in Sweden with England and Wales.[318] Infant deaths were classified by father's occupation and occupations were again coded the same way in each country. The results are shown in Figure 13.4. Deaths of babies born to single parents, which cannot be coded by father's occupation, are shown separately. Once again, the Swedish death rates are lower right across the society. (Note that as both these studies were published some time ago, the actual death rates they show are considerably higher than the current ones.)

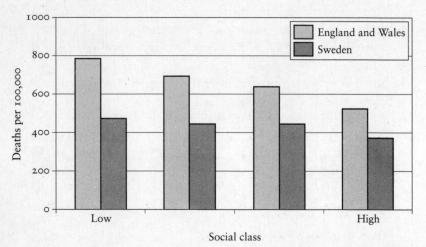

Figure 13.3 *Death rates among working-age men are lower in all occupational classes in Sweden compared to England and Wales.*[317]

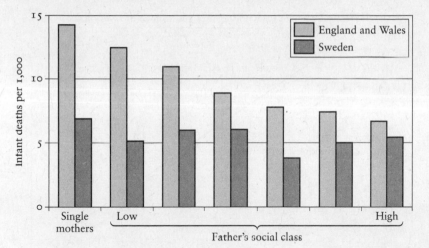

Figure 13.4 *Infant mortality rates are lower in all occupational classes in Sweden than in England and Wales.*[318]

Comparisons have also been made between the more and less equal of the fifty states of the USA. Here too the benefits of smaller income differences in the more equal states seem to spread across all income groups. One study concluded that 'income inequality exerts a comparable effect across all population subgroups', whether people are classified by education, race or income – so much so that the authors suggested that inequality acted like a pollutant spread throughout society.[319] In a study of our own, we looked at the relationship between median county income and death rates in all counties of the USA.[8] We compared the relationship between county median income and county death rates according to whether the counties were in the twenty-five more equal states or the twenty-five less equal states. As Figure 13.5 shows, in both the more and less equal states, poorer counties tended – as expected – to have higher death rates. However at all levels of income, death rates were lower in the twenty-five more equal states than in the twenty-five less equal states. Comparing counties at each level of income showed that the benefits of greater equality were largest in the poorer counties, but still existed even in the richest counties. In its essentials the picture is much like that shown in Figures 13.3 and 13.4 comparing Sweden

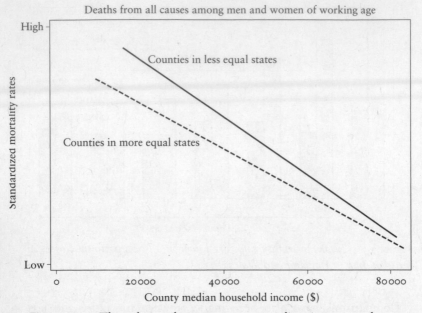

Figure 13.5 *The relation between county median income and county death rates according to whether the counties are in the twenty-five more equal states or the twenty-five less equal states.*

with England and Wales. Just as among US counties, where the benefits of greater state equality extended to all income groups, so the benefits of Sweden's greater equality extended across all classes, but were biggest in the lowest classes.

Figure 8.4 in Chapter 8, which compared young people's literacy scores across different countries according to their parents' level of education (and so indirectly according to the social status of their family of upbringing) also showed that the benefits of greater equality extend throughout society. In more equal Finland and Belgium the benefits of greater equality were, once again, bigger at the bottom of the social ladder than in less equal UK and USA. But even the children of parents with the very highest levels of education did better in Finland and Belgium than they did in the more unequal UK or USA.

A question which is often asked is whether even the rich benefit from greater equality. Perhaps, as John Donne said, 'No man is an Island' even from the effects of inequality. The evidence we have been discussing typically divides the population into three or four income or educational groups, or occasionally (as in Figure 13.4) into six occupational classes. In those analyses it looks as if even the richest groups do benefit. But if, when we talk of 'the rich', we mean millionaires, celebrities, people in the media, running large businesses or making the news, we can only guess how they might be affected. We might feel we live in a world peopled by faces and names which keep cropping up in the media, but such people actually make up only a tiny fraction of 1 per cent of the population and they are just too small a proportion of the population to look at separately. Without data on such a small minority we can only guess whether or not they are likely to escape the increased violence, drugs or mental illness of more unequal societies. The lives and deaths of celebrities such as Britney Spears, John Lennon, Kurt Cobain, Marilyn Monroe, the assassinated Kennedy brothers, Princess Diana or Princess Margaret, suggest they might not. What the studies do make clear, however, is that greater equality brings substantial gains even in the top occupational class and among the richest or best-educated quarter or third of the population, which include the small minority of the seriously rich. In short, whether we look at states or countries, the benefits of greater equality seem to be shared across the vast majority of the population. Only because the benefits of greater equality are so widely shared can the differences in the rates of problems between societies be as large as it is.

As the research findings have come in over the years, the widespread nature of the benefits of greater equality seemed at first so paradoxical that they called everything into question. Several attempts by international collaborative groups to compare health inequalities in different countries suggested that health inequalities did not differ very much from one country to another. This seemed inconsistent with the evidence that health was better in more equal societies. How could greater equality improve health unless it did so by narrowing the health differences between rich and poor? At the time this seemed a major stumbling block. Now, however, we can see how the two sets of findings are consistent. Smaller income differences improve health for everyone, but make a bigger difference to the health of the poor than the rich. If smaller income differences lead to roughly the same percentage reduction in death rates across the whole society then, when measured in relative terms, the differences in death rates between rich and poor will remain unchanged. Suppose death rates are 60 per 100,000 people in the bottom class and only 20 per 100,000 in the top one. If you then knock 50 per cent off death rates in all groups, you will have reduced the death rate by 30 in the bottom group and by 10 at the top. But although the poor have had much the biggest absolute decline in death rates, there is still a threefold relative class difference in death rates. Whatever the percentage reduction in death rates, as long as it applies right across society, it will make most difference to the poor but still leave relative measures of the difference unchanged.

We can now see that the studies which once looked paradoxical were in fact telling us something important about the effects of greater equality. By suggesting that more and less equal societies contained similar relative health differentials within them, they were telling us that everyone receives roughly proportional benefits from greater equality. There are now several studies of this issue using data for US states,[8, 319, 320] and at least five international ones, which provide consistent evidence that, rather than being confined to the poor, the benefits of greater equality are widely spread.[152, 315, 317, 318, 321]

OTHER EXPLANATIONS?

It is clear that there is something which affects how well or badly societies do across a wide range of social problems, but how sure can we be that it is inequality? Before discussing whether inequality plays a causal role, let us first see whether there might be any quite different explanations.

Although people have occasionally suggested that it is the English-speaking countries which do badly, that doesn't explain much of the evidence. For example, take mental health, where the worst performers among the countries for which there is comparable data are English-speaking. In Chapter 5 we showed that the highest rates are in the USA, followed in turn by Australia, UK, New Zealand and Canada. But even among those countries there is a very strong correlation between the prevalence of mental illness and inequality. So inequality explains why English-speaking countries do badly, *and* it explains which ones do better or worse than others.

Nor is it just the USA and Britain, two countries which do have a lot in common, which do badly on most outcomes. Portugal also does badly. Its poor performance is consistent with its high levels of inequality, but Portugal and the USA could hardly be less alike in other respects. However, the proof that these relationships are not simply a reflection of something wrong with English-speaking cultures is that even if you delete them from Figure 13.1 (p. 174) there is still a close relationship between inequality and the Index of Health and Social Problems among the remaining countries. The same applies to the dominance of the Nordic countries at the other end of the distribution. They clearly share some important cultural characteristics. But, like the English speaking countries, if you delete them from Figure 13.1, a strong relationship remains between inequality and the Index among the remaining countries.

Although that puts paid to the only obvious cultural explanations, it's worth pointing out some interesting contrasts between countries. For example, although Portugal does badly, Spain fares at least as well as the average – despite the fact that they share a border, they lived under dictators until the mid 1970s, and have many other cultural similarities. Yet all that seems to be trumped by the differences in inequality. The country which does best of all is Japan, but Japan is, in other respects, as different as it could be from Sweden, which is the next best performer. Think of the contrasting family structures and the position of women in Japan and Sweden. In both cases these two countries come at opposite ends of the spectrum. Sweden has a very high proportion of births outside marriage and women are almost equally represented in politics. In Japan the opposite is true. There is a similar stark contrast between the proportion of women in paid employment in the two countries. Even how they get their greater equality is quite different. Sweden does it through redistributive taxes and benefits and a large welfare state. As a proportion of national income, public social expenditure in Japan is, in contrast to

Sweden, among the lowest of the major developed countries. Japan gets its high degree of equality not so much from redistribution as from a greater equality of market incomes, of earnings *before* taxes and benefits. Yet despite the differences, both countries do well – as their narrow income differences, but almost nothing else, would lead us to expect.

This leads us to another important point: greater equality can be gained either by using taxes and benefits to redistribute very unequal incomes or by greater equality in gross incomes before taxes and benefits, which leaves less need for redistribution. So big government may not always be necessary to gain the advantages of a more equal society. The same applies to other areas of government expenditure. For countries in our international analysis, we collected OECD figures on public social expenditure as a proportion of Gross Domestic Product and found it entirely unrelated to our Index of Health and Social Problems. Perhaps rather counter-intuitively, it also made no difference to the association between inequality and the Index. Part of the reason for this is that governments may spend either to prevent social problems or, where income differences have widened, to deal with the consequences.

Examples of these contrasting routes to greater equality which we have seen in the international data can also be found among the fifty states of the USA. Although the states which perform well are dominated by ones which have more generous welfare provisions, the state which performs best is New Hampshire, which has among the lowest public social expenditure of any state. Like Japan, it appears to get its high degree of equality through an unusual equality of market incomes. Research using data for US states which tried to see whether better welfare services explained the better performance of more equal states found that although – in the US setting – services appear to make a difference, they do not account fully for why more equal states do so much better.[309] The really important implication is that how a society becomes more equal is less important than whether or not it actually does so.

ETHNICITY AND INEQUALITY

People sometimes wonder whether ethnic divisions in societies account for the relationship between inequality and the higher frequency of health and social problems. There are two reasons for thinking that there might be a link. First is the idea that some ethnic groups are inherently less capable and more likely to have problems. This must be rejected because it is simply an expression of racial prejudice. The other, more serious, possibility is that minorities often do worse because they are excluded from the educational and job opportunities needed to do well. In this view, prejudice against minorities might cause ethnic divisions to be associated with bigger income differences and, flowing from this, also with worse health and more frequent social problems. This would, however, produce a relation between income inequality and worse scores on our index through very much the same processes as are responsible for the relationship wherever it occurs. Ethnic divisions may increase social exclusion and discrimination, but ill-health and social problems become more common the greater the relative deprivation people experience – whatever their ethnicity.

People nearer the bottom of society almost always face downward discrimination and prejudice. There are of course important differences between what is seen as class prejudice in societies without ethnic divisions, and as racial prejudice where there are. Although the cultural marks of class are derived inherently from status differentiation, they are less indelible than differences in skin colour. But when differences in ethnicity, religion or language come to be seen as markers of low social status and attract various downward prejudices, social divisions and discrimination may increase.

In the USA, state income inequality is closely related to the proportion of African-Americans in the state's population. The states with wider income differences tend to be those with larger African-American populations. The same states also have worse outcomes – for instance for health – among both the black *and* the white population. The ethnic divide increases prejudice and so widens income differences. The result is that both communities suffer. Rather than whites enjoying greater privileges resulting from a larger and less well-paid black community, the consequence is that life expectancy is shorter among both black and white populations.

So the answer to the question as to whether what appear to be the effects of inequality may actually be the result of ethnic divisions is that the two involve most of the same processes and should not be seen as alternative explanations. The prejudice which often attaches to ethnic divisions may increase inequality and its effects. Where ethnic differences have become strongly associated with social status divisions, ethnic divisions may provide almost as good an indicator of the scale of social status differentiation as income inequality. In this situation it has been claimed that income differences are trumped, statistically speaking, by ethnic differences in the USA.[310] However, other papers examining this claim have rejected it.[311-13] The USA, with its ethnic divisions, is only one of a great many contexts in which the impact of income inequality has been tested. We reviewed 168 published reports of research examining the effect of inequality on health, and there are now around 200 in all.[10] In many of these (for example Portugal) there is no possibility that effects could be attributed to ethnic divisions. An international study which included a measure of each country's ethnic mix, found that it did not account for the tendency for more unequal societies to be less healthy.[314]

SINGLE PARENTS

As we noted near the beginning of this chapter, it is usually the same countries that do well and the same ones which do badly whatever health or social problems we look at. The fact that so many quite different problems share the same international pattern implies that they have a common underlying cause. The question is whether that common cause is inequality. Another alternative possibility is that these problems might all be rooted in the breakdown of the two-parent family as the unit in which children are brought up. There is a tendency to blame a wide range of social problems on bad parenting

– particularly resulting from the increased prevalence of single parents.

Data comparing children brought up in single parent families with those brought up by two parent families almost always shows that the children of single parents do less well. More controversial is the question of how much this reflects differences in mothers' education and maternal depression,[397] how much is due to the tendency for single parent families to be poorer, and how much results from less good parent-child relationships. Usually all these factors are found to make substantial contributions.

The proportion of parents who are single varies dramatically from one nation to another. In countries like Greece, only about 4 per cent of families with children are single parent families, but in others, like the USA, Britain and New Zealand, it rises to almost 30 per cent. Could this explain why children in some countries do less well than others? Rather than inequality, is the real issue the problems of single parenthood? To find out, we looked to see if the UNICEF index of child wellbeing was related to the proportion of parents who were single parents in each country. The surprising results are shown in Figure 13.6. There is no connection between the proportion of single parents and national standards of child wellbeing. This contrasts sharply with the strong relationship between child wellbeing and income inequality shown in Figure 2.6 (see p. 23).

That there is so little connection at the international level between child wellbeing and the proportion of single parents is probably partly a reflection of the extent to which welfare systems in some countries protect single parent families from poverty. Recent OECD figures suggest that only 6 per cent of Swedish single parents with jobs, and 18 per cent of those without, were in relative poverty, as against 36 and 92 per cent for the USA.[399] The figures for the UK are 7 per cent for single parents with jobs and 39 per cent for those without. The provision of childcare which enables single parents to work must also be important.

Given the political controversies around the provision of state support to single parents, two points are worth noting. First, that it seems to be possible to safeguard children against most of the adverse effects of being brought up by lone parents, and second, that

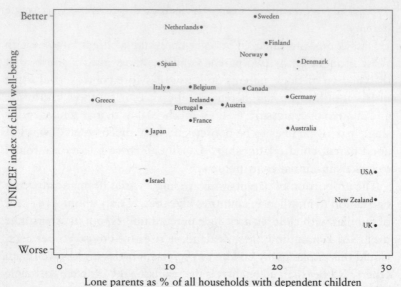

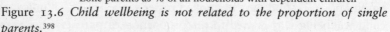

Lone parents as % of all households with dependent children

Figure 13.6 *Child wellbeing is not related to the proportion of single parents.*[398]

denying state support does not seem to reduce the proportion of single parents.

DIFFERENT HISTORIES

Another explanation sometimes suggested for why income inequality is related to health and social problems is that what matters is not the inequality itself, but the historical factors which led societies to become more or less equal in the first place – as if inequality stood, almost as a statistical monument, to a history of division. This is most often suggested in relation to the USA when people notice that the more unequal states are usually (but not always) the southern states of the Confederacy with their histories of plantation economies dependent on slave labour. However, the degree of equality or inequality in every setting has its own particular history. If we look to see how Sweden became more equal, or how Britain and a number of other countries have recently become much less so, or how the regions of Russia or China developed varying amounts of equality or inequality, we get different stories in every case. And of course these different backgrounds are important: there is no doubt that there are, in each case, specific historical explanations of why some countries, states or regions are now more or less unequal than others. But the prevalence of ill-health and of social problems in those societies is not simply a patternless reflection of so many unique histories. It is instead patterned according to the amount of inequality which has resulted from those unique histories. What seems to matter therefore is not *how* societies got to where they are now, but *where* – in terms of their level of inequality – it is that they have now got to.

That does not mean that these relations with inequality are set in stone for all time. What does change things is the stage of economic development a society has reached. In this book our focus is exclusively on the rich developed societies. But it is clear that a number of outcomes, including health and violence, are also related to inequality in less developed countries. What happens during the course of economic development is that some problems reverse their social gradients and this changes their associations with inequality. In poorer societies both obesity and heart disease are more common among the rich, but as societies get richer they tend to reverse their social distribution and become more common among the poor. As a result, we find that among poorer countries it is the more unequal ones which have more underweight people – the opposite of the pattern among the rich countries shown in Chapter 7. The age of menarche also changes its social distribution during the course of economic development. When more of the poor were undernourished they reached sexual maturity later than girls in richer families. With the rise in living standards that pattern too has reversed – perhaps contributing to the gradient in teenage pregnancies described in Chapter 9. All in all, it looks as if economic growth and social status differences are the most powerful determinants of many aspects of our lives.

CAUSALITY

The relationships between inequality and poor health and social problems are too strong to be attributable to chance; they occur independently in both our test-beds; and those between inequality and both violence and health have been demonstrated a large number of times in quite different settings, using data from different sources. But association on its own does not prove causality and, even if there is a causal relationship, it doesn't tell us what is cause and what is effect.

The graphs we have shown have all been cross-sectional – that is, they have shown relationships at a particular point in time rather than as they change in each country over time. However these cross-sectional relationships could only keep cropping up if somehow they changed together. If health and inequality went their separate ways and passed by only coincidentally, like ships in the night, we would not keep catching repeated glimpses of them in close formation. There is usually not enough internationally comparable data to track relationships over time, but it has been possible to look at changes in health and inequality. One study found that changes between 1975 and 1985 in the proportion of the population living on less than half the national average income among what were then the twelve members of the European Union were significantly related to changes in life expectancy.[81] Similarly, the decrease in life expectancy in Eastern European countries in the six years following the collapse of communism (1989–95) was shown to be greatest in the countries which saw the most rapid widening of income differences. A longer-term and particularly striking example of how income distribution and health change over time is the way in which the USA and Japan swapped places in the international league table of life expectancy in developed countries. In the 1950s, health in the USA was only surpassed by a few countries. Japan on the other hand did badly. But by the 1980s Japan had the highest life expectancy of all developed countries and the USA had slipped down the league and was well on the way to its current position as number 30 in the developed world. Crucially, Japanese income differences narrowed during the forty years after the Second World War. Its health improved rapidly, overtaking other countries, and its crime rate (almost alone among developed countries) decreased. Meanwhile, US income differences widened from about 1970 onwards.

Chapter 3 provided a general explanation of why we are so sensitive to inequality, and in each of Chapters 4–12 we have suggested causal links specific to each health and social problem. Earlier in this chapter we saw why cultural factors cannot be regarded as rival explanations of the associations with inequality. What other explanation might there be if one wanted to reject the idea of a causal relationship? Could inequality and each of the social problems be caused by some other unknown factor?

Weak relationships may sometimes turn out to be a mere mirage reflecting the influence of some underlying factor, but that is much less plausible as an explanation of relationships as close as these. The fact that our Index is not significantly related to average incomes in either our international test-bed or among the US states almost certainly rules out any underlying factor directly related to material living standards. Our analysis earlier in this chapter also rules out government social expenditure as a possible alternative explanation. As for other possible hidden factors, it seems unlikely that such an important causal factor will suddenly come to light which not only determines inequality but which also causes everything from poor health to obesity and high prison populations.

That leaves the question of which way causality goes. Occasionally when we describe our findings people suggest that instead of inequality causing everything else, perhaps it all works the other way round and health and social problems cause bigger income differences. Of course, in the real world these things do not happen in clearly defined steps which would allow us to see which comes first. The limited evidence from studies of changes over time tells us only that they tend to change together. Could it be that people who succumb to health or social problems suffer a loss of income and that tends to increase inequality? Perhaps people who are sick or very overweight are less likely to have jobs or to be given promotion. Could this explain why countries with worse health and social problems are more unequal?

The short answer is no – or at least, not much. First, it doesn't explain why societies that do badly on any particular health or social problem tend to do badly on all of them. If they are not all caused at least partly by the same thing, then there would be no reason why countries which, for instance, have high obesity rates should also have high prison populations. Second, some of the health and social problems are unlikely to lead to serious loss of income. Using the UNICEF index we showed that many childhood outcomes were worse in more unequal countries. But low child wellbeing will not have a major influence on income inequality among adults. Nor could higher homicide rates be considered as a major cause of inequality even if the numbers were much higher. Nor for that matter could expanding prison populations lead to wider income differences – rather the reverse, because measures of inequality are usually based on measures of household income which leave out institutionalized populations. Although it could be argued that teenage parents might increase inequality because they are often single and poor, we have seen that even when more equal countries have a high proportion of single parents that does not explain national differences in child wellbeing. This is partly because generous welfare systems ensure that very much smaller proportions of them are in poverty than in more unequal countries.

However, there is a more fundamental objection to the idea that causality might go from social problems to inequality. Earlier in this chapter we showed that it was people at almost all income levels, not just the poor, who do worse in more unequal societies. Even when you compare groups of people with the same income, you find that those in more unequal societies do worse than those on the same income in more equal societies. Though some more unequal societies have more poor people, most of the relationship with inequality is, as we pointed out earlier, not explained by the poor: the effects are much more widespread. So even if there is some loss of income among those who are sick or affected by some social problem, this does not begin to explain why people who remain on perfectly good incomes still do worse in more unequal societies.

Another alternative approach is to suggest that the real cause is not income distribution but something more like changes in ideology, a shift perhaps to a more individualistic economic philosophy or view of society, such as the so-called 'neo-liberal' thinking. Different ideologies will of course affect not only government policies but also decisions taken in economic institutions throughout society. They are one of very many different factors which can affect the scale of income differences. But to say that a change in ideology can affect income distribution is not at all the same as saying that it can also affect all the health and social problems we have discussed – regardless of what happens to income distribution. Although it does look as if neo-liberal policies widened income differences (see Chapter 16) there was no government intention to lower social cohesion or to increase violence, teenage births, obesity, drug abuse and everything else. So while changes in government ideology may sometimes be among the causes of changes in income distribution, this is not part of a package of policies intended to increase the prevalence of social problems. Their increase is, instead, an unintended consequence of the changes in income distribution. Rather than challenging the causal role of inequality in increasing health and social problems, if governments understood the consequences of widening income differences they would be keener to prevent them.

Economists have never suggested that poor health and social problems were the real determinants of income inequality. Instead they have concentrated on the contributions of things like taxes and benefits, international competition, changing technology and the mix of skills needed by industry. None of these is obviously connected to the frequency of health and social problems. In Chapter 16 we shall touch on the factors responsible for major changes in inequality in different countries.

A difficulty in proving causality is that we cannot experimentally reduce the inequalities in half our sample of countries and not in the others and then wait to see what happens. But purely observational research can still produce powerful science – as astronomy shows. There are, however, some experimental studies which do support causality working in the way our argument suggests. Some of them have already been mentioned in earlier chapters. In Chapter 8 on education we described experiments which show how much people's performance is affected by being categorized as socially inferior.

Indian children from lower castes solved mazes just as well as those from higher castes – until their low caste was made known. Experiments in the United States have shown that African-American students (but not white students) do less well when they are told a test is a test of ability than they do on the same test when they are told it is not a test of ability. We also described the famous 'blue-eyes' experiments with school children which showed the same processes at work.

Sometimes associations which are only observed among human beings can be shown to be causal in animal experiments. For instance, studies of civil servants show cardiovascular health declines with declining social status. But how can we tell whether the damage is caused by low social status rather than by poorer material conditions? Experiments with macaque monkeys make the answer clear. Macaques form status hierarchies but with captive colonies it is possible to ensure all animals live in the same material conditions: they are given the same diet and live in the same compounds. In addition, it is possible to manipulate social status by moving animals between groups. If you take low-status animals from different groups and house them together, some have to become high-status. Similarly, if you put high-status animals together some will become low-status. Animals which move down in these conditions have been found to have a rapid build-up of atherosclerosis in their arteries.[322] Similar experiments also suggest a causal relationship between low social status and the accumulation of abdominal fat.[323] In Chapter 5 we mentioned other animal experiments which showed that when cocaine was made available to monkeys in these conditions, it was taken more by low social status animals – as if to offset their lower dopamine activity.[59] Lastly, the primary importance of inequality has been confirmed by researchers using statistical methods designed to check the causal pathways through which inequality affects levels of trust or bullying in schools.[27, 400, 402]

Although we know of no experiments confirming the causality of the relation between inequality and violence, we invite anyone to go into a poor part of town and try randomly insulting a few people.

We have discussed the reasons for thinking that these links are causal from a number of different perspectives. But as philosophers of science, such as Sir Karl Popper, have emphasized, an essential element in judging the success of any theory is whether it makes successful predictions. A successful theory is one which predicts the existence of previously unknown phenomena or relationships which can then be verified. The theory that more equal societies were healthier arose from one set of international data. There have now been a very large number of tests (about 200) of that theory in different settings. With the exception of studies which looked at inequality in small local areas, an overwhelming majority of these tests confirmed the theory. Second, if the link is causal it implies that there must be a mechanism. The search for a mechanism led to the discovery that social relationships (as measured by social cohesion, trust, involvement in community life and low levels of violence) are better in more equal societies. This happened at a time when the importance of social relationships to health was beginning to be more widely recognized. Third, the theory that poor health might be one of a range of problems with social gradients related to inequality has been tested (initially on cause-specific death rates as described earlier in this chapter) and has since been amply confirmed in two different settings as we have described in Chapters 4–12. Fourth, at a time when there was no reason to think that inequality had psychosocial effects, the relation between health and equality seemed to imply that inequality must be affecting health through psychosocial processes related to social differentiation. That inequality does have powerful psychosocial effects is now confirmed by its links (shown in earlier chapters) with the quality of social relations and numerous behavioural outcomes.

It is very difficult to see how the enormous variations which exist from one society to another in the level of problems associated with low social status can be explained without accepting that inequality is the common denominator, and a hugely damaging force.

Accepting this does not involve a huge theoretical leap. Two points should be kept in mind. First, the evidence merely confirms the common intuition that inequality is divisive and socially corrosive. Second, everyone knows that within our societies ill health and social problems are related to social status and are most common in the most deprived neighbourhoods. Though you could once have been forgiven for thinking that this merely reflected a tendency for the vulnerable to end up at the bottom of society, it is now obvious that this fails to explain why these problems are so much more common in more unequal societies. This book simply points out that if you increase the income and status differences related to these problems, then – unsurprisingly – the problems all become more common.

14

Our social inheritance

Gifts make friends and friends make gifts.
> Marshall Sahlins, *Stone Age Economics*

LOOKING BEFORE LEAPING

Although attitudes to inequality have always been central to the disagreement between the political right and left, few would not prefer a friendlier society, with less violence, better mental health, more involvement in community life – and so on. Now that we have shown that reducing inequality leads to a very much better society, the main sticking point is whether people believe greater equality is attainable. Our analysis has not of course compared existing societies with impossibly egalitarian imaginary ones: it is not about utopias or the extent of human perfectibility. Everything we have seen comes from comparisons of existing societies, and those societies have not been particularly unusual or odd ones. Instead, we have looked exclusively at differences between the world's richest and most successful economies, all of which enjoy democratic institutions and freedom of speech. There can be no doubt whatsoever that human beings are capable of living well in societies with inequalities as small – for instance – as Japan and the Nordic countries. Far from being impractical, the implications of our findings are probably more consistent with the institutional structures of market democracy than some people – at either end of the political spectrum – would like to believe.

Some may still feel hesitant to take the evidence at face value.

"...I can therefore conclude that the primates are indeed social animals."

From the vantage point of more unequal countries, it may seem genuinely perplexing and difficult to understand how some, apparently similar, countries can function with so much less inequality. Evidence that material self-interest is the governing principle of human life seems to be everywhere. The efficiency of the market economy seems to prove that greed and avarice are, as economic theory assumes, the overriding human motivations. Even the burden of crime appears to spring from the difficulty of stopping people breaking the rules to satisfy selfish desires. Signs of a caring, sharing, human nature seem thin on the ground.

Some of this scepticism might be allayed by a more fundamental understanding of how we, as human beings, are damaged by inequality and have the capacity for something else. We need to understand how, without genetically re-engineering ourselves, greater equality allows a more sociable human nature to emerge.

TWO SIDES OF THE COIN

In our research for this book, social status and friendship have kept cropping up together, linked inextricably as a pair of opposites. First, they are linked as determinants of the health of each individual. As we saw in Chapter 6, friendship and involvement in social life are highly protective of good health, while low social status, or bigger status differences and more inequality, are harmful. Second, the two are again linked as they vary in societies. We saw in Chapter 4 that as inequality increases, sociability as measured by the strength of community life, how much people trust each other, and the frequency of violence, declines. They crop up together for a third time in people's tendency to choose friends from among their near equals: larger differences in status or wealth create a social gulf between people.

What binds social status and friendship together in these different ways? The explanation is simple. They represent the two opposite ways in which human beings can come together. Social status stratification, like ranking systems or pecking orders among animals, are fundamentally orderings based on power and coercion, on privileged access to resources, regardless of others' needs. In its most naked and animal form, might is right and the weakest eat last.

Friendship is almost exactly the opposite kind of relationship. It is about reciprocity, mutuality, sharing, social obligations, co-operation and recognition of each other's needs. Gifts are symbols of friendship because they demonstrate that the giver and receiver do not compete for access to necessities, but instead recognize and respond to each other's needs. In the well-chosen words of Marshall Sahlins, a social anthropologist, 'gifts make friends and friends make gifts'.[324] Food-sharing and eating together carry the same symbolic message, and they do so particularly powerfully because food is the most fundamental of all material necessities. In times of scarcity, competition for food has the potential to be extraordinarily socially destructive.

FRIEND OR FOE

Social status and friendship are so important to us because they reflect different ways of dealing with what is perhaps the most fundamental problem of social organization and political life among animals and humans alike. Because members of the same species have the same needs as each other, they have the potential to be each other's worst rivals, competing for almost everything – for food, shelter, sexual partners, a comfortable place to sit in the shade, a good nesting site – indeed for all scarce comforts and necessities. As a result, among very many species the most frequent conflicts take place not so much between members of different species, despite the danger of predators, but between members of the same species. A low-status baboon has to spend much more time keeping out of the way of a dominant baboon than in avoiding lions. Most of the bite marks and scars which subordinate animals bear come from more dominant members of their own species. You can see signs of rivalry within species all around us – you have only to watch birds at a garden feeder, or dogs fighting, or think of the banned sport of cock fighting: in each case the conflicts are within the species.

Human beings have to deal with the same problem. Writing in the seventeenth century, Thomas Hobbes made the danger of conflict, caused by rivalry for scarce resources, the basis of his political philosophy.[325] As we all have the same needs, competition for scarce necessities would lead to a continuous conflict of 'every man against every man'. Hobbes believed that, because of this danger, the most important task of government was simply to keep the peace. He assumed that, without the firm hand of government, life 'in a state of nature' would be 'solitary, poor, nasty, brutish, and short'.

But perhaps Hobbes missed an important part of the story. As well as the potential for conflict, human beings have a unique potential to be each other's best source of co-operation, learning, love and assistance of every kind. While there's not much that ostriches or otters can do for an injured member of their own species, among humans there is. But it's not just that we are able to give each other care and protection. Because most of our abilities are learned, we depend on others for the acquisition of our life skills. Similarly, our unique capacity for specialization and division of labour means that human beings have an unrivalled potential to benefit from co-operation. So as well as the potential to be each other's worst rivals, we also have the potential to be each other's greatest source of comfort and security.

We have become attentive to friendship and social status because the quality of social relationships has always been crucial to well-being, determining whether other people are feared rivals or vital sources of security, co-operation and support. So important are these dimensions of social life that lack of friends and low social status are among the most important sources of chronic stress affecting the health of populations in rich countries today.

Although Hobbes was right about the underlying problem of the dangers of competition between members of the same species, his view of how societies managed before the development of governments with the power to keep the peace was very wide of the mark. Now that we have much more knowledge of hunting and gathering societies it is clear that our ancestors did not live in a state of continuous conflict. Instead, as Sahlins pointed out, they had other ways of keeping the peace.[324] To avoid the 'warre of each against all', social and economic life was based on systems of gift exchange, food sharing, and on a very high degree of equality. These served to minimize animosity and keep relations sweet. Forms of exchange involving direct expressions of self-interest, such as buying and selling or barter, were usually regarded as socially unacceptable and outlawed.

These patterns demonstrate the fundamental truth: systems of material or economic relations are systems of social relations.

✓ ECONOMIC EXPERIMENTS

Economic theory has traditionally worked on the assumption that human behaviour could be explained largely in terms of an inherent tendency to maximize material self-interest. But a series of experiments using economic games have now shown how far from the truth this is.

In the 'ultimatum game', volunteers are randomly paired but remain anonymous to each other and do not meet. A known sum of money is given to the 'proposer' who then divides it as he or she pleases with the 'responder'. All the responders do is merely accept or reject the offer. If rejected, neither partner gets anything, but if it is accepted, they each keep the shares of money offered.

They play this game only once, so there is no point in rejecting a small offer to try to force the proposer to be more generous next time – they know there isn't going to be a next time. In this situation, self-interested responders should accept any offer, however derisory, and self-interested proposers should offer the smallest positive amount, just enough to ensure that a responder accepts it.

Although experiments show that this is exactly how chimpanzees behave,[326] it is not what happens among human beings. In practice, the average offer made by people in developed societies is usually between 43 and 48 per cent, with 50 per cent as the most common offer.[327] At direct cost to ourselves, we come close to sharing equally even with people we never meet and will never interact with again.

Responders tend to reject offers below about 20 per cent. Rejected offers are money which the responder chooses to lose in order to punish the proposer and prevent them benefiting from making a mean offer. The human desire to punish even at some personal cost has been called 'altruistic punishment', and it plays an important role in reinforcing co-operative behaviour and preventing people freeloading.

Although the studies of how people played the ultimatum game were not concerned with the levels of inequality in each society, they are, nevertheless, about how equally or unequally people choose to divide money between themselves and someone else. They are concerned with what people feel is a proper way to treat others (even when there is no direct contact between them and they bear the cost of any generosity). The egalitarian preferences people reveal in the ultimatum game seem to fly in the face of the actual inequalities in our societies.

CHIMPS AND BONOBOS

Some non-human primates are much more hierarchical than others. Looking at their different social systems, it often seems as if the amount of conflict, the quality of social relations and the relationship between the sexes are functions of how hierarchical they are. Human beings are not of course bound to any one social system. Our adaptability has enabled us to live in very different social structures, both very egalitarian and very hierarchical. But some of the same effects of hierarchy on other aspects of our social systems still seem to be visible – even though the behavioural patterns are driven by culture rather than by instinct. Less hierarchical societies are less male-dominated so, as we saw in Chapter 4, the position of women is better. Similarly, the quality of social relations in more equal societies is less hostile. People trust each other more and community life is stronger (Chapter 4), there is less violence (Chapter 10) and punishment is less harsh (Chapter 11).

Around six or seven million years ago the branch of the evolutionary tree from which we have emerged split from that which led to two different species of ape: chimpanzees and bonobos. Genetically we are equally closely related to both of them, yet there are striking differences in their social behaviour and they illustrate sharply contrasting ways of solving the Hobbesian problem of the potential for conflict over scarce resources.

Bands of chimpanzees are headed by a dominant male who gains his position largely on the basis of superior size, strength, and an ability to form alliances – often including support from females. Dominance hierarchies in any species are orderings of access to scarce resources, including – as far as males are concerned – reproductive access to females. Rankings within the dominance hierarchy are established and maintained through frequent contests, displays and assessments of strength. In the words of primatologists Frans de Waal and Frans Lanting:

Chimpanzees go through elaborate rituals in which one individual communicates its status to the other. Particularly between adult males, one male will literally grovel in the dust, uttering panting grunts, while the other stands bipedally performing a mild intimidation display to make clear who ranks above whom.[328, p. 30]

Bonobos, on the other hand, behave very differently. Not only is there much less conflict between neighbouring groups of bonobos than between neighbouring groups of chimps, but bonobos – again unlike chimps – have a high degree of sex equality. Females are at least as important as males, and dominance hierarchies are much less pronounced. Although males are slightly larger than females, females are usually allowed to eat first. Often dubbed the 'caring, sharing' apes, they engage in sexual activity – including mutual masturbation – frequently and in any combination of sexes and ages. Sex has evolved not only to serve reproductive functions, but also to relieve tensions in situations which, in other species, might cause conflict. As de Waal says, 'sex is the glue of bonobo society'.[329, p. 99] It eases conflict, signals friendliness, and calms stressful situations. Bonobos use sex to solve the problem of how to avoid conflict over access to scarce resources. Feeding time is apparently the peak of sexual activity. Even before food is thrown into their enclosure, male bonobos get erections and males and females invite both opposite and same-sex partners for sex. Possible conflict over non-food resources is dealt with in the same way.

Although sexual activity is not a preliminary to feeding among humans, eating is a peak of sociality – whether in the form of shared family meals, meals with friends, feasts and banquets, or even in the religious symbolism of sharing bread and wine at communion.

Summing up the behavioural difference between chimps and bonobos, de Waal and Lanting said: 'If, of the twin concepts of sex and power, the chimpanzee has an appetite for the second, the bonobo clearly has one for the first. The chimpanzee resolves sexual issues (disputes) with power; the bonobo resolves power issues with sex.'[328, p. 32] Perhaps as a result of these differences, bonobos are, as research has shown, better at co-operative tasks than chimps.

So what makes the difference? Interestingly, a section of DNA, known to be important in the regulation of social, sexual and parenting behaviour, has been found to differ between chimps and bonobos.[329] It is perhaps comforting to know that, at least in this section of DNA, humans have the bonobo rather than the chimp pattern, suggesting that our common ancestor may have had a preference for making love rather than war.

THE SOCIAL BRAIN

The fact that we can simultaneously agree with Sartre that 'hell is other people' and also recognize that other people can be heaven, shows how deeply enmeshed in social life we are. Research looking for the most potent sources of stress affecting the cardiovascular system concluded that 'conflicts and tensions with other people are by far the most distressing events in daily life in terms of both initial and enduring effects on emotional wellbeing' – more so than the demands of work, money worries or other difficulties.[330] The quality of our relations with other people has always been so crucial not only to wellbeing, but also to survival and to reproductive success, that social interaction has been one of the most powerful influences on the evolution of the human brain.

A remarkable indication of this is the impressively close relationship, first pointed out by the primatologist Robin Dunbar, between the normal group size of each species of primate (whether they are solitary, go about in pairs, or in smaller or larger troupes) and the proportion of the brain made up of the neocortex.[331] The larger the group size, the more neocortex we seem to need to cope with social life. Our Palaeolithic ancestors usually lived in larger communities than other primates, and the neocortex makes up a larger part of our brains than it does of primates' brains. Because its growth was key to the enlargement of the human brain, the relationship suggests that the reason why we became clever may have been a response to the demands of social life.

Human beings are – the world over – preoccupied with social interaction, with what people have said, what they might have been thinking, whether they were kind, off-hand, rude ..., why they behaved as they did, what their motivations were, and how we should respond. All that social processing depends on the acquisition of a basic set of social skills such as the ability to recognize and distinguish between faces, to use language, to infer each other's thoughts and feelings from body language, to recognize each other's peculiarities, to understand and heed what are acceptable and un-acceptable ways of behaving in our society, to recognize and manage the impressions others form of us, and of course a basic ability to make friends and to handle conflict. But the reasons why our brains have developed as social organs to handle social interaction is not just to provide amusement, but because of the paramount importance of getting our social relationships right. That is why we mind about them. The reason why other people can be heaven or hell is because they have the potential to be our worst rivals and competitors as well as to be our best source of co-operation, care and security.

OUR DUAL INHERITANCE

Different forms of social organization provide different selective environments. Characteristics which are successful in one setting may not be so in another. As a result, human beings have had to develop different mental tool-kits which equip them to operate both in dominance hierarchies and in egalitarian societies. Dominance and affiliative strategies are part of our deep psychological make-up.

Through them we know how to make and keep friends, how to compete for status, and when each of these two contrasting social strategies is appropriate.

Dominance strategies are almost certainly pre-human in origin. They would not have been appropriate to life in the predominantly egalitarian societies of Stone Age human hunters and gatherers. In pre-human dominance hierarchies we not only developed characteristics which help attain and express high status, but also strategies for making the best of low status if that turns out to be our lot. The danger, particularly for males in some species, is that low social status is an evolutionary dead end. To avoid that, a certain amount of risk-taking and opportunism may be desirable.

Competing effectively for status requires much more than a desire for high social status and an aversion to low status. It requires a high degree of attentiveness to status differentials and the ability to make accurate social comparisons of strength and status: it is important to be able to distinguish accurately between winnable and unwinnable status conflicts. In many species life and limb often depend on knowing when to back off and when to challenge a dominant animal for rank. Maximizing status depends on being seen as superior. This is fertile psychological ground for the development and expression of forms of downward prejudice, discrimination and snobbishness intended to express superiority. And the more we feel devalued by those above us and the fewer status resources we have to fall back on, the greater will be the desire to regain some sense of self-worth by asserting superiority over any more vulnerable groups. This is likely to be the source of the so-called 'bicycling reaction' mentioned in Chapter 12 – so called because it is as if people bow to their superiors while kicking down on inferiors.

Although it is often thought that the pursuit of status is a particularly masculine characteristic, we should not forget how much this is likely to be a response to the female preference for high-status males. As Henry Kissinger said: 'Power is the ultimate aphrodisiac.'

Despite the modern impression of the permanence and universality of inequality, in the time-scale of human history and prehistory, it is the current highly unequal societies which are exceptional. For over 90 per cent of our existence as human beings we lived, almost exclusively, in highly egalitarian societies. For perhaps as much as the last two million years, covering the vast majority of the time we have been 'anatomically modern' (that is to say, looking much as we do now), human beings lived in remarkably egalitarian hunting and gathering – or foraging – groups.[332-5] Modern inequality arose and spread with the development of agriculture. The characteristics which would have been selected as successful in more egalitarian societies would have been very different from those selected in dominance hierarchies.

Rather than reflecting an evolutionary outbreak of selflessness, studies of modern and recent hunter-gatherer societies suggest that they maintained equality not only through the institutions of food sharing and reciprocal gift exchange, but also through what have been called 'counter-dominance strategies'.[331] Sharing was what has been described as 'vigilant sharing', with people watching to see that they got their fair share. The counter-dominance strategies through which these societies maintained their equality functioned almost as alliances of everyone against anyone whose behaviour threatened people's sense of their own autonomy and equality. The suggestion is that these strategies may have developed as a generalized form of the kind of alliances which primatologists often describe being formed between two or three animals to enable them to gang up on and depose the dominant male. Observational studies of modern and recent foraging societies suggest that counter-dominance strategies normally involve anything from teasing and ridicule to ostracism and violence, which are turned against anyone who tries to dominate others. An important point about these societies is that they show that the selfish desires of individuals for greater wealth and pre-eminence can be contained or diverted to less socially damaging forms of expression.

A number of psychological characteristics would have been selected to help us manage in egalitarian societies. These are likely to include our strong conception and valuation of fairness, which makes it easier for people to reach agreement without conflict when sharing scarce resources. Visible even in young children, our concern for fairness sometimes seems so strong that we might wonder how it is that social systems with great inequality are tolerated. Similarly, the sense of indebtedness (now recognized as universal in human societies) which we experience after having received a gift, serves to prompt reciprocity and prevent freeloading, so sustaining friendship. As the experimental economic games which we discussed showed, there is also evidence that we can feel sufficiently infuriated by unfairness that we are willing to punish, even at some personal cost to ourselves.

Another characteristic which is perhaps important is our tendency to feel a common sense of identity and interdependence with those with whom we share food and other resources as equals. They form the in-group, the 'us', with whom we empathize and share a sense of identity. In various religious institutions and political organizations sharing has been used to create a sense of brotherhood or sisterhood, and whether we say a society has an 'extended' or 'nuclear' family system is a matter of the extent of the sharing group – whether more distant relations have a call on each other's resources. Writing in the middle of the nineteenth century, de Tocqueville believed that substantial differences in material living standards between people was a formidable barrier to empathy.[23] As we saw in Chapter 4, he thought the differences in material conditions prevented the French nobility from empathizing with the sufferings of the peasantry, and also explained why American slave owners were so unaffected by the suffering of their slaves. He also thought the strong community life he saw among whites on his visit to the USA in 1830 was a reflection of what he called 'the equality of conditions'.

A very important source of the close social integration in an egalitarian community is the sense of self-realization we can get when we successfully meet others' needs. This is often seen as a mysterious quality, almost as if it were above explanation. It comes of course from our need to feel valued by others. We gain a sense of being valued when we do things which others appreciate. The best way of ensuring that we remained included in the co-operative hunting and gathering group and reducing the risk of being cast out, ostracized, and preyed upon, was to do things which people appreciated. Nowadays, whether it is cooking a nice meal, telling jokes or providing for people's needs in other ways, it can give rise to a sense of self-worth. It is this capacity – now most visible in parenting – which, long before the development of market mechanisms and wage labour, enabled humans – almost uniquely – to gain the benefits of a division of labour and specialization within co-operative groups of interdependent individuals.

We have then social strategies to deal with very different kinds of social organization. At one extreme, dominance hierarchies are about self-advancement and status competition. Individuals have to be self-reliant and other people are encountered mainly as rivals for food and mates. At the other extreme is mutual interdependence and co-operation, in which each person's security depends on the quality of their relationships with others, and a sense of self-worth comes less from status than from the contribution made to the wellbeing of others. Rather than the overt pursuit of material self-interest, affiliative strategies depend on mutuality, reciprocity and the capacity for empathy and emotional bonding.

In practice, of course, god and mammon coexist in every society and the territory of each varies depending on the sphere of life, the economic system and on individual differences.

EARLY EXPERIENCE

So different are the kinds of society which humans have had to cope with that the processes which adapt us to deal with any given social system start very early in life. Growing up in a society where you must be prepared to treat others with suspicion, watch your back and fight for what you can get, requires very different skills from those needed in a society where you depend on empathy, reciprocity and co-operation. Psychologists and others have always told us that the nature of a child's early life affects the development of their personality and the kind of people they grow up to be in adult life. Examples of a special capacity in early life to adapt to local environmental circumstances exist throughout animal and even plant life. In humans, stress responses and processes shaping our emotional and mental characteristics go through a kind of tuning, or programming, process which starts in the womb and continues through early childhood. The levels of stress which women experience in pregnancy are passed on to affect the development of babies before birth. Stress hormones cross the placental barrier and affect the baby's hormone levels and growth in the womb.

Also important in influencing children's development is the stress they experience themselves in infancy. The quality of care and nurture, the quality of attachment and how much conflict there is, all affect stress hormones and the child's emotional and cognitive development. Although not yet identified in humans, sensitive periods in early life may sometimes involve 'epigenetic' processes by which early exposures and experience may switch particular genes on or off to pattern development in the longer term. Differences in nursing behaviour in mother rats have been shown to affect gene expression in their offspring, so providing ways of adapting to the environment in the light of early experience.[336]

In the past, there was a strong tendency simply to regard children who had had a very stressful early life as 'damaged'. But it looks increasingly as if what is happening is that early experience is being used to adapt the child to deal with contrasting kinds of social reality. The emotional make-up which prepares you to live in a society in which you have to fend for yourself, watch your back and fight for every bit you can get, is very different from what is needed if you grow up in a society in which (to take the opposite extreme) you depend on empathy, reciprocity and co-operation, and in which your security depends on maintaining good relations with others. Children who experience more stress in early life may be more aggressive, less empathetic, and probably better at dealing with conflict. In effect, early life serves to provide a taster of the quality of social relations you are likely to have to cope with in adulthood.

So important are these processes that we need to see parenting as part of a system for passing on the adult's experience of adversity to the child. When people talk of poor parenting, or say people lack parenting skills, the truth is often that the way parents treat their children actually serves to pass on their experience of adversity to the child. Although this is usually an unconscious process, in which the parent simply feels short-tempered, depressed or at their wit's end, it is sometimes also conscious. In a recent court case, three women were found to have encouraged their toddlers to fight –

goading them to hit each other in the face and to kick a sibling who had fallen to the ground.[337] The children's grandmother showed no remorse, insisting that it 'would harden them up'. Given their experience of life, that was clearly what they thought was needed. Many studies have shown that forms of behaviour experienced in childhood tend to be mirrored in adulthood. Children who have, for example, experienced violence or abuse are more likely to become abusing and violent when they reach adulthood.

The effects of early experience are long-lasting. Children stressed in early life, or whose mothers were stressed during pregnancy, are more likely to suffer in middle and old age from a number of stress-related diseases – including heart disease, diabetes and stroke. The result is that some of the effects of widening income differences in a society may not be short-lived. Increased inequality means that more families suffer the strains of living on relatively low incomes, and numerous studies have shown the damaging effects on child development. When parents experience more adversity, family life suffers, and the children grow up less empathetic but ready to deal with more antagonistic relationships.

Many of the problems which we have seen to be related to inequality involve adult responses to status competition. But we have also found that a number of problems affecting children are related to inequality. These include juvenile conflict, poor peer relationships and educational performance at school, childhood obesity, infant mortality and teenage pregnancy. Problems such as these are likely to reflect the way the stresses of a more unequal society – of low social status – have penetrated family life and relationships. Inequality is associated with less good outcomes of many kinds because it leads to a deterioration in the quality of relationships. An important part of the reason why countries such as Sweden, Finland and Norway score well on the UNICEF index of child wellbeing is that their welfare systems have kept rates of relative poverty low among families.

MIRROR NEURONS AND EMPATHY

To view the pursuit of greater equality as a process of shoe-horning societies into an uncomfortably tight-fitting shoe reflects a failure to recognize our human social potential. If we understood our social needs and susceptibilities we would see that a less unequal society causes dramatically lower rates of ill-health and social problems because it provides us with a better-fitting shoe.

Mirror neurons are a striking example of how our biology establishes us as deeply social beings. When we watch someone doing something, mirror neurons in our brains fire as if to produce the same actions.[338] The system is likely to have developed to serve learning by imitation. Watching a person doing a particular sequence of actions – one research paper uses the example of a curtsey – as an external observer, does not tell you how to do it yourself nearly as well as if your brain was acting *as if* you were making the same movements in sympathy. To do the same thing you need to experience it from inside.

Usually, of course, there is no visible sign of the internal processes of identification that enable us to put ourselves inside each other's actions. However, the electrical activity triggered by these specialized neurons is detectable in the muscles. It has been suggested that similar processes might be behind our ability to empathize with each other and even behind the way people sometimes flinch while watching a film if they see pain inflicted on someone else. We react as if it was happening to us.

Though equipped with the potential to empathize very closely with others, how much we develop and use this potential is again affected by early childhood.

OXYTOCIN AND TRUST

Another example of how our biology dovetails with the nature of social relations involves a hormone called oxytocin and its effects on our willingness to trust each other. In Chapter 4 we saw that people in more unequal societies were much less likely to trust each other. Trust is of course an important ingredient in any society, but it becomes essential in modern developed societies with a high degree of interdependence.

In many different species, oxytocin affects social attachment and bonding, both bonding between mother and child, and pair-bonding between sexual partners. Its production is stimulated by physical contact during sexual intercourse, in childbirth and in breastfeeding where it controls milk let-down. However, in a number of mammalian species, including humans, it also has a role in social interaction more generally, affecting approach and avoidance behaviour.

The effects of oxytocin on people's willingness to trust each other was tested in an experiment involving a trust game.[339] The results showed that those given oxytocin were much more likely to trust their partner. In similar experiments it was found that these effects worked both ways round: not only does receiving oxytocin make people more likely to trust, but being trusted also leads to increases in oxytocin. These effects were found even when the only evidence of trust or mistrust between people was the numerical decisions communicated through computer terminals.[340]

CO-OPERATIVE PLEASURE AND PAINFUL EXCLUSION

Other experiments have shown how the sense of co-operation stimulates the reward centres in the brain. The experience of mutual co-operation, even in the absence of face-to-face contact or real communication, leads reliably to stimulation of the reward centres. The researchers suggested that the neural reward networks serve to encourage reciprocity and mutuality while resisting the temptation to act selfishly.[341]

In contrast to the rewards of co-operation, experiments using brain scans have shown that the pain of social exclusion involves the same areas of the brain as are stimulated when someone experiences physical pain. Naomi Eisenberger, a psychologist at UCLA, got volunteers to play a computer bat-and-ball game with, as it seemed on the screen, two other participants.[342] The program was arranged so that after a while the other two virtual participants would start to pass the ball just between each other, so excluding the experimental subject. Brain scans showed that the areas of the brain activated by this experience of exclusion were the same areas as are activated by physical pain. In various species of monkeys these same brain areas have been found to play a role in offspring calling for, and mothers providing, maternal protection.

These connections have always been understood intuitively. When we talk about 'hurt feelings' or a 'broken heart' we recognize the connection between physical pain and the social pain caused by the breaking of close social bonds, by exclusion and ostracism. Evolutionary psychologists have shown that the tendency to ostracize people who do not co-operate, and to exclude them from the shared proceeds of co-operation, is a powerful way of maintaining high standards of co-operation.[343] And, just as the ultimatum game showed that people were willing to punish a mean allocator by rejecting – at some cost to themselves – allocations that seemed unfair, so we appear to have a desire to exclude people who do not co-operate.

Social pain is of course central to rejection and is the opposite of the pleasures – discussed earlier – of being valued or of the sense of self-realization which can come from others' appreciation of what we have done for them. The powers of inclusion and exclusion indicate our fundamental need for social integration and are, no doubt, part of the explanation of why friendship and social involvement are so protective of health (Chapter 6).

Social class and status differences almost certainly cause similar forms of social pain. Unfairness, inequality and the rejection of co-operation are all forms of exclusion. The experiments which demonstrated the performance effects of being classified as inferior (which we saw in Chapter 8 among Indian children in different castes, in experiments with school children, and among African-American students told they were doing tests of ability) indicated the social pain related to exclusion. Part of the same picture is the social pain which sometimes triggers violence (Chapter 10) when people feel they are put down, humiliated or suffer loss of face.

For a species which thrives on friendship and enjoys co-operation and trust, which has a strong sense of fairness, which is equipped with mirror neurons allowing us to learn our way of life through a process of identification, it is clear that social structures which create relationships based on inequality, inferiority and social exclusion must inflict a great deal of social pain. In this light we can perhaps begin not only to see why more unequal societies are so socially dysfunctional but, through that, perhaps also to feel more confident that a more humane society may be a great deal more practical than the highly unequal ones in which so many of us live now.

15

Equality and sustainability

The one who dies with most toys wins.

US bumper sticker

Over the next generation or so, politics seem likely to be dominated either by efforts to prevent runaway global warming or, if they fail, by attempts to deal with its consequences. Carbon emissions per head in rich countries are between two and five times higher than the world average. But cutting their emissions by a half or four-fifths will not be enough: world totals are already too high and allowances must be made for economic growth in poorer countries.

How might greater equality and policies to reduce carbon emissions go together? Given what inequality does to a society, and particularly how it heightens competitive consumption, it looks not only as if the two are complementary, but also that governments may be unable to make big enough cuts in carbon emissions without also reducing inequality.

SUSTAINABILITY AND THE QUALITY OF LIFE

Ever since the Brandt Report in 1980 people have suggested that social and environmental sustainability go together. It is fortunate that just when the human species discovers that the environment cannot absorb further increases in emissions, we also learn that further economic growth in the developed world no longer improves

health, happiness or measures of wellbeing. On top of that, we have now seen that there are ways of improving the quality of life in rich countries without further economic growth.

But if we do not need to consume more, what would be the consequences of consuming less? Would making the necessary cuts in carbon emissions mean reducing present material living standards below what people in the rich world could accept as an adequate quality of life? Is sustainability compatible with retaining our quality of life?

A starting point for answering this question is Figure 15.1. It shows life expectancy in relation to CO_2 emissions per head of population among rich and poor countries. Because carbon emissions tend to go up as societies get richer, it looks very like the relationship between life expectancy and National Income per person shown in Figure 1.1. However, what we can now see is that some countries achieve life expectancies close to 80 years at a fraction of the CO_2 emissions common in the richest countries. It should therefore be

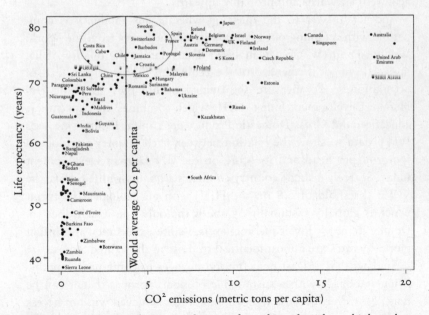

Figure 15.1 *Low infant mortality can be achieved without high carbon emissions.*[344]

possible to make dramatic reductions in emissions in most rich countries without any loss of health and wellbeing – even on the basis of current inefficient technology based mainly on non-renewable sources of energy.

The circle in the top left hand corner of Figure 15.1 shows (again on the basis of current technology) the area in which societies seem to be able to gain good health at the minimum environmental cost. As the vertical line through the centre of the circle is a rough estimate of world average CO_2 emissions, the graph suggests that all countries of the world have the potential to achieve high life expectancies without exceeding current world CO_2 emissions.

But because current global emissions are already causing such rapid global warming, we need to reduce world emissions far below current levels. That can only be achieved by more energy efficient ways of living and the development of sustainable sources of energy. Such changes would shift the circle (marking the lowest environmental costs at which high levels of health and wellbeing can be achieved) leftwards and probably upwards.

Another answer to the question whether sustainability is compatible with retaining our high quality of life comes from the World Wildlife Fund (WWF). It analysed data relating the quality of life in each country to the size of the ecological footprint per head of population.[345] To measure the quality of life they used the UN Human Development Index (HDI) which combines life expectancy, education and Gross Domestic Product per capita. Figure 15.2 uses WWF data to show the relation between each country's ecological footprint per head and its score on the UN Human Development Index. Scarcely a single country combines a quality of life (above the WWF threshold of 0.8 on the HDI) with an ecological footprint which is globally sustainable. Cuba is the only one which does so. Despite its much lower income levels, its life expectancy and infant mortality rates are almost identical to those in the United States.

The fact that at least one country manages to combine acceptable living standards with a sustainable economy, proves that it can be done. However, because the combination is achieved without access to the greenest and most fuel-efficient technology means it could be done more easily in countries with access to more advanced tech-

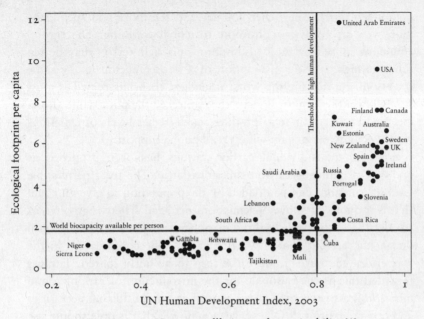

Figure 15.2 *Human wellbeing and sustainability.*[345]

nology than Cuba has. With the advantages of power generation from renewables, environmentally friendly new technologies and greater equality, we can be confident that it is possible to combine sustainability with a high quality of life. Before leaving Figure 15.2 it is worth noting that much of the reason why the highest scores on the HDI are achieved by countries with the largest ecological feet is merely a reflection of the fact that Gross Domestic Product per head is one of the components of the HDI.

REDUCING CARBON EMISSIONS FAIRLY

Improving the real quality of our lives at lower levels of consumption is only one of the contributions equality can make to reducing carbon emissions. There are two others. First, if policies to cut emissions are to gain public acceptance, they must be seen to be applied fairly. The richer you are and the more you spend, the more you are likely to contribute to global warming. The carbon emissions caused by the consumption of a rich person may be ten times as high as the consumption of a poorer person in the same society. If the rich are the worst offenders, then fair remedies must surely affect them most. Policies that squeezed the poor while allowing the rich to continue to produce much higher levels of emissions would be unlikely to gain widespread public support.

A system of individual carbon rations has been proposed as one way of reducing carbon emissions fairly. The total permissible level of emissions can be divided by the population to give an equal share, or quota, of allowable emissions per head. There is an obvious parallel here with the egalitarian policies implemented in Britain during the Second World War: to gain public co-operation in the war effort, the burden had to be seen to be fairly shared. Titmuss regarded this as the rationale for the introduction of rationing and more progressive income taxes, as well as for subsidizing necessities and taxing luxuries.[346] One suggestion now is that people should use an electronic card to cover payments for fuel, power and air travel. Those using less than their ration would be able to sell their unused allocation back to a carbon bank, from where it could then be bought by richer people wanting to use more than their allocation of fuel and power. Under such a system of 'tradeable carbon quotas' high consumers would be compensating low consumers, and income would be redistributed from rich to poor. In 2006 the then Minister for the Environment in Britain, David Miliband, proposed such a system and a small trial was begun in Manchester in 2007. To safeguard the poor it may be necessary to prevent people selling unused parts of their ration till the end of the period it covers, so only allowances already saved could be traded.

NEW TECHNOLOGY IS NOT
ENOUGH ON ITS OWN

We might hope that new technology will save us from the rigours of carbon rationing. However, although green innovations which reduce fuel consumption and carbon emissions are an essential part of the change we need to make, they cannot solve the problem on their own. Imagine that a new generation of car engines is introduced which halve fuel consumption. Driving would then be cheaper and that would save us money, but it is money which we would almost certainly spend on something else. We might spend it on driving more, or on buying a bigger car, or on more power-hungry electrical equipment – perhaps a bigger fridge-freezer. But however we spend the money put back in our pockets by more efficient car engines, our additional consumption will probably add to carbon emissions elsewhere and lose much of the original environmental benefit. The same logic applies in almost all areas. More power-efficient washing machines or better insulated houses will help the environment; but they also cut our bills, and that immediately means we lose some of the environmental gain by spending the saved money on something else. As cars have become more fuel-efficient we have chosen to drive further. As houses have become better insulated we have raised standards of heating, and as we put in energy-saving light bulbs the chances are that we start to think it doesn't matter so much leaving them on.

Because energy-saving innovations mean that we can buy more, they are like economic growth. Though they give us higher material living standards for any level of carbon emissions, much of the carbon savings get swallowed up by higher living standards. The only question is how much of the benefits of greener technology get eaten up in higher consumption. As many countries have adopted smaller, more fuel-efficient cars, national emissions have usually continued to rise despite the increased efficiency.

A STEADY-STATE ECONOMY

It is clear that we have to move to something more like the steady-state economy first proposed by economist Herman Daly.[347] But how do we do that when, as Murray Bookchin, the American social ecologist and libertarian philosopher, said, 'Capitalism can no more be "persuaded" to limit growth than a human being can be "persuaded" to stop breathing'?[348] When Daly developed the concept of a steady-state economy people were more concerned about using up the earth's finite mineral and agricultural resources than they were with global warming. He suggested that we should have physical quotas on the extraction of minerals and that the use of the world's resources should be prevented from growing. Limiting world oil and coal production might turn out to be a very effective way of limiting global warming. Innovation and change would then be concentrated on using finite resources more effectively for the benefit of humankind.

Think of material living standards as given by the stock of goods in use, rather than the rate of flow from consumption to waste. The faster things wear out and need replacing, the more they contribute to the flow and to waste. If material living standards depend on the goods we have in use, then each thing that wears out is a subtraction from that. Rather than serving as consumers, helping business to keep sales up, we need incentives to build and maintain longer-lasting goods of every kind.

Clearly any system for tackling these problems has to treat rich and poor countries differently. India, producing 1.6 tonnes of carbon per person annually, cannot be treated the same as the USA, producing 24.0 per person. Any regulatory system has to include policies for 'contraction and convergence' or 'cap and share'. Both approaches propose a year-on-year contraction in permitted emissions levels, leading to an eventual convergence on equal per capita emissions across the planet.

It would be a mistake to think that a steady-state economy would mean stagnation and lack of change. Paradoxically, the transition to a sustainable steady state economy would create huge demands for innovation and change. Trying to get more from the limited resources available has always been one of the fundamental drivers of innovation and technical change.[349] Fixing limits on resource consumption and emissions would require innovation as never before. As we shall see in the next chapter, continued rapid technological advances, such as digitization, electronic communications and virtual systems, creating 'weightless' sectors of the economy, make it very much easier to combine high living standards with low resource consumption and emissions.

It is often suggested that invention and innovation go with inequality and depend on the promise of individual financial incentives. However, Figure 15.3 suggests the contrary – that more equal societies tend to be more creative. It shows that there is a tendency for more patents to be granted per head of population in more equal societies than in less equal ones. Whether this is because talent goes undeveloped or wasted in more unequal societies, or whether hierarchy breeds conformity, is anyone's guess. But it does suggest that greater equality will not make societies less adaptable.

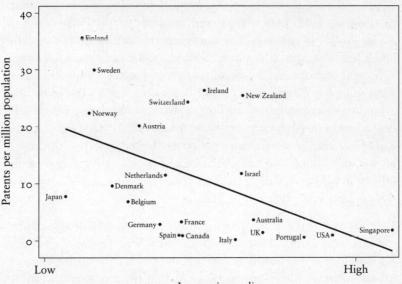

Figure 15.3 *More equal societies are more innovative.*[403]

INEQUALITY AND CONSUMERISM

The second link between greater equality and the prevention of global warming involves the consumerism which makes it so much harder to contain economic activity within sustainable levels. Our addiction to shopping and spending makes many people think that we have already lost the battle against global warming. As well as leading most of us into an ostrich-like denial of its implications for our way of life, the strength of our consumerist tendencies has reduced governments to a state of paralysis, too nervous of the electorate to implement any policy capable of making a real difference. How are we to transform this culture and make it possible to reduce the threat to the planet?

Greater equality gives us the crucial key to reducing the cultural pressure to consume. In a period when people seem to have been less guarded, Henry Wallich, a former governor of the Federal Reserve and professor of economics at Yale, said: 'Growth is a substitute for equality of income. So long as there is growth there is hope, and that makes large income differentials tolerable.'[350] But this relation holds both ways round. It is not simply that growth is a substitute for equality, it is that greater equality makes growth much less necessary. It is a precondition for a steady-state economy.

A great deal of what drives consumption is status competition. For most of us it probably feels less like being competitive and more like a kind of defensiveness; if we don't raise our standards, we get left behind and everything starts to look dowdy, shabby and out of date. Robert Frank, an economist at Cornell University, has described how standards are inherently relative and involve comparisons with others. In his book, *Falling Behind: How rising inequality harms the middle class* (2007), he puts it like this:[351]

No one denies that a car experienced in 1950 as having brisk acceleration would seem sluggish to most drivers today. Similarly, a house of given size is more likely to be viewed as spacious the larger it is relative to other houses in the same local environment. And an effective interview suit is one that compares favorably with those worn by other applicants for the same job. In short, evaluation depends always and everywhere on context. (pp. viii–ix)

The problem is that second-class goods make us look like second-class people. By comparison with the rich and famous, the rest of us appear second-rate and inferior, and the bigger the differences, the more noticeable and important they become. As inequality increases status competition, we have to struggle harder to keep up. While the rich may believe their willingness to spend huge sums on a watch, a car or some other luxury item reflects their appreciation of the 'attention to detail' or 'craftsmanship', what really makes the difference is what their purchases say about them relative to the rest of us. As every advertiser knows, it serves to set them apart as people of distinction social distinction. Only the best people can have nothing but the best.

The other side of this coin is that the consumption of the rich reduces everyone else's satisfaction with what they have, by showing it up as inferior – as less than the best. In his book, *Happiness*, Richard Layard, founder of the Centre for Economic Performance at the London School of Economics, treated this dissatisfaction as a cost which the rich impose on the rest of society.[3] Rather as if it were smoke from a factory chimney, he estimated the cost that the rich should pay for it. He was, however, unaware of the effects of inequality on the health and social problems which we have outlined. He based his calculations solely on the loss of satisfaction, or happiness, among the rest of the population and concluded that a 60 per cent tax rate on the better-off might cover that cost (presumably that should be over and above the tax rates other people pay).

The idea that inequality ratchets up the competitive pressure to consume is not just speculation. It has observable effects. While inequality has been rising in the USA and Britain, there has been a long-term decline in savings and a rise in debt. Robert Frank notes that in 1998, even though the American economy was booming as never before, one family in sixty-eight filed for bankruptcy – four times the rate in the early 1980s before the most dramatic rises in inequality.[351] By 2002, unpaid credit card debt was $9,000 for the average card-holder. Looking at changes over a ten-year period,

Frank found that bankruptcy rates rose most in parts of the USA where inequality had risen most.[154, 351] The growth of inequality made it harder for people to maintain standards relative to others. The increased pressure to consume led people to save less and borrow more to such an extent that the expansion of consumer demand became one of the main drivers of the long economic boom and financial speculation which ended in crisis. This fits well with the fact that spending on advertising also varies with inequality – in more unequal countries a higher proportion of Gross Domestic Product is spent on advertising, with the USA and New Zealand spending twice as much as Norway and Denmark.

Another indicator of how inequality increases the pressure to consume comes from the way working hours vary in different countries in relation to inequality. A study of working hours in OECD countries by Sam Bowles, professor emeritus of economics at the University of Massachusetts, showed not only that more unequal countries tend to have longer working hours, but also that differences in working hours changed in line with changes in inequality over several decades.[352] The relationship between greater inequality and longer working hours is shown in Figure 15.3. People in more unequal countries do the equivalent of two or three months' extra work a year. A loss of the equivalent of an extra eight or twelve weeks' holiday is a high price to pay for inequality.

Another study, this time using data within the USA, found that married women were more likely to go out to work if their sister's husband earned more than their own husband.[353] A similar study suggested that the decisions married women make about taking paid work are also affected by less personal inequalities: it looked at women who were married to employed men and found that they were more likely to take a job themselves if they lived in an area in which men's incomes were more unequal.[354]

The evidence we have described from a number of different sources on savings, debt, bankruptcy rates, spending on advertising and working hours, all concurs with the view that inequality does indeed increase the pressure to consume. If an important part of consumerism is driven by emulation, status competition, or simply having to run to keep up with everyone else, and is basically about

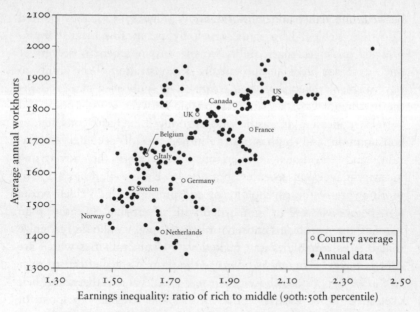

Figure 15.4 *People work longer in more unequal societies.*[352]

social appearances and position, this would explain why we continue to pursue economic growth despite its apparent lack of benefits. If everyone wants more money because it improves self-image and status in relation to others, then each person's desire to be richer does not add up to a societal desire for economic growth. How much people's desire for more income is really a desire for higher status has been demonstrated in a simple experiment. People were asked to say whether they'd prefer to be less well-off than others in a rich society, or have a much lower income in a poorer society but be better-off than others. Fifty per cent of the participants thought they would trade as much as half their real income if they could live in a society in which they would be better off than others.[355] This shows how much we value status and explains why (as we saw in Chapter 2) the income differences within rich societies matter so much more than the income differences between them. Once we have enough of the necessities of life, it is the relativities which matter.

When Bowles and Park first demonstrated the relationship

between inequality and working hours (Figure 15.3), they quoted Thorstein Veblen, who said: 'The only practicable means of impressing one's pecuniary ability on the unsympathetic observers of one's everyday life is an unremitting demonstration of the ability to pay.' Veblen's *Theory of the Leisure Class*, published in 1899, was the first major work on the relationship between consumption and social stratification. It was he who introduced the term 'conspicuous consumption' and emphasized the importance of 'pecuniary emulation' and 'invidious comparisons'.[356] Because the advertising industry plays on insecurities about how we are seen, it has made us more aware of the psychology of consumption. But Veblen wrote long before we were so bombarded with advertising. So rather than blaming these problems entirely on advertising, we should recognize that it simply amplifies and makes use of vulnerabilities which are there anyway. Economists now use the term 'Veblen effect' to refer to the way goods are chosen for their social value rather than their usefulness. And research confirms that the tendency to look for goods which confer status and prestige is indeed stronger for things which are more visible to others.

Too often consumerism is regarded as if it reflected a fundamental human material self-interest and possessiveness. That, however, could hardly be further from the truth. Our almost neurotic need to shop and consume is instead a reflection of how deeply social we are. Living in unequal and individualistic societies, we use possessions to show ourselves in a good light, to make a positive impression, and to avoid appearing incompetent or inadequate in the eyes of others. Consumerism shows how powerfully we are affected by each other. Once we have enough of the basic necessities for comfort, possessions matter less and less in themselves, and are used more and more for what they say about their owners. Ideally, our impressions of each other would depend on face-to-face interactions in the course of community life, rather than on outward appearances in the absence of real knowledge of each other. That point takes us back to the discussion in Chapter 4 of the evidence that inequality weakens community life. The weakening of community life and the growth of consumerism are related.

If, to cut carbon emissions, we need to limit economic growth severely in the rich countries, then it is important to know that this does not mean sacrificing improvements in the real quality of life – in the quality of life as measured by health, happiness, friendship and community life, which really matters. However, rather than simply having fewer of all the luxuries which substitute for and prevent us recognizing our more fundamental needs, inequality has to be reduced simultaneously. We need to create more equal societies able to meet our real social needs. Instead of policies to deal with global warming being experienced simply as imposing limits on the possibilities of material satisfaction, they need to be coupled with egalitarian policies which steer us to new and more fundamental ways of improving the quality of our lives. The change is about a historic shift in the sources of human satisfaction from economic growth to a more sociable society.

In his speech accepting the 2007 Nobel Peace Prize on behalf of the Intergovernmental Panel on Climate Change which he chairs, Rajendra Pachauri described how global warming would reduce agricultural yields, food and water supplies for hundreds of millions of people and so lead to increasing conflict. (He spoke before the contribution of biofuel crops to rising world food prices had been clearly recognized.) The task of responding adequately to the threat of global warming needs to be seen as bigger and more important than any of us. But if everyone – individuals, corporations, whole nations – feels it is almost their duty to get round regulations, to exploit whatever loopholes they can (as has long been taken as the norm with taxation) then the task is lost. As we write, tankers of biofuels are crossing the Atlantic from Europe to the USA and back in order to pick up the US government subsidy paid when small quantities of petroleum are added, which could just as well have been added in Europe without every litre crossing the Atlantic twice. Reversing the intended effect of regulations for private gain is an expression of the dominance of attitudes which make it much harder to respond adequately to the threat of global warming.

Tackling climate change depends on world co-operation like never before: we cannot succeed if in practice everyone is trying to circumvent the regulations. Cheating on regulations and the pursuit of short-term sectional or self-interest becomes not just anti-social but anti-humanity. Policies to reduce carbon emissions depend on a wider sense of social responsibility, of co-operation and public-spiritedness. Here again the evidence suggests that more equal societies do better. We have seen (Chapter 4) that they are more socially cohesive and have higher levels of trust which foster public-spiritedness. We have also seen how this carries over into inter-national relations: more equal societies give more in development aid and score better on the Global Peace Index. An indication that a greater sense of public responsibility in more equal countries might affect how societies respond to environmental issues can be seen in Figure 15.5, which shows that they tend to recycle a higher pro-portion of their waste. The data comes from Australia's Planet Ark Foundation Trust.[357] We show each country's ranking for the proportion of waste that they recycle. Another indication of a stronger sense of public responsibility comes from an international survey of opinions of business leaders. As our colleagues, Roberto De Vogli and David Gimeno, pointed out, business leaders in more

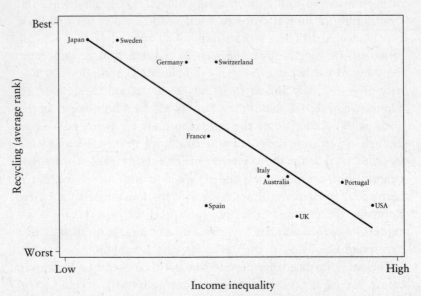

Figure 15.5 *More equal countries recycle a higher proportion of their waste.*

equal countries are more strongly in favour of their governments complying with international environmental agreements than business leaders in more unequal countries.[404, 405]

So rather than assuming that we are stuck with levels of self-interested consumerism, individualism and materialism which must defeat any attempts to develop sustainable economic systems, we need to recognize that these are not fixed expressions of human nature. Instead they reflect the characteristics of the societies in which we find ourselves and vary even from one rich market democracy to another. At the most fundamental level, what reducing inequality is about is shifting the balance from the divisive, self-interested consumerism driven by status competition, towards a more socially integrated and affiliative society. Greater equality can help us develop the public ethos and commitment to working together which we need if we are going to solve the problems which threaten us all. As wartime leaders knew, if a society has to pull together, policies must be seen to be fair and income differences have to be reduced.

ME

MORRIS

16

Building the future

Turning corporations loose and letting the profit motive
run amok is not a prescription for a more liveable world.
                    Tom Scholz, Interview with the Sierra Club

Before discussing what should be done to make our societies more
equal, it is worth pointing out that focusing attention on the inequalities within them does not mean ignoring the international
inequalities between rich and poor countries. The evidence strongly
suggests that narrowing income differences within rich countries will
make them more responsive to the needs of poorer countries. In
Chapter 4 we showed (Figure 16) that more equal countries tend to
pay a higher proportion of their national income in foreign aid.
Compared to the most unequal countries, some of the most equal
devote four times the proportion of their national income to aid.
More unequal countries also seem to be more belligerent internationally. Inequality is related to worse scores on the Global Peace
Index, which combines measures of militarization with measures of
domestic and international conflict, and measures of security, human
rights and stability. (It is produced by Visions of Humanity in
conjunction with the Economist Intelligence Unit.)[358]
  If we turn instead to the part countries play in international trade
agreements or, for instance, in negotiations on reducing carbon
emissions, we find that more equal countries take positions on these
issues which are likely to be more beneficial to developing countries.
  It looks as if the inequalities which affect the way people treat
each other within their own societies also affect the norms and

expectations they bring to bear on international issues. Growing up and living in a more unequal society affects people's assumptions about human nature. We have seen how inequality affects trust, community life and violence, and how – through the quality of early life – it predisposes people to be more or less affiliative, empathetic or aggressive. Obviously these issues are closely related to the increased status competition and consumerism we discussed in the previous chapter. It implies that if we put our own houses in order, we may look more sympathetically on developing countries.

A TRANSFORMATION

But how can we make our societies more equal? Talk about greater equality worries some people. Trying to allay these fears at a National Policy Association conference on health inequalities in Washington, one of us pointed out that as all the data came from rich developed market democracies and we were only talking about the differences between them, it surely wouldn't take a revolution to put things right. But when *It Doesn't Take a Revolution* appeared as the title of the National Policy Association's booklet from the conference, it was surprising to find a few people who thought it would.

As Bill Kerry, one of the founders of the Equality Trust, put it, if we are going to achieve a major narrowing of income differences while responding effectively to global warming, what is required amounts to a *transformation* of our societies, a transformation which will not be furthered by a departure from peaceful methods but one which is unlikely to be achieved by tinkering with minor policy options. A social movement for greater equality needs a sustained sense of direction and a view of how we can achieve the necessary economic and social changes. The key is to map out ways in which the new society can begin to grow within and alongside the institutions it may gradually marginalize and replace. That is what making change is really about. Rather than simply waiting for government to do it for us, we have to start making it in our lives and in the institutions of our society straight away. What we need is not one big revolution but a continuous stream of small changes in a consistent direction. And to give ourselves the best chance of making the necessary transformation of society we need to remember that the aim is to make a more sociable society, which means avoiding the disruption and dislocation which increase insecurity and fear and so often end in a disastrous backlash. The aim is to increase people's sense of security and to reduce fear; to make everyone feel that a more equal society not only has room for them but also that it offers a more fulfilling life than is possible in a society dominated by hierarchy and inequality.

In the past, when arguments about inequality centred on the privations of the poor and on what is fair, reducing inequality depended on coaxing or scaring the better-off into adopting a more altruistic attitude to the poor. But now we know that inequality affects so many outcomes, across so much of society, all that has changed. The transformation of our society is a project in which we all have a shared interest. Greater equality is the gateway to a society capable of improving the quality of life for all of us and an essential step in the development of a sustainable economic system.

It is often said that greater equality is impossible because people are not equal. But that is a confusion: equality does not mean being the same. People did not become the same when the principle of equality before the law was established. Nor – as is often claimed – does reducing material inequality mean lowering standards or levelling to a common mediocrity. Wealth, particularly inherited wealth, is a poor indicator of genuine merit – hence George Bernard Shaw's assertion that: 'Only where there is pecuniary equality can the distinction of merit stand out.'[359, p. 71] Perhaps that makes Sweden a particularly suitable home for the system of Nobel prizes.

We see no indication that standards of intellectual, artistic or sporting achievement are lower in the more equal societies in our analyses. Indeed, making a large part of the population feel devalued can surely only lower standards. Although a baseball team is not a microcosm of society, a well-controlled study of over 1,600 players in twenty-nine teams over a nine-year period found that major league baseball teams with smaller income differences among players do significantly better than the more unequal ones.[360] And we saw in earlier chapters that more equal countries have higher overall levels of attainment in many different fields.

THE POLICY FAILURE

Politics was once seen as a way of improving people's social and emotional wellbeing by changing their economic circumstances. But over the last few decades the bigger picture has been lost. People are now more likely to see psychosocial wellbeing as dependent on what can be done at the individual level, using cognitive behavioural therapy – one person at a time – or on providing support in early childhood, or on the reassertion of religious or 'family' values. However, it is now clear that income distribution provides policy makers with a way of improving the psychosocial wellbeing of whole populations. Politicians have an opportunity to do genuine good.

Attempts to deal with health and social problems through the provision of specialized services have proved expensive and, at best, only partially effective. Evaluations of even some of the most important services, such as police and medical care, suggest that they are not among the most powerful determinants of crime levels or standards of population health. Other services, such as social work or drug rehabilitation, exist to treat – or process – their various client groups, rather than to diminish the prevalence of social problems. On the occasions when government agencies do announce policies ostensibly aimed at prevention – at decreasing obesity, reducing health inequalities, or trying to cut rates of drug abuse – it usually looks more like a form of political window-dressing, a display of good intentions, intended to give the impression of a government actively getting to grips with problems. Sometimes, when policies will obviously fall very far short of their targets, you wonder whether even those who formulated them, or who write the official documents, ever really believed their proposals would have any measurable impact.

Take health inequalities, for example. For ten years Britain has had a government committed to narrowing the health gap between rich and poor. In an independent review of policy in different countries, a Dutch expert said Britain was ahead of other countries in implementing policies to reduce health inequalities.[361] However, health inequalities in Britain have shown little or no tendency to decline. It is as if advisers and researchers of all kinds knew, almost unconsciously, that realistic solutions cannot be given serious consideration.

Rather than reducing inequality itself, the initiatives aimed at tackling health or social problems are nearly always attempts to break the links between socio-economic disadvantage and the problems it produces. The unstated hope is that people – particularly the poor – can carry on in the same circumstances, but will somehow no longer succumb to mental illness, teenage pregnancy, educational failure, obesity or drugs.

Every problem is seen as needing its own solution – unrelated to others. People are encouraged to take exercise, not to have unprotected sex, to say no to drugs, to try to relax, to sort out their work–life balance, and to give their children 'quality' time. The only thing that many of these policies do have in common is that they often seem to be based on the belief that the poor need to be taught to be more sensible. The glaringly obvious fact that these problems have common roots in inequality and relative deprivation disappears from view.

TRENDS IN INEQUALITY

Inequality has risen in many, but not all, developed countries over the last few decades. Figures 16.1 and 16.2 show the widening gap between the incomes of rich and poor in Britain and the United States over a thirty-year period. The figures show the widening gap between the top and bottom 10 per cent in each country. Both countries experienced very dramatic rises in inequality which peaked in the early 1990s and have changed rather little since then. In both countries inequality remains at levels almost unprecedented since records began – certainly higher than it has been for several generations. Few other developed countries have shown quite such dramatic increases in inequality over this period, but only a very few

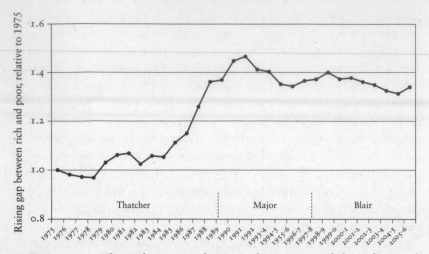

Figure 16.1 *The widening gap between the incomes of the richest and poorest 10 per cent in Britain 1975 (=1) to 2005–2006.*

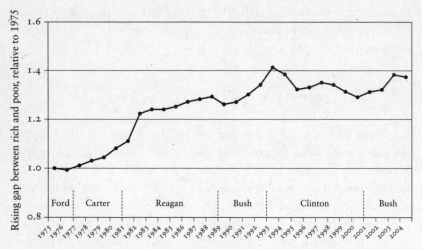

Figure 16.2 *The widening gap between the incomes of the richest and poorest 10 per cent in the USA 1975 (=1) to 2004.*

– such as The Netherlands – seem to have avoided them entirely. Others, like Sweden, which avoided them initially, have had steep rises since the early 1990s.

The figures showing widening income inequality in Britain and the United States leave no room for doubt that income differences do change substantially over time and that they are now not far short of 40 per cent greater than they were in the mid-1970s.

If things can change so rapidly, then there are good reasons to feel confident that we *can* create a society in which the real quality of life and of human relationships is far higher than it is now.

Whenever governments have really wanted to increase equality, policies to do so have not been lacking. The historical evidence confirms the primacy of political will. Rather than greater equality waiting till well-meaning governments think they can afford to make societies more equal, governments have usually not pursued more egalitarian policies until they thought their survival depended on it. In the early 1990s a World Bank report pointed out that rapid economic growth in a number of East Asian countries was underpinned by growing equality.[366] In trying to explain why governments had adopted more egalitarian policies, the report said that it was because they faced crises of legitimacy and needed to gain popular support. The governments in Taiwan and Hong Kong faced rival claims from the Communist Chinese government. South Korea faced North Korea, and the governments of Singapore and the Philippines faced guerrilla forces. Describing policy in these countries, John Page, writing in a 1994 World Bank publication, said:

Very explicit mechanisms were used to demonstrate the intent that all would have a share of future wealth. Korea and Taiwan carried out comprehensive land reform programs; Indonesia used rice and fertilizer price policies to raise rural incomes; Malaysia introduced explicit wealth sharing programs to improve the lot of ethnic Malays vis-à-vis the better off ethnic Chinese; Hong Kong and Singapore undertook massive public housing programs; in several economies, governments assisted workers' cooperatives and established programs to encourage small and medium-sized enterprises. Whatever the form, these programs demonstrated that the government intended for all to share in the benefits of growth.[367]

Japan owes its status as the most equal of the developed countries partly to the fact that the whole establishment had been humiliated by defeat in the Second World War, and partly to the support for political and economic reconstruction – including drawing up a new constitution – provided by disinterested, and remarkably far-sighted, American advisers working under General MacArthur.[95]

Other examples of increases in equality have similar origins. Bismarck's early development of forms of social insurance were part of his attempt to gain popular support for his project of unifying the German states. Britain became substantially more equal during both the First and Second World Wars as part of an attempt to gain support for the war effort by making people feel the burden of war was equally shared. As Richard Titmuss put it: 'If the cooperation of the masses was thought to be essential [to the war effort], then inequalities had to be reduced and the pyramid of social stratification had to be flattened.'[368]

Sweden's greater equality originated in the Social Democratic Party's electoral victory in 1932 which had been preceded by violent labour disputes in which troops had opened fire on sawmill workers. As prime minister almost continuously from 1932 to 1946, Per Albin Hansson was able, during Swedish rearmament and the war, to push through his aim of making Sweden 'a classless society' and 'the people's home'.

Turning now to examples of where income differences have widened rather than narrowed, the central role of politics is no less clear. In Figures 16.1 and 16.2 we saw the widening of income differences in Britain and the USA which took place particularly during the 1980s and early 1990s. Paul Krugman, the Nobel Prize winning economist, analyses the reasons for rising inequality in the USA. He says that the conventional explanation is that it was driven by a rising demand for skilled labour, resulting mainly from the spread of information technology, and by the import of cheap goods, such as textiles, replacing less skilled labour. However, he dismisses these explanations saying that econometric research suggests that they are only a small part of the picture. He also points out that factors such as these do not explain the runaway incomes at the top – for instance among CEOs – which was one of the main features of the growth in inequality, and adds that although these forces have been at work in all rich countries, income differences widened in only some of them. Countries in which inequality did not increase during the 1980s and early '90s include Canada, France, Japan, Netherlands, Spain and Switzerland.[406, 407]

Confining his attention largely to the USA, Krugman argues that, rather than market forces, rising inequality was driven by 'changes in institutions, norms and political power'. He emphasizes the weakening of trade unions, the abandonment of productivity sharing agreements, the influence of the political right, and government changes in taxes and benefits. He could also have added the failure to maintain adequate minimum wage legislation.

Despite substantial differences between countries, the basic trends in income distribution seen in the USA throughout the twentieth century can be seen in many countries. After inequalities rose to a peak just before the Great Crash of 1929, they then narrowed so dramatically in the later 1930s and early '40s that the period is sometimes referred to as the 'Great Compression'. Income differences then remained narrower until the later 1970s or the mid 1980s. They then started to widen rapidly again until just before the most recent financial crash, where they reached levels of inequality not seen since just before the 1929 crash.

Most research on changes in income distribution is concerned with dividing up the components of the overall trends: how much is due to widening differences in earnings? How much to changes in taxes and benefits? How much is due to simultaneous growth in workless and two-earner households? And then, at the next causal level down, how much of the widening differences in earnings is due to weaker trade unions and how much is due to a decline in demand for unskilled labour? But the truth is that the major changes in income distribution in any country are almost never attributable simply to market forces influencing wage rates. What we see instead is something much more like the changes in institutions, norms and the use of political power which Krugman describes in the USA. Differences in pre-tax earnings rise, tax rates are made less progressive, benefits are cut, the law is changed to weaken trade union powers and so on. Together these are a fairly clear sign of a change in norms and political outlook. If that were not so, and widening differences in earnings were politically unacceptable, governments would have acted to reduce rather than increase the differences. In Britain it was not until after the change of government in 1997 that any such attempts were made.

There can be even less doubt about the political nature of the compression of income differences before and during the Second World War. Against a backdrop of the Depression, unprecedented levels of unemployment and growing signs of social unrest, coupled, presumably, with a fear of the spread of communism, governments took action. In the USA President Roosevelt inaugurated the New Deal in the early 1930s and, with the coming of war, many governments reduced income differences even more dramatically.

If 'market forces' were the real drivers of inequality, it is unlikely that the post-war settlement would have remained intact for three or four decades before income differences began to widen again more rapidly in the 1980s. The ending of that consensus was very clearly related to a rightward shift in political opinion. The triumph of the new right extolling the benefits of the free market and the dominance of monetarist economics were enshrined in the political leadership of Reagan in the USA and Thatcher in Britain. Communism had ceased to be a realistic threat and many governments privatized what had been state owned public utilities.

To recognize how political attitudes sweep across the international scene, we have only to look at the way revolutionary upheavals of 1848 shook half a dozen different European countries, or remember the radicalism of the 1960s, or how many communist governments collapsed in 1989–90. An indicator that the widening income differences of the 1980s resulted from another such change in the political wind is that, with the exception of Canada, they widened most rapidly in English speaking countries – in Britain, the USA, New Zealand and Australia – accompanied in each case by a free-market ideology and by policies designed to create a more 'flexible' labour force. Stronger linguistic and ideological connections meant that English speaking countries caught the disease quickly from each other and caught it badly.

A study which analysed trends in inequality during the 1980s and

1990s in Australia, Canada, Germany, Japan, Sweden, the United Kingdom and the United States, found that the most important single factor was trade union membership.[370] Although high levels of unemployment weaken the bargaining power of labour, in this study, declines in trade union membership were most closely associated with widening income differences.

Not only the extent of unionization but provisions for labour representation in companies are also likely to affect wage settlements. The Commission of the European Union requires minimum standards of representation and consultation for all larger companies but it is not clear how far practice in different countries conforms to what was intended. In Japan, however, there is often a much closer relationship between management and unions. Indeed, the Japanese Federation of Employers Association found that 15 per cent of the directors of large companies were former trade union officials.[371] In the countries of the European Union the earnings of some 70 per cent of employees are covered by collective agreements, compared to only 15 per cent in the USA. At 35 per cent, the figure for the UK is among the lowest in the EU.

DIFFERENT ROUTES TO GREATER EQUALITY

Rather than suggesting a particular route or set of policies to narrow income differences, it is probably better to point out that there are many different ways of reaching the same destination. In Chapter 13 we showed that although the more equal countries often get their greater equality through redistributive taxes and benefits and through a large welfare state, countries like Japan manage to achieve low levels of inequality *before* taxes and benefits. Japanese differences in gross earnings (before taxes and benefits) are smaller, so there is less need for large-scale redistribution. This is how Japan manages to be so much more equal than the US, even though its social security transfers were a smaller proportion of GDP than social security transfers in the USA.[362] Although, of all the countries included in our analyses, the USA and Japan are at opposite extremes in terms of inequality, the proportion of their GDP taken up by government social expenditure is small in both cases: they come second and third lowest of the countries in our analysis.

Similar evidence that there are very different routes to greater equality can also be seen among the American states.[363] The total tax burden in each state as a percentage of income is completely unrelated to inequality. Because Vermont and New Hampshire are neighbouring New England states, the contrast between them is particularly striking. Vermont has the highest tax burden of any state of the union, while New Hampshire has the second lowest – beaten only by Alaska. Yet New Hampshire has the best performance of any state on our Index of Health and Social Problems and is closely followed by Vermont which is third best. They both also do well on equality: despite their radically different taxation, they are the fourth and sixth most equal states respectively. The need for redistribution depends on how unequal incomes are before taxes and benefits.

Both the international and US state comparisons send the same message: there are quite different roads to the greater equality which improves health and reduces social problems. As we said in Chapter 13, what matters is the level of inequality you finish up with, not how you get it. However, in the figures there is also a clear warning for those who might want to place low public expenditure and taxation at the top of their list of priorities. If you fail to avoid high inequality, you will need more prisons and more police. You will have to deal with higher rates of mental illness, drug abuse and every other kind of problem. If keeping taxes and benefits down leads to wider income differences, the need to deal with the ensuing social ills may force you to raise public expenditure to cope.

There may be a choice between using public expenditure to cope with social harm where inequality is high, or to pay for real social benefits where it is low. An example of this balance shifting in the wrong direction can be seen in the USA during the period since 1980, when income inequality increased particularly rapidly. During that period, public expenditure on prisons increased six times as fast as public expenditure on education, and a number of states have now reached a point where they are spending as much public money on prisons as on higher education.[364]

Not only would it be preferable to live in societies where money can be spent on education rather than on prisons, but policies to support families in early childhood would have meant that many of those in prison would have been earning and paying taxes instead of being a burden on public funds. As we saw in Chapter 8, pre-school provisions can be a profitable long-term investment: children who receive these services are less likely to need special education and, when they reach adulthood, they are more likely to be earning and less likely to be dependent on welfare or to incur costs through crime.[365]

It is tempting to say that there are two quite different paths to greater equality, one using taxes and benefits to redistribute income from the rich to the poor, and the other achieving narrower differences in gross market incomes before any redistribution. But the two strategies are not mutually exclusive or inconsistent with each other. In the pursuit of greater equality we should use both strategies: to rely on one without the other would be to fight inequality with one arm tied behind your back. Nevertheless, it is worth remembering that the argument for greater equality is not necessarily an argument for big government. Given that there are many different ways of diminishing inequality, what matters is creating the necessary political will to pursue any of them.

POLITICAL WILL

So if it all boils down to politics, how can we create the necessary political will to narrow income differences? The strength of the evidence that a more equal society is a better society has a key role to play in changing public opinion. Many people have a strong personal belief in greater equality and fairness, but these values have remained private intuitions which they fear others do not share. The advantage of the growing body of evidence of the harm inflicted by inequality is that it turns what were purely personal intuitions into publicly demonstrable facts. This will substantially increase the confidence of those who have always shared these values and encourage them to take action. In addition, some people will change their views in the light of the new evidence. Many people are seriously worried about the many signs of social failure in our societies and search for explanations.

Political differences are more a reflection of different beliefs about the solution to problems than of disagreements about what the problems are. Almost everyone, regardless of their politics, would prefer to live in a safer and more friendly society. Everyone will agree that a good society would have fewer of all the health and social problems we have looked at. The argument is therefore about solutions. Although people have suggested many ways of helping individuals facing particular difficulties, the evidence presented in this book suggests that greater equality can address a wide range of problems across whole societies. And if greater equality is also an important component of policies to tackle global warming, there is much to recommend it. Recent research in Britain using focus groups has shown that an understanding of the effects of inequality can have a powerful influence on people's attitudes to it.[408] Participants drawn from across the social and political spectrum were shown the evidence provided in this book on how inequality affects trust, child conflict, and mental illness. As well as finding the relationships intuitively plausible, they were also moved by them. Many of those previously opposed to greater equality changed their minds. Even people who rejected appeals for greater fairness were in favour of greater equality when it was presented as part of a social vision around improving the quality of life for everyone. In terms of creating the necessary political will, the evidence was regarded as one of the most important reasons for reducing inequality.

For several decades progressive politics have been seriously weakened by the loss of any concept of a better society. People have argued for piecemeal improvements in different areas of life, campaigned against new environmental threats or for better treatment of asylum seekers, and have demonstrated against military interventions. But nowhere is there a popular movement capable of inspiring people with a vision of how to make society a substantially better place to live for the vast majority. Without that vision politics will rarely provoke more than a yawn.

Yet most people do want change. In the first chapter of this book we referred to a research report called *Yearning for Balance*, which showed that three-quarters or more of Americans felt that society had lost touch with what really mattered.[1] Consumerism and materialism, they felt, were winning out over more important values to do with friends, family and community. Although politicians recognize a deep-seated malaise, and so campaign for votes, saying that they stand for 'change', they sometimes seem to have few ideas for change which go deeper than differences in the personal images they project. There is no suggestion that they have any view of how to begin changing daily life into something more joyful and fulfilling.

Public opinion polls suggest that there is a substantial desire for narrower income differences. In Britain over the last twenty years polls have shown that the proportion of the population who think that income differences are too big has averaged around 80 per cent and has rarely dipped below 75 per cent – even though most people underestimate how big income differences actually are. In the USA, the 2005 Maxwell Poll on Civic Engagement reported that over 80 per cent of the population thought the extent of inequality was a problem, and almost 60 per cent thought the government should try to reduce it. Gallup polls between 1984 and 2003 which asked Americans whether income and wealth were fairly distributed or should be more evenly distributed, found that over 60 per cent of the population thought they should be more evenly distributed.[369]

CORPORATE POWER – THE ELEPHANT IN THE LIVING ROOM

Part of the problem of political will is the feeling that we do not have the means to make any difference. We may all decry the vast wealth of the super-rich, but what can we do? Unions can, as the evidence suggests, make some difference, but it is hard to escape the conclusion that the high levels of inequality in our societies reflect the concentrations of power in our economic institutions. The institutions in which we are employed are, after all, the main source of income inequality. It is there that value is created and divided between the various gradations of employees. It is there that the inequities which necessitate redistribution are set up. And it is there that we are most explicitly placed in a rank-ordered hierarchy, superiors and inferiors, bosses and subordinates.

In 2007 chief executives of 365 of the largest US companies received well over 500 times the pay of their average employee, and these differences were getting bigger. In many of the top companies the chief executive is paid more in each day than the average worker is in a year. Among the Fortune 500 companies the pay gap in 2007 was close to ten times as big as it was in 1980, when the long rise in income inequality was just beginning.

Because the ratio of CEO pay to average worker pay varies somuch between large and small companies and from one sector to another, it is difficult to compare like with like when making international comparisons. However, an attempt (from a respected source) to make such comparisons, suggests that ratios of CEO compensation to the pay of production workers in manufacturing might be 16:1 in Japan, 21:1 in Sweden, 31:1 in the UK and 44:1 in the USA.[372]

According to the annual survey of chief executives' pay carried out by the *Guardian*, boardroom pay in the 100 companies included in the Financial Times Stock Exchange index in Britain has risen in successive years by 16 per cent, 13 per cent, 28 per cent and most recently (2006–2007) by 37 per cent at a period when inflation was rarely more than 2 per cent.[373] The average pay (including bonuses) for the chief executives of top companies stood at just under £2.9 million. After reviewing empirical research, the International Labour Organization concluded that there is little or no evidence of a relationship between executive pay and company performance and suggested that these excessive salaries are likely to reflect the dominant bargaining position of executives.[374]

Top business pay has far outstripped anything in the public sector. In the USA, the twenty highest-paid people working in public traded corporations received almost 40 times as much as the twenty highest-paid people in the non-profit sector, and 200 times more than the twenty highest-paid generals or cabinet secretaries in the Federal Government.[375]

It seems likely that the denationalization of major industries and the privatization of large numbers of friendly societies, mutuals, building societies, provident societies and credit unions, which had been controlled by their members, may have made a substantial contribution to the widening income differences shown in Figures 16.1 and 16.2. It was common practice for CEOs and other senior managers to receive huge salary increases shortly after conversion to profit-making corporations. This probably explains some of the sharp rise in inequality which Figure 16.1 shows took place in Britain around the mid-1980s. British Telecom was privatized in 1983, British Gas in 1986, followed by a flood of major companies in 1987. The international extent of the widening of income inequality is also consistent with a contribution from privatization.

Numerous corporations are now bigger than many nation states. In the words of the United Nations Conference on Trade and Development (UNCTAD):[376]

Twenty-nine of the world's 100 largest economic entities are transnational corporations (TNCs), according to a new UNCTAD list that ranks both countries and TNCs on the basis of value added. Of the 200 TNCs with the highest assets abroad in 2000, Exxon is the biggest in terms of value added ($63 billion). It ranks 45th on the new list, making it comparable in economic size to the economies of Chile or Pakistan. Nigeria comes in just between DaimlerChrysler and General Electric, while Philip Morris is on a par with Tunisia, Slovakia and Guatemala.

Using different measures, other estimates suggest that half of the world's largest economies are multinationals, and that General Motors is bigger than Denmark, that DaimlerChrysler is bigger than Poland; Royal Dutch/Shell bigger than Venezuela, and Sony bigger than Pakistan. Like the aristocratic ownership of huge tracts of land, which in 1791 Tom Paine attacked in his *The Rights of Man*,[377] these productive assets remain effectively in the hands of a very few, very rich people, and make our claims to real democracy look pretty thin.

In Tom Paine's lifetime the capitalist system was in its infancy. As an advocate of equality and democracy, he focused his attack on the landed aristocracy, the nobility, the monarchy, and on their ownership of huge swathes of land. He seems to have assumed that the market system, then involving mainly small traders and craftsmen, would remain small-scale, fairly egalitarian, and so compatible with democracy. Had he foreseen how the development of huge multinational corporations would surpass the concentrations of wealth and undemocratic power of his day, he would surely have included them in his sights. It is not possible to discuss ways of reducing income differences without discussing what can be done about these bastions of wealth, power and privilege.

The failed experiment with state ownership in the centrally planned economies of the former Soviet Union and Eastern Europe was intended, among other things, to provide a solution to the problem of the growing concentration of productive power in private hands. But concentrating that power into the hands of the state was not only sometimes hugely inefficient, but invited corruption, led to the denial of important basic freedoms and harmed public life. That failure seems to have made us feel there are no workable alternatives to the standard capitalist model and prevented us thinking creatively about other more democratic and egalitarian methods. We blinker ourselves to the fact that there are lots of alternatives, many of which are already part of our lives and flourishing all around us.

ALTERNATIVES

In his book, *America Beyond Capitalism: Reclaiming our Wealth, our Liberty and our Democracy*, Gar Alperovitz, a professor of political economy at the University of Maryland, summarizes the variety and scale of the alternatives operating in the USA.[378] He emphasizes the huge size of the non-profit sector. In the twenty largest US cities almost 40 per cent of the 200 largest enterprises are non-profit organizations like universities and medical institutions. He mentions the 2,000 municipal electric utilities which supply 40 million Americans with electricity. Largely because they are not having to make profits for shareholders they are often cheaper – an average of 11 per cent cheaper, Alperovitz says – than profit-making companies, and many pay particular attention to sustainability and the development of renewable sources of power. Also at the local level, he discusses organizations like the 4,000 or so Community Development Corporations which support local communities by setting up low-income housing schemes, providing finance for local businesses which they sometimes own and control. There are 48,000 co-ops in the US and some 120 million people are members of them. There are around 10,000 credit unions, with assets totalling $600 billion, providing financial services for 83 million Americans. Around 1,000 mutual insurance companies are owned by their policy-holders, and 30 per cent of American farm products are marketed through co-operatives.

In Britain institutions like universities, hospitals and local government are also often the largest local employers. Because medical care and universities – like the rest of education – are almost entirely publicly funded, they are governed by bodies accountable to the public. The governing bodies of Oxford and Cambridge colleges are democratically comprised of all fellows. Despite a stampede to cash in the profits to be made by selling off friendly societies and mutuals, there are still 63 building societies (with over 2,000 branches and 38,000 employees), 650 credit unions, 70 mutual insurance companies as well as 250 friendly societies in Britain, providing various financial services to their members. There are almost 170,000 charities with a combined annual income of over £44 billion. In 2007 the Co-operative Bank, with £40 billion of assets, was recognized as the most corporately responsible company in the UK, according to Business in the Community, an influential charitable association of British companies. The recently revamped 6,300 Co-op shops still have a market share of about 5 per cent of all food retailing and they remain the UK's largest 'neighbourhood' retailer with a share of almost 8 per cent of that market. Even Britain's experience of nationalized industries (which once covered electricity, gas, water, telephones, railways) was not all bad. Throughout the 1950s and 1960s, as the economist and journalist Will Hutton has pointed out, productivity in the nationalized industries matched or exceeded the private sector.[379] He says they began to get a bad name when governments raided their profits and held down their prices to help reduce inflationary pressures in the national economy.

The variety and vast scale of this organizational experience leaves no doubt that profit-making business is not the only effective way people can work together to provide important services. It is a truism – but nevertheless an important one – to say that the key difference between the kinds of organization we have listed and profit-making corporations is simply whether or not their primary purpose is to make money or to provide a service while remaining economically viable. Although some profit-making businesses have high ethical standards, the institutional framework (and often cut-throat market pressures) seem to invite them into an exploitative relationship with society – hence perhaps why we have needed a 'fair trade' movement. Presumably because of the motivational difference, there is a strong impression that many of the other forms of organization allow institutions to develop a service ethic and to see their purpose as the furthering of environmental and community interests. The fact that top salaries in the profit-making sector are several hundred times top political, judicial or military salaries is no doubt partly a reflection of the profit-making motive.

WHAT CAN BE DONE?

So how can the inequality-generating forces in the profit-making sector be contained and democratized? How can they be adapted to fit in with the need to make our societies more equal? What can we do which cannot be easily reversed by an incoming government with opposing interests? When thinking about this we should keep in mind just how fundamental a turning point we have reached in human history. As we showed in Chapters 1 and 2, further improvements in the quality of life no longer depend on further economic growth: the issue is now community and how we relate to each other.

One approach to tackling runaway pay rates at the top might be to plug loopholes in the tax system, limit 'business expenses', increase top tax rates, and even legislate to limit maximum pay in a company to some multiple of the average or lowest paid. While such solutions may seem to be the only short-term option, they are very vulnerable to changes in government: even if effective tax changes were devised and introduced, a new government with different political allegiances could simply reverse them all. Given the importance of keeping inequality down, we need to find ways of ensuring that greater equality is more deeply rooted in the fabric of our societies and less vulnerable to the whim of successive governments. We need to address the concentrations of power at the heart of the economic life.

An approach which would solve some of the problems is democratic employee-ownership. It not only avoids concentrating power in the hands of the state, but evaluations suggest that it has major economic and social advantages over organizations owned and controlled by outside investors in whose interests they act.

In many countries, governments use tax concessions to encourage employee share-ownership systems. They do so because it is assumed that share ownership improves company performance by reducing the opposition of interests between employers and employees. In the UK, share-ownership schemes now cover almost a quarter of all employees and some 15 or 20 per cent of all UK companies.[380-81] In the US, the 2001 Tax Law increased the tax advantages of Employee Stock Ownership Plans (ESOPs), and they now cover 8 million employees in 10,000 firms with an average employee-ownership of 15–20 per cent.[382]

However, many share-ownership schemes amount to little more than incentive schemes, intended to make employees more compliant with management and sometimes to provide a nest-egg for retirement. As a result, they are often seen as tokenism, rather than as a key to transforming the structure of employment. This is why research shows that employee share-ownership, on its own, is not enough to make much difference to company performance. Patrick Rooney, an economist at the universities of Indiana and Purdue, found that employee share-ownership did not necessarily mean that employees were more involved in the running of the companies in which they worked.[383] He compared the extent of employee participation in a wide range of decisions in companies with and without employee share-ownership schemes. In general, employee involvement was low, but even in companies with employee share-ownership schemes staff members were often not informed or consulted, and the majority of these companies did not enable employees to have a significant input into decision making.

To make a reliable difference to company performance, share-ownership has to be combined with more participative management methods.[384-5] There have now been a number of large and well-controlled studies – including those using before-and-after performance data for several hundred matched pairs of companies[386] – which demonstrate the economic benefits of the combination of employee share-ownership and participation.[385, 387] The studies show repeatedly that substantial performance benefits come only when employee share-ownership schemes are accompanied by more participatory management methods.[380, 383, 388-9] Research that looked at a large number of British companies during the 1990s found that employee share-ownership, profit-sharing and participation each make an independent contribution to increased productivity.[380] A review of research concluded: [385]

We can say with certainty that when ownership and participative management are combined, substantial gains result. Ownership alone and participation alone, however, have at best, spotty or short-lived results. (p. 11)
... the impact of participation in the absence of (share) ownership is short-lived ... Ownership seems to provide the cultural glue to keep participation going. (p. 3)

Studies of how work affects health point in the same direction: as we saw in Chapter 6, people seem to thrive where they have more control over their work. Having control at work was the most successful single factor explaining threefold differences in death rates between senior and junior civil servants working in the same government offices in Britain.[64] In practice, this probably has a lot to do with a sense of autonomy and not feeling so directly subordinated. The importance of control at work is now understood to involve a greater degree of workplace democracy.[390] There is, in addition, growing evidence that a sense of unfairness at work is an important risk factor for poor health.[391]

The concept of a company being owned by outside investors has implications which look increasingly anachronistic. A smaller and smaller part of the value of a company is the value of its buildings, equipment and marketable assets. It is instead the value of its employees. When companies are bought and sold, what is actually being bought and sold is, above all, its staff as a group of people, with their assembled skills, abilities, and knowledge of company systems and production methods. Only they have the ability to make the company tick. And of course the concept of a group of people being bought and sold, and belonging to anyone but its own members, is a concept which is the very opposite of democratic.

Should employees not have full control over their work and the distribution of its earnings? And should external shareholders really receive unearned income beyond agreed interest on capital? Participation, commitment, control and profit-sharing would be maximized if companies were 100 per cent employee-owned. Companies could raise capital through loans or mortgages, retaining control themselves. At the moment, only a tiny proportion of the money gambled on the Stock Exchange makes any contribution to helping companies buy productive assets. Indeed, over time the payment of dividends to external shareholders is a major drain on company profits which might have been used to improve their technology and equipment.

Robert Oakeshott, a British authority on employee-ownership, says that employee-ownership 'entails a movement from business as a piece of property to business as a working community'.[388, p. 104] Companies change from being property to being communities when employees own a majority of shares and so control the business. That is when management becomes responsible, not to outside shareholders with little interest in the company beyond returns on capital, but to the body of employees. Then company meetings become occasions when management reports back to employees and has to deal with questions and discussion among people who have an intimate knowledge of what has gone right and what has gone wrong in the preceding period, and what the remedies might be. The transformation after an employee buy-out from the usual top-down mentality can involve a long slow process of people's emancipation from the usual assumptions round class and ability which make those in more junior positions feel themselves to be inferior human beings. We discussed in Chapter 8 some of the experimental evidence using race and caste to show how attributions of inferior status can affect performance.

This process of adjustment and emancipation is described in *Local Heroes*, David Erdal's account of the employee buy-out of Loch Fyne Oysters in Scotland.[392] It is in part a process of undoing the damage of class inequality, a process presumably made more difficult by the fact that such assumptions remain entrenched all around people in the rest of their lives. However, the structures in which we work are pivotal.

Co-operatives and employee buy-outs have often originated as responses to desperate circumstances in which traditional systems of ownership and management have failed. Employees have used them to avoid closures and unemployment in the most difficult market circumstances. Even then they have sometimes succeeded beyond expectations – as did Tower Colliery in South Wales when, in 1995, miners used their redundancy money to buy the pit and ran it successfully until the coal was worked out thirteen years later. Many fully employee-owned companies have a proud record. Examples include, or have included, the London Symphony Orchestra, Carl Zeiss, United Airlines, Gore-tex, the Polaroid Corporation, and the John Lewis Partnership (one of Britain's most successful retailers with 68,000 employee-partners and annual sales of £6.4bn). In the USA, among the largest majority employee-owned companies are Publix Supermarkets, Hy-vee Supermarkets, Science Applications International Corporation (SAIC), the international engineering and construction company CH2M Hill and Tribune which, among other media operations, publishes the *Los Angeles Times* and *Chicago Tribune*. These companies average 55,000 employees each.

One of the best-known co-operative groups is the Mondragon Corporation in the Basque region of Spain. Over half a century it has developed into a group of over 120 employee-owned co-operatives with 40,000 worker-owners and sales of $4.8 billion US dollars. Mondragon co-operatives are twice as profitable as other Spanish firms and have the highest labour productivity in the country.[388] It is hard to explain some of the successes unless a combination of ownership and participation does indeed have the potential to improve productivity by reducing the conflict of interests.

For most of the employed population it is at work that they interact most closely with people other than family and have the potential to feel part of a community. In Chapter 3 we saw evidence of the huge rises in anxiety which have taken place over the last fifty or so years as community life has weakened under the impact of growing geographical and social mobility. While greater equality is associated with more cohesive communities and higher levels of trust (see Chapter 4) and so may be expected to improve life in residential neighbourhoods, in the near future we are unlikely to regain the benefits of the very close-knit residential communities of the past. But at work there is the potential for people to find a nucleus of friendships and to feel valued. This potential is usually undermined by the hierarchical stratification of people into various gradations of order-givers and order-takers, which ensure that employees act not as a community, but as property, brought together and used to earn a return on other people's capital. One of us recently visited two small companies soon after they had been bought by their employees. When staff were asked what difference it had made, the first thing office staff in both companies said in reply was that, when they went on to the shop floor, 'people look you in the eye'. Under the old system, eye contact had been avoided.

Employee-ownership has the advantage of increasing equality specifically by extending liberty and democracy. It is bottom-up rather than top-down. Although we don't know what scale of income differences people would think fair, it seems likely that they might agree that the chief executive of the company they work for should be paid a salary several times as big as their own – maybe three, or perhaps even ten, times as big. But it is unlikely that they would say several hundred times as big. Indeed, such huge differentials can probably only be maintained by denying any measure of economic democracy.

As long as the employee-owned sector remains only a small part of the whole economy, it cannot use very different pay scales from other companies. If employee-owned companies paid junior workers more than other companies, and the most senior staff less, then the junior staff would never leave and senior ones would be harder to recruit. However, as the employee-owned sector became larger, people's norms and values about what are appropriate rates of pay for different jobs, and what differentials are acceptable, would change. We might at least move towards the norms of the public and non-profit sector. And if there was no longer a set of hugely wealthy private sector bosses inviting comparisons and making people think such salaries could be justified, the non-profit sector might itself become more egalitarian. Perhaps it is time we moved away from a world in which people regard maximizing personal gains as a laudable aim in life.

David Erdal, former chair of the Tullis Russell Group and Director of the Baxi Partnership, once studied the effects of employment in co-operatives on the communities in which they were situated.[393] He compared three towns in northern Italy: Imola, which has 25 per cent of its workforce employed in co-operatives, Faenza, where 16 per cent work in co-operatives, and Sassuolo where there are no co-operatives. On the basis of rather a small survey and low response rates, he concluded that health, education, crime and social participation were all better in the towns with a larger proportion of the population employed in co-operatives.

As a way of creating a more egalitarian society, employee-ownership and control have many advantages. First, it enables a process of social emancipation as people become members of a team. Second, it puts the scale of earning differentials ultimately under democratic control: if the body of employees want big income differentials they could choose to keep them. Third, it involves a very substantial redistribution of wealth from external shareholders to employees and a simultaneous redistribution of the income from that wealth. In this context, that is a particularly important advantage. Fourth, it improves productivity and so has a competitive advantage. Fifth, it increases the likelihood that people will regain the experience of being part of a community. And sixth, it is likely to improve sociability in the wider society. The real reward however, is not simply to have a few employee-owned companies in a society still dominated by a hierarchical ideology and status-seeking, but to have a society of people freer of those divisions. And that can only be achieved by a sustained campaign over several decades.

Rather than being compatible with just one system of management and work organization, employee-ownership is highly flexible. It merely puts ultimate authority in the hands of employees to develop whatever systems they find work best. This enables systems to evolve to suit any situation. Systems of work teams, of directors elected for longer or shorter periods, of departmental representatives, of company trustees, of anything from weekly to annual company meetings, could all be tried from place to place. Power could be delegated, or exercised directly by the body of voting employees. Gradually people would learn the strengths and weaknesses of different structures and what forms of democracy best fitted the public and private sectors and how to represent the interests of consumers and local communities.

However, to ensure that the number of employee-owned workplaces increases, it is essential that they are constituted – as they easily can be – in ways which prevent employees from selling their companies back to external shareholders. Although most are adequately protected, there have also been cases of sell-outs in which companies have been lost to employee-ownership and control.

As a means of transforming our societies, employee-ownership has the advantage that it can (and does) exist side by side with conventional business structures. New and old forms of business can coexist: with the right legal support and tax incentives the transformation of society can start straight away. It enables us to embark on a fundamental transformation of our society through an orderly transition, making the new society grow within the old. Governments can give additional incentives and support to encourage employee share-ownership. Companies might be required to transfer a proportion of shares each year, and retiring owners might sometimes be willing to pass their companies to employees.

Although employee-owned and controlled industry need not involve local community and consumer representatives on the governing body, that is a fault which can easily be remedied. It might also be said in opposition to employee-ownership, that it does nothing about the basic amorality of the market. The desire to earn a bigger profit would still lead companies to act in anti-social ways, however they were controlled. As well as some highly ethical companies operating in the market supporting fair trade, the environment, giving to local communities, etc., there are, at the same time, also companies trying to expand markets for tobacco in the developing world in the sure knowledge that they will cause millions of extra deaths. There are companies which have caused needless deaths by encouraging mothers in developing countries to buy powdered baby milk instead of breast feeding, despite lack of access to clean water or basic hygiene. There are others which continue to destroy ecosystems, land and water supplies, to exploit mineral resources where governments are too weak or corrupt to stand up to them, and still others use their patents to prevent life-saving drugs being sold at affordable prices in poorer countries.

There are reasons to think that employee-owned companies might maintain higher standards of morality even with the profit motive. In conventional employment people are specifically hired to work for purposes which are not their own. They are paid to use their expertise to whatever purpose their employer chooses. You might disagree with the purpose to which your work is being put, you might not even know what the purpose is, but you are not employed to have opinions about such things and certainly not to express them. Such issues are not your concern. If you are hired to advise on how your company can expand its markets, improve profits, avoid press attention, the chances are that you are not being asked for an ethical opinion. You are hired to put your expertise to work to serve someone else's purpose. Not only are the purposes not your responsibility, but as an employee you are likely to feel absolved from responsibility for them. This is why people have so often disclaimed responsibility for what they were doing by saying that they were 'only carrying out orders'. The famous Milgram experiments showed that we have such a strong tendency to obey authority that it can result in us doing some pretty awful things. In what was presented as a 'learning' experiment, Milgram showed that people were willing to deliver what they believed were not only very painful, but also life-threatening electric shocks to a learning partner whenever the partner gave the wrong answer to a question. They did this at the request of a man in a white coat conducting the experiment, despite hearing what they thought were the screams caused by the shocks they delivered.[394]

However, within a framework of employee-ownership and control, people specifically regain ownership and control of the purposes of their work. If, for instance, you get to know that some aspect of a design or manufacturing process is harming children's health, you would want to change it and would probably start by finding out what colleagues thought about it. There would not be the same pressure to keep your doubts to yourself. Nor would you be able to shrug it off, dismissing it as none of your business. Neither would you fear that your job would be in jeopardy if you raised awkward questions. Although employee-owned firms would not be above all anti-social behaviour, it is likely that they would succeed in making it at least a little less common.

FREEDOM AND EQUALITY

The idea that we can't have both liberty and equality seems to have emerged during the Cold War. What the state-owned economies of Eastern Europe and the Soviet Union seemed to show was that greater equality could only be gained at the expense of freedom. An important ideological cost of the Cold War was that America gave up its historical commitment to equality. For the first Americans, as for Tom Paine, you couldn't have true liberty without equality. Without one you could not have the other. Slavery, as the simultaneous denial of both, proved that rule. Equality was the bastion against arbitrary power. This was expressed in the historical demand for 'No taxation without representation', and 'No legislation without representation'. The American Declaration of Independence says that all men are born equal and endowed with liberty as an inalienable right, just as the French revolutionaries demanded liberty, equality, fraternity. The complementarity of liberty and equality has been proclaimed in the writings of many democratic thinkers, including the social philosopher L. T. Hobhouse, who believed that liberty depended, in all its domains, on equality – equality before the law, equality of opportunity, equality of parties to a contract.[395]

The scale of economic inequality which exists today is less an expression of freedom and democracy as of their denial. Who, apart from the super-rich, would vote for multi-million dollar bonuses for the corporate and financial elite while denying adequate incomes to people who undertake so many essential and sometimes unpleasant tasks – such as caring for the elderly, collecting the trash, or working in emergency services? The truth is that modern inequality exists because democracy is excluded from the economic sphere. It needs therefore to be dealt with by an extension of democracy into the workplace. We need to experiment with every form of economic democracy – employee ownership, producer and consumer co-operatives, employee representatives on company boards and so on.

RUNNING WITH THE TECHNOLOGICAL TIDE

In her book, *The Weightless World*, Diane Coyle points out that although people in most industrialized countries experienced something like a twentyfold increase in their real incomes during the twentieth century, the weight of all that was produced at the end of the century was roughly the same as it had been at the beginning.[396] She also says that the average weight of one dollar's worth of US exports (adjusted for inflation) fell by a half between 1990 and 1996. While the trend towards 'weightlessness' is partly a reflection of the growth of the service sector and the 'knowledge' economy, it is also a reflection of changing technology and the trend towards miniaturization. That so much of modern consumption is actually lighter on the use of material resources than it was, is presumably good news for the environment. But the underlying nature of the changes contributing to weightlessness may also have important implications for equality.

Introductory economics courses teach students the distinction between the 'fixed' costs of production on the one hand, and 'marginal' or variable costs on the other. Fixed costs are the costs of the factory buildings and machinery, and the variable costs are the additional costs of making one more unit of output – traditionally made up largely of the costs of the additional labour and materials needed, on the assumption that the plant and equipment are already there. Economic theory says that prices in a competitive market should fall until they equal marginal (or variable) costs. Prices higher than that would mean that by producing and selling more, a manufacturer could still earn a little more profit, whereas at a lower price making even one more item would add more to costs than it gained in income from sales.

Throughout large swathes of the modern economy technological change is rapidly reducing variable costs. For everything that can be copied digitally, additional copies cost little or nothing either to produce or to distribute over the internet. This applies to all music, to all computer software and games, to films, to all books and to the written word in any form, to all information and to pictures. That covers a large part of what is produced for entertainment and leisure, for education at all levels, and for many economic and professional applications of computer software – whether for stock control, statistical analysis or computer-aided design.

So low are marginal costs of digital products that there is a growing 'free' sector. Efforts are made to enforce patents and copyright protection in an attempt to restrict access and enable companies to hold on to profits; but the logic of technological progress is difficult to resist. Systems of copy protection codes are cracked and goods 'liberated'. In some cases free access is supported by advertising, in others it is genuinely free, as with 'freeware' or 'shareware' computer programmes. The internet has already provided free access to almost unlimited information, not only books, encyclopaedias, dictionaries, newspapers, but increasingly to on-line journals. Whether legally or not, music and films are downloaded free. Some service providers now provide unlimited free storage space. Phone calls can cost only a fraction of what they used to and, when using computer links, are increasingly free. Emails and instant messaging also provide effectively free communications.

Though less dramatic than in the digital economy, the trend towards rapidly diminishing variable costs may also apply to many other areas of technology, including the products of nano-technology, biotechnology, electronically printed components and genetic engineering. These new technologies hold out possibilities of more efficient solar power, cheaper medicines and more economical new materials.

From the point of view of many of the companies producing digital products, the changes have not appeared as new opportunities for enhancing human life and enjoyment, but as profound threats to profits. Instead of maximizing the benefits of the new technologies, we find ourselves with institutional structures which have fought to restrict this new potential. The dramatic lowering of variable costs puts a rapidly widening gap between the maximization of profit and the maximization of public benefit. In this situation it is important that governments use their powers to aid the development of new institutional structures, not to prop up and defend the restrictions of the old ones.

It used to be argued that goods for which the marginal costs were close to zero were inherently public goods and should be made publicly available. Before the digital era, bridges and roads were commonly used examples. Once society has incurred the capital costs of making a bridge or road, maximum benefit from the initial investment is gained only if use is unrestricted by charging. Hence, people should be allowed free access. The need to provide unrestricted free access in order to maximize the public benefit was offered as an economic explanation of why roads and bridges were in public ownership – until governments began to try to recoup the costs of road building by charging tolls.

Once the capital cost has been incurred, the more people sharing the benefits the better. Where municipal investment provides local internet access, there is no need to restrict access to it. When the Victorians established free public libraries they recognized the same logic: a book can be read repeatedly at no extra cost. Perhaps we need public bodies and non-profits, funded from public revenue, able to negotiate a price at which to buy access or copyrights for the nation. Perhaps we need international bodies able to negotiate free access to educational and business resources throughout the world. From the point of view of society as a whole, the tendency for technological change to reduce marginal costs is rapidly tipping the balance of advantage away from allowing profit-maximizing corporations to control the distribution of goods. Increasingly they can only rely on the remnants of monopolistic power provided by patents or copyright. We need to find new ways of paying organizations and individuals for life-enhancing research, creativity and innovation – the geese which lay the golden eggs – which does not then restrict access to the benefits. Perhaps we need charities to fund the development of software for free worldwide use. We certainly need a complete revision of copyright and patent laws so that those who produce valuable goods and services can be paid in ways which do not restrict access to their products.

The question for politicians and the public is whether it is possible to find ways of paying corporations for their research and development without trying to police a pricing system which restricts access to the benefits of what they have produced – benefits which may include life-saving drugs, agricultural innovations which could feed the hungry, and access to scientific and academic journals for universities in the developing world. If it is correct to think that new technology tends increasingly to lower variable costs, then this problem will become increasingly pressing.

Perhaps the logic moves us towards a society in which access to an ever-increasing range of goods is no longer tightly rationed by income, and our possessions cease to play such an important role in social differentiation. We might hope that we will start to experience ourselves primarily as unranked members of the same society brought together in different combinations according to our various shared interests.

THE FUTURE OF EQUALITY

Caught up in day-to-day events, it is easy to forget that a longer view reveals an almost unstoppable historical trend towards greater equality. It runs like a river of human progress from the first constitutional limitations on the 'divine' (and arbitrary) right of kings, and continues on through the slow development of democracy and the establishment of the principle of equality before the law. It swells with the abolition of slavery and is strengthened by the extension of the franchise to include non-property-owners and women. It picks up pace with the development of free education, health services and systems of minimum income maintenance covering periods of unemployment and sickness. It runs on to include legislation to protect the rights of employees and tenants, and legislation to prevent racial discrimination. It includes the decline of forms of class deference. The abolition of capital and corporal punishment is also part of it. So too is the growing agitation for greater equality of opportunity – regardless of race, class, gender, sexual orientation and religion. We see it also in the increasing attention paid by lobby groups, social research and government statistical agencies to poverty and inequality over the last fifty years; and most recently we see it in the attempt to create a culture of mutual respect.

All are different manifestations of growing equality. And, despite differences in political opinion, there are few people who, when looking back on these historical developments, would not regard them all as welcome. The historical forces underlying them ensure that these are changes which a large majority will want to continue. That this river of human progress is occasionally briefly dammed up, or we experience eddying currents, should not blind us to its existence.

The relationships between inequality and the prevalence of health and social problems shown in earlier chapters suggest that if the United States was to reduce its income inequality to something like the average of the four most equal of the rich countries (Japan, Norway, Sweden and Finland), the proportion of the population feeling they could trust others might rise by 75 per cent – presumably with matching improvements in the quality of community life; rates of mental illness and obesity might similarly each be cut by almost two-thirds, teenage birth rates could be more than halved, prison populations might be reduced by 75 per cent, and people could live longer while working the equivalent of two months less per year.

Similarly, if Britain became as equal as the same four countries, levels of trust might be expected to be two-thirds as high again as they are now, mental illness might be more than halved, everyone would get an additional year of life, teenage birth rates could fall to one-third of what they are now, homicide rates could fall by 75 per cent, everyone could get the equivalent of almost seven weeks extra holiday a year, and the government could be closing prisons all over the country.

What is essential if we are to bring a better society into being is to develop a sustained movement committed to doing that. Policy changes will need to be consistently devoted to this end over several decades and that requires a society which knows where it wants to go. To help with this we provide – and will continue to provide – our research findings, graphs and other information on the Equality Trust's web site (www.equalitytrust.org.uk).

The initial task is to gain a widespread public understanding of what is at stake. But rather than allowing this to be just one more idea that briefly gains attention before fashionable opinion moves on, we need to build a social movement committed to its realization. It must be taken up and pursued by a network of equality groups meeting to share ideas and action everywhere, in homes and offices, in trade unions and political parties, in churches and schools. It needs also to be pursued by the pressure groups, charities and services concerned with the various issues which are related to equality, whether health or teenage births, prison populations or mental health, drugs or educational standards. And they need to be coupled with the urgent task of dealing with global warming. In all these settings we must speak out and explain the advantages of a more equal society.

Nor should we allow ourselves to be cowed by the idea that higher taxes on the rich will lead to their mass emigration and economic catastrophe. We know that more egalitarian countries live well, with high living standards and much better social environments. We know also that economic growth is not the yardstick by which everything else must be judged. Indeed we know that it no longer contributes to the real quality of our lives and that consumerism is a danger to the planet. Nor should we allow ourselves to believe that the rich are scarce and precious members of a superior race of more intelligent beings on whom the rest of us are dependent. That is merely the illusion that wealth and power create.

Rather than adopting an attitude of gratitude towards the rich, we need to recognize what a damaging effect they have on the social fabric. The financial meltdown of late 2008 and the resulting recession show us how dangerous huge salaries and bonuses at the top can be. As well as leading those in charge of our financial institutions to adopt policies which put the wellbeing of whole populations in jeopardy, the very existence of the super-rich increased the pressure to consume as everyone else tried to keep up. The long speculative boom which preceded the financial crash was fuelled substantially by the growth of consumers' expenditure. Increased inequality led people to reduce their savings, increase their bank overdrafts and credit card debt, and arrange second mortgages to fund consumption. By adding to the speculative element in the cycles of economic boom and bust, great inequality shifts our attention from the pressing environmental and social problems and makes us worry about unemployment, insecurity, and 'how to get the economy moving again'. Reducing inequality would not only make the economic system more stable, it would also make a major contribution to social and environmental sustainability.

Modern societies will depend increasingly on being creative, adaptable, inventive, well-informed and flexible communities, able to respond generously to each other and to needs wherever they arise. Those are characteristics not of societies in hock to the rich, in which people are driven by status insecurities, but of populations used to working together and respecting each other as equals. And, because we are trying to grow the new society within the old, our values and the way we work must be part of how we bring a new society into being. But we must also try to bring about a shift in public values so that instead of inspiring admiration and envy, conspicuous consumption is seen as part of the problem, a sign of greed and unfairness which damages society and the planet.

Martin Luther King said, 'The moral arc of the universe is long, but it bends towards justice.' Given that in human prehistory we lived in remarkably equal societies, maintaining a steady state – or sustainable – way of life in what some have called 'the original affluent society',[324] it is perhaps right to think of it as an arc, curving back to very basic human principles of fairness and equality which we still regard as good manners in any normal social interaction.[349]

But at all stages, creating a more equal society involves people speaking their minds, making the case, organizing and campaigning.

It is impossible for governments not to influence income differences. Not only are they the largest employer in most countries, but almost every area of economic and social policy affects income distribution. Tax and benefit policies are the most obvious way. Other influential areas of policy include minimum wage legislation, education policies, the management of the national economy, whether unemployment is kept to low levels, whether different rates of VAT and sales taxes are applied to necessities and luxuries, provision of public services, pension policies, inheritance taxes, negative income tax, basic income policies, child support, progressive consumption taxes,[351] industrial policy, retraining schemes, and many more. But in this chapter we have also suggested more fundamental changes to ensure that income differences are subject to democratic control and greater equality becomes more deeply rooted in the social fabric.

At this stage, creating the political will to make society more equal is more important than pinning our colours to a particular set of policies to reduce inequality. Political will is dependent on the development of a vision of a better society which is both achievable and inspiring. We hope we have shown that there is a better society to be won: a more equal society in which people are less divided by status and hierarchy; a society in which we regain a sense of community, in which we overcome the threat of global warming, in which we own and control our work democratically as part of a community of colleagues, and share in the benefits of a growing non-monetized sector of the economy. Nor is this a utopian dream: the evidence shows that even small decreases in inequality, already a reality in some rich market democracies, make a very important difference to the quality of life. The task is now to develop a politics based on a recognition of the kind of society we need to create and committed to making use of the institutional and technological opportunities to realize it.

A better society will not happen automatically, regardless of whether or not we work for it. We can fail to prevent catastrophic global warming, we can allow our societies to become increasingly anti-social and fail to understand the processes involved. We can fail to stand up to the tiny minority of the rich whose misplaced idea of self-interest makes them feel threatened by a more democratic and egalitarian world. There will be problems and disagreements on the way – as there always have been in the struggle for progress – but, with a broad conception of where we are going, the necessary changes can be made.

After several decades in which we have lived with the oppressive sense that there is no alternative to the social and environmental failure of modern societies, we can now regain the sense of optimism which comes from knowing that the problems can be solved. We know that greater equality will help us rein in consumerism and ease the introduction of policies to tackle global warming. We can see how the development of modern technology makes profit-making institutions appear increasingly anti-social as they find themselves threatened by the rapidly expanding potential for public good which new technology offers. We are on the verge of creating a qualitatively better and more truly sociable society for all.

To sustain the necessary political will, we must remember that it falls to our generation to make one of the biggest transformations in human history. We have seen that the rich countries have got to the end of the really important contributions which economic growth can make to the quality of life and also that our future lies in improving the quality of the social environment in our societies. The role of this book is to point out that greater equality is the material foundation on which better social relations are built.

Postscript – Research Meets Politics

THE SPIRIT LEVEL DEBATE

This book was first published in March 2009, about six months after the start of the worst financial crisis since the Second World War. Much of the blame for the crisis was rightly attributed to the extraordinary risks taken by people in the financial sector whose excesses were matched only by their grotesquely high salaries. Though our research predates the crisis by many years, and its validity is unaffected by the crisis, the book's generally positive reception clearly owes something to its timing. Many people who, before the crash, had assumed that huge salaries and bonuses reflected the unique contributions and brilliance of their recipients, changed their minds as they learned about the lack of relationship between performance and rewards.[408]

AN IDEA WHOSE TIME HAS COME?

But the reception of the book cannot be wholly attributed to the moment at which it appeared. Since publication, we have – between us – given well over 350 lectures, in many different countries. We have spoken to civil servants, health authorities, academics, charities, faith groups, think tanks, professional associations, arts and literary festivals, trade unions, senior business people, community groups, royal societies, international agencies and political parties across the ideological spectrum. Although we have often been invited to speak to groups which were pre-disposed to be sympathetic to the idea of greater equality, that has not always been the case. Yet audiences have been so uniformly positive and appreciative that we have sensed there is an intellectual vacuum, a hunger for the evidence we present – as if under the surface the world was full of closet egalitarians.

Three things seem likely to have contributed to this. First is a desire for an explanation of why, amidst such unprecedented affluence, our societies are beset by such a worrying array of social problems. Why are rates of depression and anxiety so high? Why is there such widespread reliance on drugs and alcohol? And why is violence so common? The second component is the evidence with which we started the book – that a very large majority of the population feels that 'consumerism' or 'materialism' is something we get caught up in despite feeling it runs counter to our values and our desire for more time with family and friends or in our community. Third, our analysis seems to confirm people's intuition that inequality is divisive and socially corrosive. Again and again, people tell us they feel they have gained from the book a picture of the world which is both quite new to them and yet somehow also immediately recognizable, a picture they feel they have been waiting for and which changes how they see what is going on around them.

A recent report confirms empirically the impression we have received so strongly – that the general public is averse to the high levels of inequality in very unequal countries. In a random sample of over 5,500 Americans, researchers from Duke University and Harvard University investigated views of the distribution of wealth (rather than income) in society.[409] People were shown three pie charts illustrating three different distributions of wealth – one in which each fifth of the population got the same, another which showed (unlabelled) the distribution of wealth in the USA and another (also unlabelled) based on the distribution in Sweden. Ninety-two per cent said they would prefer to live in a society with the Swedish distribution – and the percentage only varied from 89 to 93 per cent depending on whether they were rich or poor, Democrats or Republicans. When asked what they thought the distribution of wealth is in the USA, the average estimate was that the richest 20 per cent of Americans control 59 per cent of the wealth. In reality, they control 84 per cent. Asked what they thought the ideal distribution would be, people preferred the top 20 per cent to have 32 per cent of all wealth.

Nevertheless, as well as its very positive reception, the book has attracted both thoughtful criticism and strident political attacks. The main purpose of this chapter is to respond to these before going on to discuss some new research findings. But before doing cither, we would like to address a criticism made by several commentators which seems to be based on a misunderstanding.

WHO BENEFITS FROM GREATER EQUALITY?

Some reviewers of the book were not convinced that we had shown that the vast majority of the population benefited from greater equality. They seemed to think that the evidence did no more than establish that *average* performance across the whole population is worse in more unequal societies.[410]

In a section running from p. 175 to p.182 we show no fewer than five sets of data (and refer to another shown on p.109) illustrating that, whether you classify people by education, social class or income, people in each category are healthier (or have higher literacy scores) if they are in a more equal society than people in the *same* category of income, education or class in a less equal society. We also refer to studies which reach the same conclusions using statistical models which enable researchers to look at the effects of inequality after controlling for the effects of all individual incomes throughout society.

We do *not* argue that everyone in a more equal society does better than everyone in a less equal one. We are not saying that even the lowest social class or the least well paid or educated category in a more equal society does better than the highest category in a less equal society. Rather, we show that when people in the *same* social class, at the same level of income or education, are compared across countries, those in more equal societies do better. So at any given level of personal income or education, someone's quality of life will be higher if he or she has the same level of income or education but lives in a more equal society. That is what is shown in Figures 8.4, 13.2, 13.3, 13.4 and 13.5. The conclusion is that greater equality usually makes most difference to the least well off, but still produces some benefits for the well off.

As we pointed out on p.176, the very large differences between more and less equal societies in the prevalence of other social problems – including mental health, teenage births, trust, homicide and imprisonment – suggest that this picture is not confined to the areas of health and literacy. The differences are usually much larger than would result if greater equality benefited only the least well off.

INEQUALITY, CLASS AND STATUS

Academic sociologists have sometimes been surprised that the book focuses so exclusively on income inequality and pays little attention to the vast amount of careful work now available on social class classifications.[411] We have great regard for much of this work, but it does not feature here because social class classifications have two weaknesses for the kind of analyses this book undertakes. First, because almost every country uses a different socioeconomic classification system, it is difficult to make comparisons between countries. For example, in early studies of how health differences across the social hierarchy in Sweden compared with those in England and Wales, Swedish researchers had to re-classify the occupations of many thousands of Swedes according to the British occupational class classification. We showed the results in Figures 13.3 and 13.4. But even if social comparisons could be made consistently across many different countries, there is a second more fundamental problem: few, if any, social class classifications would allow an assessment of whether the gaps between groups are bigger or smaller in one country than another. Income differences, on the other hand, allow us not simply to categorize people into different classes, they also allow us to measure the *size* of the differences within the population. For all its imperfections as a measure of status differentiation, income inequality tells us a lot about a society.

Answers to a number of other points which are often raised when we give presentations on the book (including questions on ethnicity, immigration, the size of countries, local inequalities and many more) are listed under Frequently Asked Questions on The Equality Trust web site at www.equalitytrust.org.uk.

FAIR CRITICISM AND FOUL ATTACKS

Public health, with epidemiology at its centre, has a long record of political battle, from the nineteenth-century conflicts over the provision of sewers and clean water, to modern legislation protecting people from dangerous exposures at work or in the environment more widely. The political battles come when the scientific evidence runs up against vested interests of many different kinds – industrial, social and economic.

It is now almost universally accepted amongst scholars and practitioners of public health that the most important determinants of health are social and economic circumstances. Geoffrey Rose, who was one of the most highly influential and respected epidemiologists of the second half of the twentieth century, said, 'medicine and politics cannot and should not be kept apart'. Our growing understanding of how human health and wellbeing are so deeply affected by social structure inevitably pushes science into politics.

Academics in every field of course criticize each other's work all the time: that is part of the normal process of scientific progress. Attacks clearly made for ideological reasons are quite different. Rather than controversies about research methods or interpretations of the evidence being hammered out between colleagues who know the subject area, suddenly people who do not know the extensive research literature and have never made a contribution to it, use the media to try to convince the public that research findings are misleading rubbish.

Attempts to overthrow large bodies of scientific evidence that seem to have important political implications are now a well-established phenomenon. Two American academics, Naomi Oreskes and Erik

Conway, have recently described these tactics in their book, *Merchants of Doubt: How a Handful of Scientists Obscured the Truth on Issues from Tobacco Smoke to Global Warming*.[412] They describe the techniques used – often by the same people operating in a number of quite different subjects – to give the impression that crucial areas of science affecting public policy are controversial, long after the implications of the science were quite clear. As a result, there have sometimes been substantial delays in the public response to pesticides, tobacco marketing, acid rain, the hole in the ozone layer, exposure to secondary smoke, and of course global warming. It is characteristic of the tactics of these 'merchants of doubt', that one of the attacks on our book was written by someone who had recently written a diatribe against tobacco control and what is now the well-established evidence that secondary smoke is harmful to health. Fortunately the bans on smoking in public places (implemented in Scotland, parts of the USA and Canada, Rome, Ireland, and England); which in each case have been followed by declines in death rates and have saved thousands of lives, seem unlikely to be lifted in the light of his work.

WHY THE ATTACKS FAIL

On the web site of The Equality Trust we have provided a point-by-point rebuttal of all the criticisms made by The Tax Payers' Alliance, The Democracy Institute and the Policy Exchange.[413] As much of it is rather tedious, in this chapter we will describe only the broad outlines of the criticism and our responses.

Much the most important strategy of our critics has been to treat the relationships we show between inequality and social problems as if we were the only people ever to suggest such links. They then set about trying to cast doubt, one by one, on the relationships we show in our graphs, suggesting that they are a combination of statistical flukes, the result of a cunning selection of countries, or of choosing problems to suit our argument. For example, they argue that the USA should be excluded from one analysis, Japan or the Scandinavian countries from another, or that another relationship disappears if you add in poorer countries, and so on.

Regardless of their merits in relation to our work, this strategy means that these criticisms are largely piecemeal, *ad hoc*, and irrelevant to the many other demonstrations of similar relationships in different settings published in academic journals by other researchers. Because there are around 200 papers in peer-reviewed academic journals testing the relationship between income inequality and health in many different settings,[10] more than 50 papers on violence and inequality,[210, 211, 414] and quite a number on inequality in relation to trust and social capital,[400, 415] it is now extremely difficult to argue credibly that these relationships don't exist. Indeed, those who do so are almost always those who are making political attacks rather than any kind of academic criticism.

Academic discussion among those who know the literature in the field is now very largely confined to how the relationships should be interpreted. That is why (chapter 13, from p.182 onwards) we discussed the strengths and weaknesses of possible alternative interpretations, before concluding that these relationships must reflect the damage done by inequality. With few exceptions, we have previously subjected to peer review and published in academic journals almost everything we have shown in this book.

So what are the criticisms and how do we respond to them?

PICKING AND CHOOSING?

Some critics have suggested that we are selective in the choice of health and social problems that we examine.[416]

The Spirit Level does not claim to explain every kind of social problem: it is specifically a theory of problems that have social gradients, gradients which make them more common further down the social ladder. So, for example, we would not expect alcohol use to increase with inequality because, in most countries, alcohol use does not increase lower down the social ladder. In contrast, alcohol abuse (for example binge drinking and alcoholism) does have a social gradient, and deaths from alcoholic liver disease are more common in more unequal US states.[8] We have also shown that death rates such as breast and prostate cancer, which do not tend to become more common lower down the social ladder, are not related to inequality.[8] This contrasts sharply with deaths from causes such as heart disease which do have a strong social gradient.

The reason we included (in chapter 2) an analysis of the relationship between the UNICEF Index of Child Wellbeing in Rich Countries and income inequality was to show that our results were not a result of selecting problems to suit our argument. The UNICEF Index combines 40 different aspects of child wellbeing which we played no part in selecting, yet it behaves exactly like our own Index of Health and Social Problems – showing strong relationships with income inequality and none with average national income.

WHICH COUNTRIES?

Critics have also suggested that we selected countries arbitrarily to suit our argument and should have included more, and poorer, countries.[416-7]

The countries in our analyses result from the application of a strict set of criteria, applied with no departures or exceptions. Our source was the World Development Indicators Database, World Bank, April 2004. We took the richest 50 countries for which the bank publishes figures on Gross National Income per capita, ranked according to the 'Atlas method' used by the World Bank to classify countries into Low, Medium and High Income categories. From that list we excluded countries with no internationally comparable data on income inequality and those with populations with fewer than 3 million (to avoid tax havens). That gave us our final dataset of 25 rich countries. We looked exclusively at the richest countries not because these relationships only exist among them, but because these countries are on the flat part of the curve at the top right in Figure 1.1 on p.7, where life expectancy is no longer related to differences in Gross National Income per head (GNIpc) and it is therefore easier to distinguish the effects of relative and absolute levels of income.

If we had also studied poorer countries two problems would have arisen. First, comparable data on teenage births, mental illness, social mobility, social cohesion etc., are very rarely available for much poorer countries. Second, if we had included countries in which many people continue to have inadequate material resources so that increasing GNIpc is still important, we would have had to control statistically for the log trans-formation of GNIpc in order to show the effect of inequality. In a book which we hope will be widely understood, this would have been a substantial increase in complexity for little gain. Nevertheless, if we had included poorer countries it would have made little difference to our results. Studies of life expectancy, infant mortality and homicide – for which data is usually available for poorer countries – show that greater equality is beneficial at all levels of economic development.[10, 418]

To have 'cherry-picked' countries – as our critics suggest we did – according to whether their data for this or that social problem did or did not fit our thesis, would have made the book a pointless exercise. Instead we had an absolute rule that we used the most reputable data sources and took the data for as many of our 25 countries as were available – warts and all. For example, we include Singapore in our analysis of infant mortality although it is a very significant outlier: it claims the lowest infant mortality in the world despite being the most unequal country in our dataset (see Fig 6.4 on p.82).

If we had shown graphs of data collected by other researchers we would often have been able to show even stronger and more dramatic associations with inequality than already appear in the book.[207, 419] But had we done so we would necessarily have been referring to different groups of countries in studies which use different measures of income inequality and that would properly have raised questions of comparability. On the contrary, we wanted to show that there is a consistent pattern running through the data for quite different problems. Our purpose was to analyse every health and social problem using the same inequality measures with reference to the same set of countries, and then, to make quite sure, to double-check our findings by repeating the analyses on the 50 states of the USA.

The book therefore tries to show the relationships between income inequality and various health and social problems as simply and transparently as possible. The scatter graphs can be understood without any knowledge of mathematics or statistics. We point out in each chapter that our findings cannot be attributed to chance. Most readers should not feel any sense that there are mysterious areas where they cannot tell quite what is going on but, for those who want it, we provide more data and statistical detail at www.equalitytrust.org.uk

CULTURAL DIFFERENCES?

It has been suggested that the relationships we show reflect differences in national culture rather than the effects of inequality.[416]

This criticism has been made in two forms. One is the suggestion that income differences are an expression of underlying cultural differences, and it is these which are the real determinants of the health and social problems we examine. The other is that particular countries should be excluded from one or other analysis because they are culturally different from the others.

Rather than varying from better to worse on a single scale as income inequality does, national cultures differ in an infinite number of quantitative and qualitative ways. In chapter 13 we mention the huge cultural differences between Sweden and Japan which, despite both performing well in our analyses, are poles apart in other ways – including the extent of women's participation in the labour force and in politics, the dominance of the nuclear family, and whether their narrower income differences result from redistribution or narrower differences in earnings before taxes and benefits.

In contrast, Spain and Portugal have many cultural similarities and were both dictatorships until the mid 1970s. Yet as we have seen throughout the book, Portugal is now much more unequal than Spain and consistently suffers more from most of the health and social problems we discuss. So it looks as if cultural differences (Sweden and Japan) don't necessarily make societies perform differently in our analyses, and cultural similarities (Spain and Portugal) do not necessarily make them perform similarly. What matters is the scale of income differences almost regardless of other aspects of culture.

In addition, we know that in the second half of the twentieth century the USA and Japan came close to swapping positions in the international league tables of life expectancy and income inequality. In the 1950s the USA was more equal than Japan and had better health. But as the USA became more unequal, Japan became less unequal, and Japanese life expectancy outstripped that in the USA to become the best in the world. If what matters is culture rather than inequality, how is it that the plethora of cultural changes which took place in these two nations did nothing to alter the relation between each countries' burden of health and social problems and its income inequality?

The more you think about the suggestion that the relationships we show are merely a mirage created by some underlying dimension of cultural difference, the less plausible it becomes. This unknown dimension of culture would not only have to cause physical and mental ill-health, school bullying, more punitive sentencing, obesity, teenage births and so on, but it would have to do so in proportion to the scale of income inequality.

The second use to which critics put the notion of cultural differences is to justify removing groups of countries at either the more or the less equal end of our analyses on the grounds that they are 'culturally different' from the others. For example, arguments have been made for removing the Scandinavian or English-speaking countries, or sometimes even both groups.[416] Such wholesale deletions would remove crucial information which looks as if it might explain why some English-speaking countries do better on some social measures than others – for example why the USA has more mental illness and teenage pregnancies than the UK, which in turn has more of both than New Zealand (and of course all the US states are English speaking). More fundamentally, however, national cultures are themselves powerfully determined by inequality because of its corrosive effects on trust, cohesion and community life.

OUTLIERS, DAMN OUTLIERS AND STATISTICS

Some critics have suggested that the relationships we show are dependent on 'outliers'.[416]

As well as excluding countries on the grounds of cultural differences, it has also been suggested that some countries should be removed for the purely statistical reason that they are 'outliers'. In any of the graphs in our book, an outlier is a country or US state that is a long way from the line of best fit between the countries or states. Good examples are Singapore in Figure 6.4 on p.82 (showing the relationship between income inequality and infant mortality) or Italy in Figure 5.1 on p.67 (showing levels of mental illness). There are established methods to calculate the influence a single data point has on the line of best fit on a graph, but no hard and fast statistical rules as to when outliers should be left out. We decided to keep all countries and states in our analyses for three reasons: first, they represent real variation in population levels of health and social problems; second, because removing occasional data points would have invited the accusation that we were picking and choosing data points; and lastly because, as we said earlier, we wanted to show the consistency of the effects of inequality on different problems across the same group of countries.

Having mistakenly accused us of picking and choosing countries for each analysis, our critics have also attempted to discredit some of the relationships we show by selectively removing countries on the grounds that they are outliers. For example, one critic said that the Scandinavian countries were outliers in our analysis of inequality and foreign aid, but did not suggest removing Japan which, on that graph (Fig 4.6, p.61), is actually more of an outlier.[416] Removing the Scandinavian countries would mean the relationship was no longer statistically significant, but removing Japan as well would restore its significance.

The same thing happens in the case of obesity. A critic suggested that we should remove the USA from the analysis on the grounds that it is an outlier and doing so reduces the relationship to non-significance.[416] But Greece is a more distant outlier: remove Greece as well and the significant link between inequality and obesity is restored. For overweight children, the same critic removes the USA, but not Canada, which is again a more distant outlier. Remove both and once again the relationship is statistically significant.

Our results are, of course, sometimes sensitive to exclusions simply because we are looking at a limited number of countries, but the fact that so many relationships with inequality are statistically significant, despite the limits to the data, is an indication of how powerful the underlying relationships actually are.

These criticisms of the evidence that inequality affects wellbeing fail on two grounds: they do nothing to dent either the hundreds of other published analyses of health and income inequality, nor our analyses of the 50 American states; and ultimately the suggested exclusions do not remove the associations we show. In Figure 13.1 (p.174) we summarize our international evidence by combining all the health and social problems into one index. Sweden, Norway, Finland, Japan, USA and UK – all the most equal and unequal societies – can be removed all at once, and *still* there is a highly significant relationship between social health and inequality among the remaining countries.

In short, we believe that our data are very robust – and, as we said earlier, some of these relationships have been demonstrated many, many times before by other researchers in quite different settings. Research reports have shown for instance that income inequality is related to health in the regions of Russia,[420] the provinces of China[421] or Japan,[422] the counties of Chile,[423] or among rich and poor countries combined.[418] Those who dislike our conclusions would no doubt want to remove various provinces, counties or countries from these reports too.

OTHER FACTORS?

It is sometimes suggested that we should control for, or take account of, other factors that might explain the associations between income inequality and health or social problems – such as National Income per head, poverty, ethnicity, or welfare services.[416]

There were several reasons why we chose not to include other factors. First, we wished to present the simplest and most understandable picture of the correlation between income inequality and health and social problems, so that readers could see the strength of the relationship for themselves. Second, it is a fundamental methodological principle of epidemiological analysis that you should not control for factors which form part of the causal chain – in this case explaining *how* inequality causes a particular problem. For example, if we think – as we do – that societies with greater income inequality have worse health because poorer social relations increase chronic stress, then we would need to be cautious about how to analyse that particular causal sequence. Simply including measures of trust and social cohesion in a statistical model could remove the association between income inequality and health,[400] even though it is likely that inequality actually leads to poorer health *because* it is socially divisive. Third, including factors that are unrelated to inequality, or to any particular problem, would simply create unnecessary 'noise' and be methodologically incorrect.

Nevertheless, many other studies of health and income inequality *have* controlled for poverty, average income, or each person's individual income. Still others have made careful explorations of the interplay between income inequality and public spending, social capital and the ethnic composition of populations. We discussed these in chapter 13 and will return to some of them in the section below on recent advances in research.

A point which can hardly be made too often is that the relationships between inequality and various health and social problems are not reducible to the direct effects of people's material living standards independent of inequality. No one doubts that health is compromised when a substantial proportion of the population of poorer countries lack basic necessities. But when it comes to explaining the tendency for health to improve all the way up the social hierarchy even in rich countries (see Figure 1.4) the causes are less clear. The concept of 'neomaterialism' was invented as a counter to psychosocial explanations of this pattern. The idea was that health may continue to benefit from higher levels of comfort and luxury all the way up the social scale. Even if that were true, it would not explain why more equal societies are healthier. But Figure 1.3 shows life expectancy is no longer sensitive to living standards among the rich countries, Figure 2.3 shows that this is also true of our Index of Health and Social Problems, and Figure 2.7 shows the same is true of the UNICEF index of child wellbeing. Chapter 6 references a review of studies which have controlled not only for poverty but also for the effect of each person's income on their health before going on to test for an effect of inequality. An important new review of such studies is also mentioned below. Although it is easy to slip back into the conventional view that material standards are of primary importance and must somehow explain all that we attribute to inequality, we must bear in mind that this runs counter to a substantial body of evidence.

THE PROOF OF THE PUDDING

An important strength of the evidence we present in this book is its remarkable consistency, which provides a coherent picture at two levels. It is not simply that almost all health and social problems which are related to social status show the same tendency to get worse when

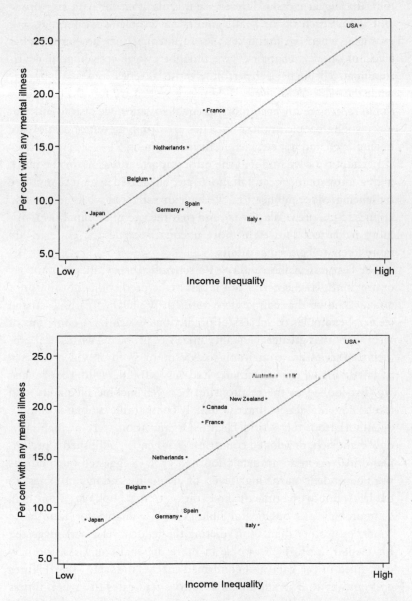

Figures 17.1 and 17.2 *The relationship between income inequality and mental illness in 8 rich countries (Fig 17.1) was confirmed when new data become available for 4 additional countries (Fig 17.2).*

there are bigger income differences: it is also that the data are consistent *within* each of the health and social problems we look at. For example, when we found that more unequal societies have higher levels of obesity (chapter 7) we thought calorie consumption levels should also be higher per person in those societies; and that indeed is what the evidence showed.[114] Similarly, when we found that educational scores are lower in more unequal societies, we also found that more young people in those societies are dropping out of school, are unemployed and not engaged in further training.[424]

In chapter 11 we said that the most important reason for the much higher imprisonment rates in more unequal societies is more punitive sentencing. Since publication, we have investigated whether this also applies to children. We have found that the age of criminal responsibility tends to be lower in more unequal societies, so children are more likely to be tried as adults.

The best test of the validity of a scientific theory, indeed a theory of any kind, is whether or not it can make predictions of things not already known that can later be verified. We have already discussed (p. 195) examples of successful predictions which have come out of our theory that greater inequality increases problems with social gradients. We can draw attention to two more, both of which concern relationships where we initially had very little data. In 2006, when we first looked at the relationship between income inequality and levels of mental illness, internationally comparable estimates of mental illness from the World Health Organization were available for only eight rich, developed countries.[425] When we published a preliminary analysis in an academic journal, critics suggested our findings were dependent on the high levels of inequality and mental illness in the USA. But by the time the first edition of this book was published, comparable data on mental illness were available for four more countries. Rather than contradicting the tendency we had suggested for mental health to be worse in more unequal countries, the new data filled in the gaps and confirmed that relationship – see Figures 17.1 and 17.2. The additional countries had rates of mental illness close to those which their levels of inequality would have predicted.

The same thing has happened in relation to measures of social mobility. When *The Spirit Level* was first published, we had comparable

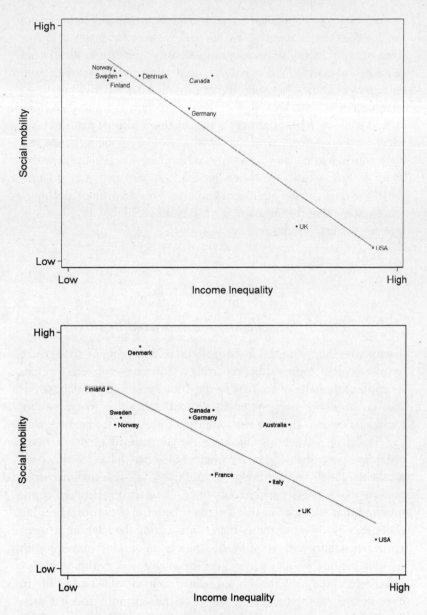

Figures 17.3 and 17.4 *The relationship between income inequality and social mobility in 8 rich countries (Fig 17.2) was confirmed when new data became available for 3 additional countries (Fig 17.4).*

measures of social mobility for only eight countries and some critics claimed that the relationship we showed between inequality and low levels of social mobility was spurious because we had too few countries to justify an analysis. We included it, despite initially having data from only eight countries, not only because it was a statistically significant relationship, but also because research reports show that social mobility slowed while income differences widened, and it seemed plausible that wider income differences would tend to reduce mobility. Since this book was published, new data on social mobility has become available which include a further three countries.[426] As Figures 17.3 and 17.4 show, the data for the additional countries provide a fuller and more robust estimate of the impact of inequality on social mobility, and confirm our original conclusions.

NEW EVIDENCE

Death rates versus self-reported health

Since we finished writing *The Spirit Level* in the spring of 2008, there have been many more studies reporting relationships between inequality and health. Nine of the new studies look specifically at rich, developed countries.[427-435] Seven find, as we do, that health is worse in more unequal societies. The two that differ both look at income inequality in relation to *self-reported* health – where, instead of death rates, people are typically asked to say whether their health has recently been excellent, good, fair or poor.[432-3] Although self-reported health is predictive of longevity within a country, comparisons between countries find that self-rated health is actually better in countries where life expectancy is lower: so rather than contradicting the relation between greater inequality and worse health, the studies of self-reported health tell us something about the way people *perceive* their health.[436-7]

But why is self-rated health not related to levels of actual health in cross-country comparisons? Could it be that in more unequal societies, with more status competition, asserting that one has excellent or very good health might be part of maintaining a hardier self-image? Or perhaps people in more equal societies are less inclined to rate themselves at the top of a scale? We can only guess. Such questions show the importance of using objective measures of health and social problems in international comparisons.

Causal pathways

Three other important new pieces of evidence have appeared recently, which tell us more about how the relation between income inequality and health works. One is a review of what are called multi-level studies published in the *British Medical Journal*.[438] Multi-level studies look at income and health in two stages: first in terms of the relation between each person's individual income and health, and second to see if there is an additional effect of inequality across each society as a whole. This review combines data from 26 multi-level studies with individual data for over 60 million people. It shows unequivocally that inequality has a damaging effect on health which cannot be attributed to how rich or poor people are in absolute terms, and concludes that even after controlling for individual incomes (including poverty) or education, reducing inequality in the OECD countries alone would prevent upwards of 1.5 million deaths per year (almost 1 in 10 deaths among adults aged 15–60). This is likely to be a conservative estimate because controlling for individual income will also control for individual social status which affects health and is a key component of inequality.

The second new piece of evidence, published in *Social Science and Medicine*, adds to the small number of studies looking at changes in inequality and health over time. All over the world, life expectancy continues to increase, but this study showed that those US states that had the biggest increases in income inequality between 1970 and 2000 had smaller improvements in life expectancy than other states.[439]

The third piece of evidence, published in *The American Journal of Public Health*, is a study that tests how far the link between income inequality and health results from different levels of trust or from different levels of government spending on health services.[415] This study confirmed what we suggested in chapter 6: that levels of trust are indeed part of the explanation, whereas spending on health care is not. Wider income differences seem to erode trust, which in turn seems to compromise healthy ageing.

Friendship and health

Throughout *The Spirit Level*, we discuss the vital importance of social relationships to human health and wellbeing and show that higher levels of income inequality damage the social fabric which contributes so much to healthy societies. Now, a major new review of the evidence from almost 150 studies confirms the important influence of social relationships on health.[440] People with stronger social relationships were half as likely to die during a study's period of follow-up as those with weaker social ties. The authors of the report found that the influence of social relations on survival was at least as important as that of smoking, and much more important than heavy drinking, physical activity or obesity. The effects were strongest when researchers combined measures of different kinds of relationships, such as marital status, feeling lonely, size of social network, participation in social activities, and so on.

Violence

As we described in Chapter 10, there is a large and consistent body of evidence on income inequality and violence. More recent studies continue to confirm this link. One study of 33 countries, published in 2010, also showed that social cohesion – as measured by levels of trust – seemed to provide the causal link between income inequality and homicide rates, whereas public spending on health and education did not.[415]

Martin Daly at McMaster University in Canada has published an analysis of whether the relation between inequality and violence among the 50 states of the USA could – as some have suggested – be due to 'southern culture' or ethnicity, rather than to inequality. He showed that on the contrary, violence was related to inequality among the southern and northern states considered separately, and that rates of violence rose along with inequality amongst both black and white perpetrators of violence.[414]

When we wrote *The Spirit Level*, we knew of no other studies of income inequality and child conflict, but a recent study of 37 countries finds higher levels of bullying in more unequal countries. Support from family and friends was associated with less bullying, but neither this nor differences in family wealth trumped the effect of income inequality.[402]

EQUALITY AND SUSTAINABILITY

The intertwined issues of equality, social justice, sustainability and economic balance are now receiving a great deal of attention all over the world. Environmental organizations such as Friends of the Earth and the World Wildlife Fund now campaign on inequality issues, including human rights and the fair distribution of natural resources, and the UK's Green Party placed economic equality at the heart of its election manifesto in 2010.

Evidence continues to accumulate that more equal societies seem to have lower carbon footprints and are in a better position to cope with the challenges of climate change. More unequal countries have higher ecological footprints, produce more waste, consume more water and fly more air miles per capita.[441] This may be because more equal societies seem to foster a greater sense of collective responsibility which is crucial for political action to address climate change. Business leaders in more equal countries are more likely to agree that their governments should cooperate with international environmental agreements than those in less equal countries.[442] Leading policy specialists now suggest that global inequalities stand in the way of cooperation on climate change.[443]

INEQUALITY, THE MARKET AND DEMOCRACY

The weight of the evidence – our own and that of many others – and its continued rapid accumulation, make the important link between income inequality and social dysfunction inescapable. But ill-founded and politically motivated criticism can muddy the waters and leave people with the impression that the evidence is less clear than it is. Imagine if someone were to assert (with no justification whatsoever) that climate science had not taken account of, say, the effects of variations in the salinity of different oceans. Unable to evaluate this claim, the inexpert listener might assume that this was an important factor, and that perhaps it had not been properly considered.

What often appear to be 'balanced' discussions in the media can be misleading. This happens even in areas of science where the accumulation of evidence leaves little legitimate room for doubt. For example, if 98 per cent of climate change scientists agree on an issue, and 2 per cent disagree, then inviting one person from each camp to take part in a news programme or public debate can leave people with an impression that an issue is much more controversial than it is. Only those viewers or readers who are particularly diligent or highly motivated will be able to pursue the issues in detail. Rather than considering our replies to the political attacks on our work, we expect some who are opposed to greater equality will simply be content to imagine that the issue is 'controversial' and can now be safely ignored.

Perhaps the best tactic in this situation is to address the beliefs that motivate the attacks. In *Merchants of Doubt*, Oreskes and Conway suggest that the defence of a kind of free market fundamentalism is the most plausible explanation of why the same individuals and institutions are often involved in attacks on research in areas as diverse as tobacco control and the evidence on climate change. As well as defending the free market, they see themselves as countering tendencies to big government and protecting democracy.[412] The same beliefs are likely to guide the attacks on the evidence of the socially damaging effects of inequality.

If that is the motivation, then it is based on a serious misconception, one which is almost the opposite of the truth. Greater inequality actually *increases* the need for big government – for more police, more prisons, more health and social services of every kind. Most of these services are expensive and only very partially effective, but we shall need them for ever if we continue to have the high levels of inequality that create the problems they are designed to deal with. Several states of the USA now spend more on prisons than on higher education. In fact, one of the best and most humane ways of achieving small government is by reducing inequality. Similarly, the assumption that greater equality can only be achieved through higher taxes and benefits, which presumably led The Tax Payers' Alliance to publish its criticism of *The Spirit Level*, is also a mistake. We have been at pains to point out (in chapter 13) that some societies achieve greater equality with unusually low taxation because they have smaller earnings differences before taxes.

There are few things more corrosive of a properly functioning democracy and of the market than corruption and unbridled greed. Although the international measures of corruption currently available were designed primarily to assess levels of corruption in poorer countries, they strongly suggest that one of the likely costs of greater inequality is increased corruption in government and society more widely.[444] In chapter 4 we saw that trust and the strength of community life are weakened by inequality, and this is true not only of interpersonal trust, but also of trust in government – the difference between the attitude of Americans and Scandinavians to their governments is well known. In addition, international data and data for the American states suggest people trust government less in more unequal states.[401, 445] There is also evidence from societies where voting is not compulsory (as it is for instance in Australia) that voter turn-out may be lower in more unequal countries.[446] Whether or not this reflects a greater separation of interests and an increasing sense of 'us and them' between people at opposite ends of the social ladder, it certainly suggests that too much inequality is a threat to democracy.

Economists sometimes suggest that the market is like a democratic voting system: our expenditure pattern is, in effect, our vote on how productive resources should be allocated between competing demands. If this is true, someone with twenty times the income of another effectively gets twenty times as many votes. As a result inequality seriously distorts the ability of economies to provide for human needs: because the poor cannot afford better housing, their demand for it is 'ineffective', yet the spending of the rich ensures scarce productive assets are devoted instead to the production of luxuries.

INEQUALITY, DEBT AND THE FINANCIAL CRASH

As well as these more general effects of large income differences, there is now evidence that inequality played a central causal role in the financial crashes of 1929 and of 2008.

We suggested (p.228, 270) that inequality leads to increases in debt. It turns out that they are intimately related. Using figures for the 40 years from 1963 to 2003, Matteo Iacoviello, an economist at the Federal Reserve Board and Boston College, has recently shown a very close correlation between increasing debt and increasing inequality in the USA and concludes that the longer term increases in debt can only be explained by the rise in inequality.[447] Using the latest international data from OECD on debt, we have also found that both short-term household debt as a proportion of household assets, as well as government National Debt as a

Figure 17.5 *The financial crashes of 1929 and 2008 took place at high points in inequality (continuous line on graph) and debt (two broken lines on graph).*[452]

proportion of Gross Domestic Product, are higher in more unequal countries.[448]

Aided by some of the world's most respected economists, the story of the way rising inequality and debt led to the financial crashes of 1929 and 2008 is well told in a documentary film called *The Flaw*.[449] Both crashes happened at the two peaks of inequality in the last hundred years after long periods of rising inequality which had led to rapid increases in debt.[450-1] As Figure 17.5 shows, their trends over time are strikingly similar. Robert Wade, professor of political economy at the London School of Economics, estimates that growing inequality meant that in the years before the 2008 crash about 1.5 trillion dollars per year were being siphoned from the bottom 90 per cent of the US population to the top ten per cent.[449] As a result, the richest people had more and more money to invest and to lend, but people outside the very wealthiest category found it increasingly difficult to maintain their relative incomes or realize their aspirations. Both for speculators and for ordinary householders rising property prices made investment in property look like a band wagon everyone had to get onto. People bought into the housing market wherever they could and remortgaged precariously as prices rose. The financial sector handling and speculating on these debts found its share of all US corporate profits rising from 15 per cent in 1980 to 40 per cent in 2003. As the bubble grew bigger, the worse its eventual and inevitable burst became.

MAKING DEMOCRACY WORK

Rather than being a threat to democracy and the market, reductions of inequality are surely an essential part of their defence. Greater equality will benefit even those who would deny the evidence.

Near the beginning of this chapter we mentioned research that showed that over 90 per cent of the American population say they would prefer to live in a society with the income distribution which actually exists in Sweden rather than that of the USA. Research in Britain also shows that people think income differences should be smaller, even though they dramatically underestimate how large they actually are. The world really is full of people who have much more egalitarian preferences and a stronger sense of justice than we tend to assume. Part of the reason for this is that in recent decades most people in the world's richest societies have been persuaded to doubt the validity and relevance of egalitarian values. The rise of neo-liberal political and economic thinking in the 1980s and 1990s meant that egalitarian ideas disappeared from public debate and those with a strong sense of justice became – in effect – closet egalitarians.

It is now time egalitarians returned to the public arena. We need to do so confident that our intuitions have been validated and found to be truer than most of us ever imagined. Because the evidence shows that few people are aware of the actual scale of inequality and injustice in our societies, or recognize how it damages the vast majority of the population, the first task is to provide education and information.

Understanding these issues is already changing attitudes to inequality among politicians. In Britain *The Spirit Level* has been endorsed across the political spectrum. In a major speech at the end of 2009, David Cameron, now the Conservative prime minister, said *The Spirit Level* showed 'that among the richest countries, it's the more unequal ones that do worse according to almost every quality of life indicator . . . per capita GDP is much less significant for a country's life expectancy, crime levels, literacy and health than the size of the gap between the richest and poorest in the population . . . We all know, in our hearts, that as long as there is deep poverty living systematically side by side with great riches, we all remain the poorer for it.'[453] In September 2010, in his first major speech as leader of the Labour Party, Ed Miliband said 'I do believe this country is too unequal and the gap between rich and poor doesn't just harm the poor, it harms us all'[454] and 'if you look round the world – at the countries that are healthier, happier, more secure – they are the more equal countries.'[455] As Liberal Democrat ministers in the coalition government, Vince Cable and Lynne Featherstone have signed a pledge committing themselves to reducing inequalities.[456]

Words are a start, but changing policies and politics, changing the way our societies organize themselves, will require the evidence to be recognized even more widely. Few tasks are more worthwhile than this: as we think *The Spirit Level* shows, the health of our democracies, our societies and their people, is truly dependent on greater equality.

The Equality Trust

If reading this book leaves you wanting to do something to help reduce inequality, then please visit The Equality Trust web site at www.equalitytrust.org.uk. There you will find downloadable slides which we hope you will use, a downloadable lecture on DVD, short summaries of the evidence, answers to frequently asked questions, and suggestions for campaigning.

Having discovered how seriously societies are damaged by great inequality we felt we had to do what we could to make the evidence better known. The Trust was set up as a not-for-profit organization to educate and campaign on the benefits of a more equal society. Its work depends on donations from individuals and organizations sharing our vision.

We hope you will sign the Equality Charter, put your name down to receive the newsletter, make a donation, give us your ideas and join or form a local equality group. Most of all we hope you will use the evidence we have started to put together to spread the word and convince others of the need to reduce inequality. In politics, words are action.

The Equality Trust is not a large organization able to implement policies, run campaigns and orchestrate things on your behalf. Instead it aims to make people better informed and provide resources to stimulate and strengthen their own political and educational activities – whether through talking to friends and colleagues, passing on our web address, writing blogs, local campaigning, sending letters to newspapers and politicians, or raising the issues in the mass media.

Our aim is to create a groundswell of opinion in favour of great equality. Without that politicians can do very little. Egalitarian sentiments are hidden close to the hearts of vast numbers of people of all shades of political opinion. Most people know how much we sacrifice to consumerism and know that there are few things nicer than relaxing with friends and equals. They also know that it is family, friends and community that matter to happiness and know that our present way of life is ruining the planet. The culture of the last few decades has reduced us to closet egalitarians: it is time we came out of the woodwork and set a course for sanity.

Appendix

HOW WE CHOSE COUNTRIES FOR OUR INTERNATIONAL COMPARISONS

First, we obtained a list of the 50 richest countries in the world from the World Bank. The report we used was published in 2004 and is based on data from 2002.

Then we excluded countries with populations below 3 million, because we didn't want to include tax havens like the Cayman Islands and Monaco. And we excluded countries without comparable data on income inequality, such as Iceland.

That left us with 23 rich countries:

Australia	Greece	Portugal
Austria	Ireland	Singapore
Belgium	Israel	Spain
Canada	Italy	Sweden
Denmark	Japan	Switzerland
Finland	Netherlands	United Kingdom
France	New Zealand	United States of America
Germany	Norway	

THE 50 AMERICAN STATES

In our figures, we label each American state with the two-letter abbreviation used by the US Postal Service. As these will be unfamiliar to some international readers, here is a list of the states and their labels:

ALABAMA	AL	MONTANA	MT
ALASKA	AK	NEBRASKA	NE
ARIZONA	AZ	NEVADA	NV
ARKANSAS	AR	NEW HAMPSHIRE	NH
CALIFORNIA	CA	NEW JERSEY	NJ
COLORADO	CO	NEW MEXICO	NM
CONNECTICUT	CT	NEW YORK	NY
DELAWARE	DE	NORTH CAROLINA	NC
FLORIDA	FL	NORTH DAKOTA	ND
GEORGIA	GA	OHIO	OH
HAWAII	HI	OKLAHOMA	OK
IDAHO	ID	OREGON	OR
ILLINOIS	IL	PENNSYLVANIA	PA
INDIANA	IN	RHODE ISLAND	RI
IOWA	IA	SOUTH CAROLINA	SC
KANSAS	KS	SOUTH DAKOTA	SD
KENTUCKY	KY	TENNESSEE	TN
LOUISIANA	LA	TEXAS	TX
MAINE	ME	UTAH	UT
MARYLAND	MD	VERMONT	VT
MASSACHUSETTS	MA	VIRGINIA	VA
MICHIGAN	MI	WASHINGTON	WA
MINNESOTA	MN	WEST VIRGINIA	WV
MISSISSIPPI	MS	WISCONSIN	WI
MISSOURI	MO	WYOMING	WY

INCOME INEQUALITY DATA

In this book, for all international comparisons, we use the 20:20 ratio measure of income inequality from the United Nations Development Programme Human Development Indicators, 2003–6. As survey dates vary for different countries (from 1992 to 2001), and as the lag time for effects will vary for the different outcomes we examine, we took the average across the reporting years 2003–6. For the US comparisons we use the 1999 state-level Gini coefficient based on household income produced by the US Census Bureau.

Data Sources

United Nations Development Program. *Human development report.* New York: Oxford University Press, 2003, 2004, 2005, 2006.
US Census Bureau. *Gini ratios by state.* 1969, 1979, 1989, 1999. Washington, DC: US Census Bureau, 1999 (table S4).

DEVELOPING THE INDEX OF HEALTH AND SOCIAL PROBLEMS

The International Index

The International Index has 10 components:

- Life expectancy (reverse coded)
- Teenage births
- Obesity
- Mental illness
- Homicides
- Imprisonment rates
- Mistrust
- Social mobility (reverse coded)
- Education (reverse coded)
- Infant mortality rate

Sixteen countries had at least nine of these ten measures. A further five countries had eight out of ten. Two countries (Israel and Singapore) with fewer measures were excluded from the index but included in analyses of individual measures.

- Countries with data on all ten measures: Canada, Germany, USA
- Countries with data on nine out of ten measures, but no data on social mobility: Australia, Belgium, France, Italy, Japan, Netherlands, New Zealand, Spain
- Countries with data on nine out of ten measures, but no data on mental health: Denmark, Finland, Norway, Sweden
- Countries with data on nine out of ten measures, but no data on education: UK
- Countries with data on eight out of ten measures, but no data on social mobility or mental illness: Austria, Greece, Ireland, Portugal, Switzerland

The Index of Health and Social Problems was created by taking the mean of the z-scores for each measure (averaged over the number of measures available for that particular country).

The Index of Health and Social Problems for the 50 states of the USA

The US Index has nine components:

- Trust (reverse coded)
- Life expectancy (reverse coded)
- Teenage births
- Obesity
- Homicides
- Imprisonment
- Education (reverse coded)
- Infant mortality rate
- Mental illness

Of the 50 states, 40 have data for all eight measures.

Nine states are missing data on trust from the General Social Survey:

- Alaska, Delaware, Hawaii, Idaho, Maine, Nebraska, New Mexico, Nevada, South Dakota

Wyoming has data on trust, but not on homicides

The Index of Health and Social Problems for the USA was created by taking the mean of the z-scores for each measure (averaged over the number of measures available for that particular state).

Sources of Data for the Indices of Health and Social Problems

Component	International data	US state data
Trust	Per cent of people who respond positively to the statement 'most people can be trusted' 1999–2001 World Values Survey[1] *Reverse-coded*	Per cent of people who respond positively to the statement 'most people can be trusted' 1999 General Social Survey[2] *Reverse-coded*
Life expectancy	Life expectancy at birth for men and women 2004 United Nations Human Development Report[3] *Reverse-coded*	Life expectancy at birth for men and women 2000 US Census Bureau, Population Division[4] *Reverse-coded*
Infant mortality	Deaths in the first year of life per 1,000 live births 2000 World Bank[5]	Deaths in the first year of life per 1,000 live births 2002 US National Center for Health Statistics[6]
Obesity	Percentage of the population with BMI >30, averaged for men and women 2002 International Obesity TaskForce[7, 8]	Percentage of the population with BMI >30, averaged for men and women 1999–2002 Corrected estimates from Prof Majid Ezzati, Harvard University, based on NHANES and BRFSS surveys[9]

Component	International data	US state data
Mental illness	Prevalence of mental illness 2001–2003 WHO[10]	Average number of days in past month when mental health was not good 1993–2001 BRFSS[11]
Education scores	Combined average of maths literacy and reading literacy scores of 15-year-olds 2000 OECD PISA[12] *Reverse-coded*	Combined average of maths and reading scores for 8th graders 2003 US Department of Education, National Center for Education Statistics[13, 14] *Reverse-coded*
Teenage birth rate	Births per 1,000 women aged 15–19 years 1998 UNICEF[15]	Births per 1,000 women aged 15–19 years 2000 US National Vital Statistics[16]
Homicides	Homicide rate per 100,000 Period average for 1990–2000 United Nations[17]	Homicide rate per 100,000 1999 FBI[18]
Imprisonment	Prisoners per 100,000 United Nations[17]	Prisoners per 100,000 1997–8 US Department of Justice[19]
Social mobility	Correlation between father and son's income 30-year period data from 8 cohort studies London School of Economics[20]	N/A

Data Sources

1. European Values Study Group and World Values Survey Association. European and World Values Survey Integrated Data File, 1999–2001, Release 1. Ann Arbor, MI: Inter-university Consortium for Political and Social Research, 2005.

2. National Opinion Research Center. *General Social Survey*. Chicago: NORC, 1999.

3. United Nations Development Program. *Human Development Report*. New York: Oxford University Press, 2004.

4. US Census Bureau. Population Division, Interim State Population Projections, Table 2. Internet release date: April 21, 2005.

5. World Bank. World Development Indicators (WDI) September 2006: ESDS International, (MIMAS) University of Manchester.

6. US National Center for Health Statistics. Table 105, Statistical abstract of the United States. Washington, DC: CDC, 2006.

7. International Obesity TaskForce. *Obesity in Europe*. London: International Obesity TaskForce in collaboration with the European Association for the Study of Obesity Task Forces, 2002.

8. International Obesity TaskForce. *Overweight and obese*. London: International Obesity Taskforce, 2002.

9. M. Ezzati, H. Martin, S. Skjold, S. Vander Hoorn, C. J. Murray. 'Trends in national and state-level obesity in the USA after correction for self-report bias: analysis of health surveys'. *J R Soc Med* 2006; 99(5): 250–7.

10. K. Demyttenaere, R. Bruffaerts, J. Posada-Villa, I. Gasquet, V. Kovess, J. P. Lepine, et al. 'Prevalence, severity, and unmet need for treatment of mental disorders in the World Health Organization World Mental Health Surveys'. *Jama* 2004; 291(21): 2581–90.

11. H. S. Zahran, R. Kobau, D. G. Moriarty, M. M. Zack, J. Holt, R. Donehoo. 'Health-related quality of life surveillance – United States, 1993–2002'. *MMWR Surveill Summ* 2005; 54(4): 1–35.

12. OECD. *Education at a glance*. OECD Indicators, 2003.

13. US Department of Education NCfES. *The Nation's Report Card: Reading Highlights 2003*. Washington, DC, 2004.

14. US Department of Education NCfES. *The Nation's Report Card: Mathematics Highlights 2003*. Washington, DC, 2004.

15. UNICEF Innocenti Research Centre. *A league table of teenage births in rich nations*. Florence: Innocenti Report Card, 2001.

16. US Census Bureau. *Statistical Abstract of the United States: 2000* (120th Edition). Washington: Census Bureau, 2000.

17. United Nations Crime and Justice Information Network. *Survey on Crime Trends and the Operations of Criminal Justice Systems* (Fifth, Sixth, Seventh, Eighth): United Nations, 2000.

18. Federal Bureau of Investigation. *Crime in the United States 1999.* Washington, DC: US Government Printing Office, 1999.

19. US Department of Justice BoJS. *Incarceration rates for prisoners under State or Federal jurisdiction.* File: corpop25.wk1.

20. J. Blanden, P. Gregg, S. Machin. *Intergenerational mobility in Europe and North America.* London: Centre for Economic Performance, London School of Economics, 2005.

Statistics

Pearson Correlation Coefficients (*r*) and Statistical Significance (*p-value*) for Associations with Income Inequality.

Indicator	International data		US data	
	r	*p-value*	*r*	*p-value*
Trust	−0.66	<0.01	−0.70	<0.01
Life expectancy	−0.44	0.04	−0.45	<0.01
Infant mortality	0.42	0.04	0.43	<0.01
Obesity	0.57	<0.01	0.47	<0.01
Mental illness	0.73	<0.01	0.18	0.12
Education score	−0.45	0.04	−0.47	.01
Teenage birth rate	0.73	<0.01	0.46	<0.01
Homicides	0.47	0.02	0.42	<0.01
Imprisonment	0.75	<0.01	0.48	<0.01
Social mobility	0.93	<0.01	–	–
Index	**0.87**	**<0.01**	**0.59**	**<0.01**
Overweight children	0.59	0.01	0.57	<0.01
Drugs index	0.63	<0.01		
Calorie intake	0.46	0.03		
Public expenditure on health care	−0.54	0.01		
Child well-being	−0.71	<0.01	−0.51	<0.01
Triple education score	−0.44	0.04		

Indicator	International data		US data	
	r	p-value	r	p-value
Child conflict	0.62	<0.01		
Spending on foreign aid	−0.61	<0.01		
Recycling	−0.82	<0.01		
Peace index	−0.51	0.01		
Paid maternity leave	−0.55	0.01		
Advertising	0.73	<0.01		
Police	0.52	0.04		
Social expenditure	−0.45	0.04		
Women's status	−0.44	0.04	−0.30	0.03
Patents per capita	−0.49	0.02		
Juvenile homicides			0.29	<0.05
High school drop-outs			0.79	<0.01
Child mental illness			0.36	0.01
Pugnacity			0.47	<0.01

References

1. The Harwood Group, *Yearning for Balance: Views of Americans on consumption, materialism, and the environment.* Takoma Park, MD: Merck Family Fund, 1995.

2. United Nations Development Program, *Human Development Report.* New York: Oxford University Press, 2006.

3. R. Layard, *Happiness.* London: Allen Lane, 2005.

4. World Bank, *World Development Report 1993: Investing in health.* Oxford: Oxford University Press, 1993.

5. European Values Study Group and World Values Survey Association, European and World Values Survey Integrated Data File, 1999–2001, Release 1. Ann Arbor, MI: Inter-university Consortium for Political and Social Research, 2005.

6. United Nations Development Program, *Human Development Report.* New York: Oxford University Press, 2004.

7. G. D. Smith, J. D. Neaton, D. Wentworth, R. Stamler and J. Stamler, 'Socioeconomic differentials in mortality risk among men screened for the Multiple Risk Factor Intervention Trial: I. White men', *American Journal of Public Health* (1996) 86 (4): 486–96.

8. R. G. Wilkinson and K. E. Pickett, 'Income inequality and socio-economic gradients in mortality', *American Journal of Public Health* (2008) 98 (4): 699–704.

9. L. McLaren, 'Socioeconomic status and obesity', *Epidemiologic Review* (2007) 29: 29–48.

10. R. G. Wilkinson and K. E. Pickett, 'Income inequality and population health: a review and explanation of the evidence', *Social Science and Medicine* (2006) 62 (7): 1768–84.

11. J. M. Twenge, 'The age of anxiety? Birth cohort change in anxiety and neuroticism, 1952–1993', *Journal of Personality and Social Psychology* (2007) 79 (6): 1007–21.

12. M. Rutter and D. J. Smith, *Psychosocial Disorders in Young People: Time trends and their causes.* Chichester: Wiley, 1995.

13. S. Collishaw, B. Maughan, R. Goodman and A. Pickles, 'Time trends in adolescent mental health', *Journal of Child Psychology and Psychiatry* (2004) 45 (8): 1350–62.

14. B. Maughan, A. C. Iervolino and S. Collishaw, 'Time trends in child and adolescent mental disorders', *Current Opinion in Psychiatry* (2005) 18 (4): 381–5.

15. J. M. Twenge, *Generation Me.* New York: Simon & Schuster, 2006.

16. S. S. Dickerson and M. E. Kemeny, 'Acute stressors and cortisol responses: a theoretical integration and synthesis of laboratory research', *Psychological Bulletin* (2004) 130 (3): 355–91.

17. T. J. Scheff, 'Shame and conformity: the defense-emotion system', *American Sociological Review* (1988) 53: 395–406.

18. H. B. Lewis, *The Role of Shame in Symptom Formation.* Hillsdale, NJ: Erlbaum, 1987.

19. R. W. Emerson, *Conduct of Life.* New York: Cosimo, 2007.

20. A. Kalma, 'Hierarchisation and dominance assessment at first glance', *European Journal of Social Psychology* (1991) 21 (2): 165–81.

21. F. Lim, M. H. Bond and M. K. Bond, 'Linking societal and psychological factors to homicide rates across nations', *Journal of Cross-Cultural Psychology* (2005) 36 (5): 515–36.

22. S. Kitayama, H. R. Markus, H. Matsumoto and V. Norasakkunkit, 'Individual and collective processes in the construction of the self: self-enhancement in the United States and self-criticism in Japan', *Journal of Personal and Social Psychology* (1997) 72 (6): 1245–67.

23. A. de Tocqueville, *Democracy in America.* London: Penguin, 2003.

24. National Opinion Research Center, *General Social Survey.* Chicago: NORC, 1999–2004.

25. R. D. Putnam, *Bowling Alone: The collapse and revival of American community.* New York: Simon & Schuster, 2000.

26. R. D. Putnam, 'Social capital: measurement and consequences', *ISUMA: Canadian Journal of Policy Research* (2001) 2 (1): 41–51.

27. E. Uslaner, *The Moral Foundations of Trust.* Cambridge: Cambridge University Press, 2002.

28. B. Rothstein and E. Uslaner, 'All for all: equality, corruption and social trust', *World Politics* (2005) 58: 41–72.

29. J. C. Barefoot, K. E. Maynard, J. C. Beckham, B. H. Brummett,

K. Hooker and I. C. Siegler, 'Trust, health, and longevity', *Journal of Behavioral Medicine* (1998) 21 (6): 517–26.

30. S. V. Subramanian, D. J. Kim and I. Kawachi, 'Social trust and self-rated health in US communities: a multilevel analysis', *Journal of Urban Health* (2002) 79 (4, Suppl. 1): S21–34.

31. E. Klinenberg, *Heat Wave: A social autopsy of disaster in Chicago*. Chicago: University of Chicago Press, 2002.

32. J. Lauer, 'Driven to extremes: fear of crime and the rise of the sport utility vehicle in the United States', *Crime, Media, Culture* (2005) 1: 149–68.

33. K. Bradsher, 'The latest fashion: fear-of-crime design', *New York Times*, 23 July 2000.

34. M. Adams, *Fire and Ice. The United States, Canada and the myth of converging values*. Toronto: Penguin (Canada), 2003.

35. E. J. Blakely and M. G. Snyder, *Fortress America: Gated communities in the United States*. Washington, DC: Brookings Institute Press, 1997.

36. I. Kawachi, B. P. Kennedy, V. Gupta and D. Prothrow-Stith, 'Women's status and the health of women and men: a view from the States', *Social Science and Medicine* (1999) 48 (1): 21–32.

37. H. J. Jun, S. V. Subramanian, S. Gortmaker and I. Kawachi, 'A multilevel analysis of women's status and self-rated health in the United States', *Journal of the American Medical Women's Association* (2004) 59 (3): 172–80.

38. OECD, International Development Statistics Online. OECD. Stat: http://www.oecd.org/dataoecd/50/17/5037721.htm, 2005.

39. L. Clark and A. Dolan, 'The disturbed generation', *Daily Mail*, 20 June 2007.

40. C. Donnellan, *Mental Wellbeing*. Cambridge: Independence Educational Publishers, 2004.

41. *The Good Childhood Inquiry. Evidence Summary 5 - Health*. London: Children's Society, 2008.

42. J. M. Perrin, S. R. Bloom and S. L. Gortmaker, 'The increase of childhood chronic conditions in the United States', *Journal of the American Medical Association* (2007) 297 (24): 2755–9.

43. Child and Adolescent Health Measurement Initiative. National Survey of Children's Health. Data Resource Center on Child and Adolescent Health: http://www.childhealthdata.org (accessed 17 August 2006).

44. Office for National Statistics, *Psychiatric Morbidity among Adults Living in Private Households, 2000*. London: HMSO, 2001.

45. *Hansard* (House of Commons Daily Debates). Written answers to questions. (2005) 439: 22 Nov. 2005: Column 1798W.

46. R. C. Kessler, W. T. Chiu, O. Demler, K. R. Merikangas and E. E. Walters, 'Prevalence, severity, and comorbidity of 12-month DSM-IV disorders in the National Comorbidity Survey Replication', *Archives of General Psychiatry* (2005) 62 (6): 617–27.

47. T. L. Mark, K. R. Levit, J. A. Buck, R. M. Coffey and R. Vandivort-Warren, 'Mental health treatment expenditure trends, 1986–2003', *Psychiatric Services* (2007) 58 (8): 1041–8.

48. D. Rowe, *How to Improve your Mental Well-being*. London: Mind, 2002.

49. K. Demyttenaere, R. Bruffaerts, J. Posada-Villa, I. Gasquet, V. Kovess, J. P. Lepine, M. C. Angermeyer, S. Bernert, G. de Girolamo, P. Morosini, G. Polidori, T. Kikkawa, N. Kawakami, Y. Ono, T. Takeshima, H. Uda, E. G. Karam, J. A. Fayyad, A. N. Karam, Z. N. Mneimneh, M. E. Medina-Mora, G. Borges, C. Lara, R. de Graaf, J. Ormel, O. Gureje, Y. Shen, Y. Huang, M. Zhang, J. Alonso, J. M. Haro, G. Vilagut, E. J. Bromet, S. Gluzman, C. Webb, R. C. Kessler, K. R. Merikangas, J. C. Anthony, M. R. von Korff, P. S. Wang, T. S. Brugha, S. Aguilar-Gaxiola, S. Lee, S. Heeringa, B. E. Pennell, A. M. Zaslavsky, T. B. Ustun and S. Chatterji, 'Prevalence, severity, and unmet need for treatment of mental disorders in the World Health Organization World Mental Health Surveys', *Journal of the American Medical Association* (2004) 291 (21): 2581–90.

50. J. E. Wells, M. A. Oakley Browne, K. M. Scott, M. A. McGee, J. Baxter and J. Kokaua, 'Te Rau Hinengaro: the New Zealand Mental Health Survey: overview of methods and findings', *Australian and New Zealand Journal of Psychiatry* (2006) 40 (10): 835–44.

51. Australian Bureau of Statistics. *National Health Survey, Mental Health, 2001*. Canberra: Australian Bureau of Statistics, 2003.

52. WHO International Consortium in Psychiatric Epidemiology, 'Cross-national comparisons of the prevalences and correlates of mental disorders', *Bulletin of the World Health Organization* (2000) 78 (4): 413–26.

53. Center for Disease Control and Prevention, 'Self-reported frequent mental distress among adults – United States, 1993–2001' (2004) 53: 963–6.

54. O. James, *Affluenza*. London: Vermilion, 2007.

55. A. de Botton, *Status Anxiety*. London: Hamish Hamilton, 2004.

56. R. H. Frank, *Luxury Fever*. New York: Free Press, 1999.

57. United Nations Office on Drugs and Crime, *World Drug Report*. Vienna: UN Office on Drugs and Crime, 2007.

58. Centers for Disease Control and Prevention. Compressed Mortality Files 1999–2002. http://wonder.cdc.gov/mortSQL.html (accessed 9 September 2008)

59. D. Morgan, K. A, Grant, H. D. Gage, R. H. Mach, J. R. Kaplan, O. Prioleau, S. H. Nader, N. Buchheimer, R. L. Ehrenkaufer and M. A. Nader, 'Social dominance in monkeys: dopamine D2 receptors and cocaine self-administration', *Nature Neuroscience* (2002) 5 (2): 169–74.

60. M. Susser and E. Susser, 'Choosing a future for epidemiology: I. Eras and paradigms', *American Journal of Public Health* (1996) 86 (5): 668–73.

61. M. Susser and E. Susser, 'Choosing a future for epidemiology: II. From black box to Chinese boxes and eco-epidemiology', *American Journal of Public Health* (1996) 86 (5): 674–7.

62. M. G. Marmot, A. M. Adelstein, N. Robinson and G. A. Rose, 'Changing social-class distribution of heart disease', *British Medical Journal* (1978) 2 (6145): 1109–12.

63. M. G. Marmot, G. Rose, M. Shipley and P. J. Hamilton, 'Employment grade and coronary heart disease in British civil servants', *Journal of Epidemiology and Community Health* (1978) 32 (4): 244–9.

64. H. Bosma, M. G. Marmot, H. Hemingway, A. C. Nicholson, E. Brunner and S. A. Stansfeld, 'Low job control and risk of coronary heart disease in Whitehall II (prospective cohort) study', *British Medical Journal* (1997) 314 (7080): 558–65.

65. M. G. Marmot, G. D. Smith, S. Stansfeld, C. Patel, F. North, J. Head, I. White, E. Brunner and A. Feeney, 'Health inequalities among British civil servants: the Whitehall II study', *Lancet* (1991) 337 (8754): 1387–93.

66. Council of Civil Service Unions/Cabinet Office, *Work, Stress and Health: The Whitehall II Study*. London: Public and Commercial Services Union, 2004.

67. G. D. Smith, M. J. Shipley and G. Rose, 'Magnitude and causes of socioeconomic differentials in mortality: further evidence from the Whitehall Study', *Journal of Epidemiology and Community Health* (1990) 44 (4): 265–70.

68. R. G. Wilkinson and M. Marmot, *Social Determinants of Health: The Solid Facts* (2nd edition). Copenhagen: World Health Organization, Regional Office for Europe, 2006.

69. E. Durkheim, *Suicide*. London: Routledge, 1952.

70. L. Berkman and T. Glass, 'Social integration, social networks, social support, and health', in L. Berkman and I. Kawachi, (eds), *Social Epidemiology*. New York: Oxford University Press, 2000.

71. S. A. Stansfeld, 'Social support and social cohesion', in M. Marmot and R. G. Wilkinson (eds), *Social Determinants of Health*. Oxford: Oxford University Press, 2006.

72. S. Cohen, 'Keynote Presentation at the Eighth International Congress of Behavioral Medicine: The Pittsburgh common cold studies: psychosocial predictors of susceptibility to respiratory infectious illness', *International Journal of Behavioral Medicine* (2005) 12 (3): 123–31.

73. J. K. Kiecolt-Glaser, T. J. Loving, J. R. Stowell, W. B. Malarkey, S. Lemeshow, S. L. Dickinson and R. Glaser, 'Hostile marital interactions, proinflammatory cytokine production, and wound healing, *Archives of General Psychiatry* (2005) 62 (12): 1377–84.

74. W. T. Boyce, 'Stress and child health: an overview', *Pediatric Annals* (1985) 14 (8): 539–42.

75. M. C. Holmes, 'Early life stress can programme our health', *Journal of Neuroendocrinology* (2001) 13 (2): 111–12.

76. R. H. Bradley and R. F. Corwyn, 'Socioeconomic status and child development', *Annual Review of Psychology* (2002) 53: 371–99.

77. M. Wilson and M. Daly, 'Life expectancy, economic inequality, homicide, and reproductive timing in Chicago neighbourhoods', *British Medical Journal* (1997) 314 (7089): 1271–4.

78. M. K. Islam, J. Merlo, I. Kawachi, M. Lindstrom and U. G. Gerdtham, 'Social capital and health: does egalitarianism matter? A literature review', *International Journal for Equity in Health* (2006) 5: 3.

79. I. Kawachi, B. P. Kennedy, K. Lochner and D. Prothrow-Stith, 'Social capital, income inequality, and mortality', *American Journal of Public Health* (1997) 87 (9): 1491–8.

80. C. McCord and H. P. Freeman, 'Excess mortality in Harlem', *New England Journal of Medicine* (1990) 322 (3): 173–7.

81. R. G. Wilkinson, 'Income distribution and life expectancy', *British Medical Journal* (1992) 304 (6820): 165–8.

82. Editor's Choice, 'The Big Idea', *British Medical Journal* (1996) 312 (7037): 0.

83. Department of Health, *The NHS Plan: A plan for investment, a plan for reform*. London: HMSO, 2000.

84. Office for National Statistics. 'Trends in ONS Longitudinal Study estimates of life expectancy, by social class 1972–2005'. http://www.statistics.gov.uk/StatBase/Product.asp?vlnk=8460&More=Y (accessed 9 September 2008).

85. C. J. Murray, S. C. Kulkarni, C. Michaud, N. Tomijima, M. T. Bulzacchelli, T. J. Iandiorio and M. Ezzati, 'Eight Americas: investigating

mortality disparities across races, counties, and race-counties in the United States', *Public Library of Science Medicine* (2006) 3 (9): e260.

86. A. T. Geronimus, J. Bound, T. A. Waidmann, C. G. Colen and D. Steffick, 'Inequality in life expectancy, functional status, and active life expectancy across selected black and white populations in the United States', *Demography* (2001) 38 (2): 227–51.

87. G. K. Singh and M. Siahpush, 'Widening socioeconomic inequalities in US life expectancy, 1980–2000', *International Journal of Epidemiology* (2006) 35 (4): 969–79.

88. P. M. Lantz, J. S. House, J. M. Lepkowski, D. R. Williams, R. P. Mero and J. Chen, 'Socioeconomic factors, health behaviors, and mortality: results from a nationally representative prospective study of US adults', *Journal of the American Medical Association* (1998) 279 (21): 1703–8.

89. P. Makela, T. Valkonen and T. Martelin, 'Contribution of deaths related to alcohol use to socioeconomic variation in mortality: register based follow up study', *British Medical Journal* (1997) 315 (7102): 211–16.

90. G. Rose and M. G. Marmot, 'Social class and coronary heart disease', *British Heart Journal* (1981) 45 (1): 13–19.

91. R. G. Wilkinson, *Unhealthy Societies: The afflictions of inequality*. London: Routledge, 1996.

92. R. Sapolsky, 'Sick of poverty', *Scientific American* (2005) 293 (6): 92–9.

93. L. Vitetta, B. Anton, F. Cortizo and A. Sali, 'Mind–body medicine: stress and its impact on overall health and longevity', *Annals of the New York Academy of Sciences* (2005) 1057: 492–505.

94. S. V. Subramanian and I. Kawachi, 'Income inequality and health: what have we learned so far?' *Epidemiologic Review* (2004) 26: 78–91.

95. S. Bezruchka, T. Namekata and M. G. Sistrom, 'Improving economic equality and health: the case of postwar Japan', *American Journal of Public Health* (2008) 98: 216–21.

96. P. Walberg, M. McKee, V. Shkolnikov, L. Chenet and D. A. Leon, 'Economic change, crime, and mortality crisis in Russia: regional analysis', *British Medical Journal* (1998) 317 (7154): 312–18.

97. K. M. Flegal, M. D. Carroll, C. L. Ogden and C. L. Johnson, 'Prevalence and trends in obesity among US adults', *Journal of the American Medical Association* (2002) 288: 1723–7.

98. International Obesity TaskForce, *Obesity in Europe*. London: International Obesity TaskForce in collaboration with the European Association for the Study of Obesity Task Forces, 2002.

99. World Health Organization, *Report of a Joint WHO/FAO Expert Consultation. Diet, nutrition and the prevention of chronic diseases.* Geneva: WHO Technical Report Series no. 916. WHO, 2002.

100. C. L. Ogden, M. D. Carroll, L. R. Curtin, M. A. McDowell, C. J. Tabak and K. M. Flegal, 'Prevalence of overweight and obesity in the United States, 1999–2004', *Journal of the American Medical Association* (2006) 295 (13): 1549–55.

101. S. J. Olshansky, D. J. Passaro, R. C. Hershow, J. Layden, B. A. Carnes, J. Brody, L. Hayflick, R. N. Butler, D. B. Allison and D. S. Ludwig, 'A potential decline in life expectancy in the United States in the 21st century', *New England Journal of Medicine* (2005) 352 (11): 1138–45.

102. CBS News, 'Teen slims down with gastric bypass: Surgery a growing trend among obese teenagers', CBS Broadcasting Inc. http://www. cbsnews.com/stories/2007/05/21/earlyshow/health/main2830891.shtm/ ?Source=Search–story (accessed 15 September 2008).

103. G. Rollings, '14st boy – is this child abuse?' *Sun*, 26 February 2007.

104. B. Ashford and V. Wheeler, 'Sam, aged 9, is 14st and size 18', *Sun*, 28 February 2007.

105. A. Parker, 'Daryl is 20 stone, aged just 12', *Sun*, 2 March 2007.

106. E. Brunner, M. Juneja and M. Marmot, 'Abdominal obesity and disease are linked to social position', *British Medical Journal* (1998) 316: 308.

107. A. Molarius, J. C. Seidell, S. Sans, J. Tuomilehto and K. Kuulasmaa, 'Educational level, relative body weight and changes in their association over 10 years: an international perspective from the WHO MONICA project', *American Journal of Public Health* (2000) 90: 1260–86.

108. P. Toynbee, 'Inequality is fattening', *Guardian*, 28 May 2004.

109. International Obesity Taskforce, *Overweight and Obese.* London: International Obesity Taskforce, 2002.

110. UNICEF Innocenti Research Centre. *Child Poverty in Perspective: An overview of child well-being in rich countries.* Florence: Innocenti Report Card, 2007.

111. H. S. Kahn, A. V. Patel, E. J. Jacobs, E. E. Calle, B. P. Kennedy and I. Kawachi, 'Pathways between area-level income inequality and increased mortality in U.S. men', *Annals of the New York Academy of Sciences* (1999) 896: 332–4.

112. A. V. Diez-Roux, B. G. Link and M. E. Northridge, 'A multilevel analysis of income inequality and cardiovascular disease risk factors', *Social Science and Medicine* (2000) 50 (5): 673–87.

113. M. Ezzati, H. Martin, S. Skjold, S. vander Hoorn and C. J. Murray,

'Trends in national and state-level obesity in the USA after correction for self-report bias: analysis of health surveys', *Journal of the Royal Society of Medicine* (2006) 99 (5): 250–7.

114. K. E. Pickett, S. Kelly, E. Brunner, T. Lobstein and R. G. Wilkinson, 'Wider income gaps, wider waistbands? An ecological study of obesity and income inequality', *Journal of Epidemiology and Community Health* (2005) 59 (8): 670–4.

115. K. Ball, G. D. Mishra and D. Crawford, 'Social factors and obesity: an investigation of the role of health behaviours', *International Journal of Obesity and Related Metabolic Disorders* (2003) 27 (3): 394–403.

116. E. J. Brunner, T. Chandola and M. G. Marmot, 'Prospective effect of job strain on general and central obesity in the Whitehall II Study', *American Journal of Epidemiology* (2007) 165 (7): 828–37.

117. L. R. Purslow, E. H. Young, N. J. Wareham, N. Forouhi, E. J. Brunner, R. N. Luben, A. A. Welch, K. T. Khaw, S. A. Bingham and M. S. Sandhu, 'Socioeconomic position and risk of short-term weight gain: prospective study of 14,619 middle-aged men and women', *BioMed Central Public Health* (2008) 8: 112.

118. S. P. Wamala, A. Wolk and K. Orth-Gomer, 'Determinants of obesity in relation to socioeconomic status among middle-aged Swedish women', *Preventive Medicine* (1997) 26 (5 Pt 1): 734–44.

119. P. Bjorntorp, 'Do stress reactions cause abdominal obesity and comorbidities?' *Obesity Reviews* (2001) 2 (2): 73–86.

120. V. Drapeau, F. Therrien, D. Richard and A. Tremblay, 'Is visceral obesity a physiological adaptation to stress?' *Panminerva Medica* (2003) 45 (3): 189–95.

121. J. Laitinen, E. Ek and U. Sovio, 'Stress-related eating and drinking behavior and body mass index and predictors of this behavior', *Preventive Medicine* (2002) 34 (1): 29–39.

122. M. F. Dallman, N. Pecoraro, S. F. Akana, S. E. La Fleur, F. Gomez, H. Houshyar, M. E. Bell, S. Bhatnagar, K. D. Laugero and S. Manalo, 'Chronic stress and obesity: a new view of "comfort food"', *Proceedings of the National Academy of Sciences USA* (2003) 100 (20): 11696–701.

123. A. M. Freedman, 'Deadly diet', *Wall Street Journal*, 18–20 December 1990.

124. C. C. Hodgkins, K. S. Cahill, A. E. Seraphine, K. Frost-Pineda and M. S. Gold, 'Adolescent drug addiction treatment and weight gain', *Journal of Addictive Diseases* (2004) 23 (3): 55–65.

125. G. A. James, M. S. Gold and Y. Liu, 'Interaction of satiety and reward response to food stimulation', *Journal of Addictive Diseases* (2004) 23 (3): 23–37.

126. K. D. Kleiner, M. S. Gold, K. Frost-Pineda, B. Lenz-Brunsman, M. G. Perri and W. S. Jacobs, 'Body mass index and alcohol use', *Journal of Addictive Diseases* (2004) 23 (3): 105–18.

127. J. H. Gao, 'Neuroimaging and obesity', *Obesity Reviews* (2001) 9 (11): 729–30.

128. K. Sproston and P. Primatesta (eds), *Health Survey for England 2003. Vol. 2: Risk Factors for Cardiovascular Disease.* London: HMSO, 2004.

129. C. Langenberg, R. Hardy, D. Kuh, E. Brunner and M. Wadsworth, 'Central and total obesity in middle aged men and women in relation to lifetime socioeconomic status: evidence from a national birth cohort', *Journal of Epidemiology and Community Health* (2003) 57 (10): 816–22.

130. R. M. Viner and T. J. Cole, 'Adult socioeconomic, educational, social, and psychological outcomes of childhood obesity: a national birth cohort study', *British Medical Journal* (2005) 330 (7504): 1354.

131. S. L. Gortmaker, A. Must, J. M. Perrin, A. M. Sobol and W. H. Dietz, 'Social and economic consequences of overweight in adolescence and young adulthood', *New England Journal of Medicine* (1993) 329 (14): 1008–12.

132. J. D. Sargent and D. G. Blanchflower, 'Obesity and stature in adolescence and earnings in young adulthood. Analysis of a British birth cohort', *Archives of Pediatric and Adolescent Medicine* (1994) 148 (7): 681–7.

133. D. Thomas, 'Fattism is the last bastion of employee discrimination', *Personnel Today*, 25 October 2005.

134. J. Wardle and J. Griffith, 'Socioeconomic status and weight control practices in British adults', *Journal of Epidemiology and Community Health* (2001) 55 (3): 185–90.

135. J. Sobal, B. Rauschenbach and E. A. Frongillo, 'Marital status changes and body weight changes: a US longitudinal analysis', *Social Science and Medicine* (2003) 56 (7): 1543–55.

136. T. Smith, C. Stoddard and M. Barnes, 'Why the Poor Get Fat: Weight Gain and Economic Insecurity', School of Economic Sciences Working Paper, Washington State University: http://ideas.repec.org/p/wsu/wpaper/tgsmith-2.html (accessed 15 September 2008).

137. B. Fisher, D. Dowding, K. E. Pickett and F. Fylan, 'Health promotion at NHS breast cancer screening clinics in the UK', *Health Promotion International* (2007) 22 (2): 137–45.

138. J. R. Speakman, H. Walker, L. Walker and D. M. Jackson,

'Associations between BMI, social strata and the estimated energy content of foods', *Journal of Obesity and Related Metabolic Disorders* (2005) 29 (10): 1281–8.

139. N. E. Adler, E. S. Epel, G. Castellazzo and J. R. Ickovics, 'Relationship of subjective and objective social status with psychological and physiological functioning: preliminary data in healthy white women', *Health Psychology* (2000) 19 (6): 586–92.

140. E. Goodman, N. E. Adler, S. R. Daniels, J. A. Morrison, G. B. Slap and L. M. Dolan, 'Impact of objective and subjective social status on obesity in a biracial cohort of adolescents', *Obesity Reviews* (2003) 11 (8): 1018–26.

141. B. Martin, 'Income inequality in Germany during the 1980s and 1990s', *Review of Income and Wealth* (2000) 46 (1): 1–19.

142. V. Hesse, M. Voigt, A. Salzler, S. Steinberg, K. Friese, E. Keller, R. Gausche and R. Eisele, 'Alterations in height, weight, and body mass index of newborns, children, and young adults in eastern Germany after German reunification', *Journal of Pediatrics* (2003) 142 (3): 259–62.

143. S. Baum and K. Payea, *Education Pays: The benefits of higher education for individuals and society*. Washington, DC: College Board, 2004.

144. Bureau of Labor Statistics, *Weekly and Hourly Earnings Data from the Current Population Survey*. Washington, DC: US Department of Labor, 2007.

145. M. Benn and F. Millar, *A Comprehensive Future: Quality and equality for all our children*. London: Compass, 2006.

146. J. D. Teachman, 'Family background, educational resources, and educational attainment', *American Sociological Review* (1987) 52: 548–57.

147. OECD and Statistics Canada, *Literacy in the Information Age: Final report of the International Adult Literacy Survey*. Paris: Organization for Economic Co-Operation and Development, 2000.

148. R. Wilkinson and K. E. Pickett, 'Health inequalities and the UK Presidency of the EU', *Lancet* (2006) 367 (9517): 1126–8.

149. R. G. Wilkinson and K. E. Pickett, 'The problems of relative deprivation: why some societies do better than others', *Social Science and Medicine* (2007) 65 (9): 1965–78.

150. J. D. Willms, 'Quality and inequality in children's literacy: the effects of families, schools, and communities', in D. P. Keating and C. Hertzman (eds), *Developmental Health and the Wealth of Nations*. New York: Guilford Press, 1999.

151. J. D. Willms, 'Literacy proficiency of youth: evidence of converging socioeconomic gradients', *International Journal of Educational Research* (2003) 39: 247–52.

152. A. Siddiqi, I. Kawachi, L. Berkman, S. V. Subramanian and C. Hertzman, 'Variation of socioeconomic gradients in children's developmental health across advanced capitalist societies: analysis of 22 OECD nations', *International Journal of Health Services* (2007) 37 (1): 63–87.

153. Centre for Longitudinal Studies, *Disadvantaged Children up to a Year Behind by the Age of Three*. London: Institute of Education, 2007.

154. R. H. Frank and A. S. Levine, *Expenditure Cascades*. Cornell University mimeograph. Ithaca: Cornell University, 2005.

155. G. W. Evans and K. English, 'The environment of poverty: multiple stressor exposure, psychophysiological stress, and socioemotional adjustment', *Child Development* (2002) 73 (4): 1238–48.

156. P. Garrett, N. Ng'andu and J. Ferron, 'Poverty experiences of young children and the quality of their home environments', *Child Development* (1994) 65 (2, Spec. no.): 331–45.

157. V. C. McLoyd, 'The impact of economic hardship on black families and children: psychological distress, parenting, and socioemotional development', *Child Development* (1990) 61 (2): 311–46.

158. V. C. McLoyd and L. Wilson, 'Maternal behavior, social support, and economic conditions as predictors of distress in children', *New Directions for Child and Adolescent Development* (1990) 46: 49–69.

159. A. Lareau, 'Invisible inequality: social class and childrearing in black families and white families', *American Sociological Review* (2002) 67: 747–76.

160. J. Currie, *Welfare and the Well-being of Children*. Reading: Harwood Academic Publishers, 1995.

161. L. G. Irwin, A. Siddiqi and C. Hertzman, *Early Childhood Development: A powerful equalizer*. Geneva: World Health Organization Commission on Social Determinants of Health, 2007.

162. UNICEF Innocenti Research Centre, *A League Table of Educational Disadvantage in Rich Nations*. Florence: Innocenti Report Card, 2002.

163. K. Hoff and P. Pandey, *Belief Systems and Durable Inequalities: An experimental investigation of Indian caste*. Policy Research Working Paper. Washington, DC: World Bank, 2004.

164. C. M. Steele and J. Aronson, 'Stereotype threat and the intellectual test performance of African-Americans', *Journal of Personality and Social Psychology* (1995) 69: 797–811.

165. S. J. Spencer, C. M. Steele and D. M. Quinn, 'Stereotype threat and women's math performance', *Journal of Experimental Social Psychology* (1999) 35 (1): 4–28.

166. W. Peters, *A Class Divided: Then and now*. New Haven: Yale University Press, 1987.

167. J. Zull, *The Art of Changing the Brain: Enriching the practice of teaching by exploring the biology of learning*. Sterling: Stylus Publishing, 2002.

168. G. Evans. *Educational Failure and Working Class White Children in Britain*. Basingstoke: Palgrave, 2006.

169. L. Atkinson, 'Sorry, Mum, we're all pregnant!' *Sneak* (2005) Issue no. 162.

170. J. Askill, 'Meet the kid sisters', *Sun*, 23 May 2005.

171. S. Carroll, 'These girls' babies are the real victims', *Daily Mirror*, 25 May, 2005.

172. Committee on Adolescence AAoP, 'Adolescent pregnancy – current trends and issues', *Pediatrics* (1998) 103: 516–20.

173. Social Exclusion Unit, *Teenage Pregnancy*. London: HMSO, 1999.

174. D. A. Lawlor and M. Shaw, 'Too much too young? Teenage pregnancy is not a public health problem', *International Journal of Epidemiology* (2002) 31 (3): 552–4.

175. A. T. Geronimus, 'The weathering hypothesis and the health of African-American women and infants: evidence and speculations', *Ethnicity and Disease* (1992) 2 (3): 207–21.

176. A. T. Geronimus, 'Black/white differences in the relationship of maternal age to birthweight: a population-based test of the weathering hypothesis', *Social Science and Medicine* (1996) 42 (4): 589–97.

177. J. Hobcraft and K. Kiernan, 'Childhood poverty, early motherhood and adult social exclusion', *British Journal of Sociology* (2001) 52 (3): 495–517.

178. J. Rich-Edwards, 'Teen pregnancy is not a public health crisis in the United States. It is time we made it one', *International Journal of Epidemiology* (2002) 31 (3): 555–6.

179. S. Cater and L. Coleman, *'Planned' Teenage Pregnancy: Views and experiences of young people from poor and disadvantaged backgrounds*. Bristol: Policy Press for the Joseph Rowntree Foundation, 2006.

180. K. Luker, *Dubious Conception. The politics of teenage pregnancy*. Cambridge, MA: Harvard University Press, 1996.

181. J. Ermisch and D. Pevalin, *Who Has a Child as a Teenager?* ISER Working Papers, Number 2003–30. Institute for Economic and Social Research, University of Essex, 2003.

182. UNICEF Innocenti Research Centre, *A League Table of Teenage Births in Rich Nations*. Florence: Innocenti Report Card, 2001.

183. S. J. Ventura, T. J. Mathews and B. E. Hamilton, 'Teenage births in the United States: trends, 1991–2000, an update', *National Vital Statistics Reports* (2002) 50 (9).

184. Alan Guttmacher Institute, *US Teenage Pregnancy Statistics Overall Trends, Trends by Race and Ethnicity and State-by-state Information*. New York: AGI, 2004.

185. K. E. Pickett, J. Mookherjee and R. G. Wilkinson, 'Adolescent birth rates, total homicides, and income inequality in rich countries', *American Journal of Public Health* (2005) 95 (7): 1181–3.

186. R. Gold, I. Kawachi, B. P. Kennedy, J. W. Lynch and F. A. Connell, 'Ecological analysis of teen birth rates: association with community income and income inequality', *Maternal and Child Health Journal* (2001) 5 (3): 161–7.

187. S. Ryan, K. Franzetta and J. Manlove, *Hispanic Teen Pregnancy and Birth Rates: Looking behind the numbers*. Washington, DC: Child Trends, 2005.

188. M. Dickson, *Latina Teen Pregnancy: Problems and prevention. Executive summary*. Washington, DC: Population Resource Center, 2001.

189. J. Bynner, P. Elias, A. McKnight, H. Pan and G. Pierre, *Young People's Changing Routes to Independence*. York: Joseph Rowntree Foundation, 2002.

190. H. Graham and E. McDermott, 'Qualitative research and the evidence base of policy: insights from studies of teenage mothers in the UK', *Journal of Social Policy* (2005) 35: 21–37.

191. J. Belsky, L. Steinberg and P. Draper, 'Childhood experience, interpersonal development, and reproductive strategy: an evolutionary theory of socialization', *Child Development* (1991) 62 (4): 647–70.

192. R. Gold, B. Kennedy, F. Connell and I. Kawachi, 'Teen births, income inequality, and social capital: developing an understanding of the causal pathway', *Health and Place* (2002) 8 (2): 77–83.

193. D. A. Coall and J. S. Chisholm, 'Evolutionary perspectives on pregnancy: maternal age at menarche and infant birth weight', *Social Science and Medicine* (2003) 57 (10): 1771–81.

194. T. E. Moffitt, A. Caspi, J. Belsky and P. A. Silva, 'Childhood experience and the onset of menarche: a test of a sociobiological model', *Child Development* (1992) 63 (1): 47–58.

195. 'American Academy of Pediatrics Committee on Adolescence: Adolescent pregnancy', *Pediatrics* (1989) 83 (1): 132–4.

196. B. J. Ellis, J. E. Bates, K. A. Dodge, D. M. Fergusson, L. J. Horwood, G. S. Pettit and L. Woodward, 'Does father absence place daughters at special risk for early sexual activity and teenage pregnancy?' *Child Development* (2003) 74 (3): 801–21.

197. J. Borger, 'Gunned down: the teenager who dared to walk across his neighbour's prized lawn', *Guardian*, 22 March 2006.

198. J. Allen, *Worry about Crime in England and Wales: Findings from the 2003/04 and 2004/05 British Crime Survey*. London: Research Development and Statistics Directorate, Home Office, 2006.

199. C. Hale, 'Fear of crime: a review of the literature', *International Review of Victimology* (1996) 4: 79–150.

200. H. Cronin, *The Ant and the Peacock*. Cambridge: Cambridge University Press, 1991.

201. J. Gilligan, *Preventing Violence*. New York: Thames & Hudson, 2001.

202. J. Gilligan, *Violence: Our deadly epidemic and its causes*. New York: G. P. Putnam, 1996.

203. R. Wilkinson, 'Why is violence more common where inequality is greater?' *Annals of the New York Academy of Sciences* (2004) 1036: 1–12.

204. M. Wilson and M. Daly, *Homicide*. Piscataway, NJ: Aldine Transaction, 1988.

205. M. Daly and M. Wilson, 'Crime and conflict: homicide in evolutionary psychological perspective', *Crime and Justice* (1997) 22: 51–100.

206. M. Daly and M. Wilson, 'Risk-taking, intrasexual competition, and homicide', *Nebraska Symposium on Motivation* (2001) 47: 1–36.

207. M. Daly, M. Wilson and S. Vasdev, 'Income inequality and homicide rates in Canada and the United States', *Canadian Journal of Public Health – Revue canadienne de criminologie* (2001) 43 (2): 219–36.

208. M. Wilson and M. Daly, 'Competitiveness, risk-taking and violence: the young male syndrome', *Ethology and Sociobiology* (1985) 6: 59–73.

209. D. M. Buss, *The Evolution of Desire: Strategies of human mating*. New York: Basic Books, 1994.

210. P. Fajnzylber, D. Lederman and N. Loayza, 'Inequality and violent crime', *Journal of Law and Economics* (2002) 45: 1–40.

211. C.-C. Hsieh and M. D. Pugh, 'Poverty, income inequality, and violent crime: A meta-analysis of recent aggregate data studies', *Criminal Justice Review* (1993) 18: 182–202.

212. United Nations Crime and Justice Information Network, *Survey on Crime Trends and the Operations of Criminal Justice Systems (Fifth, Sixth, Seventh, Eighth)*. New York: United Nations, 2000.

213. Federal Bureau of Investigation, *Crime in the United States*. Washington, DC: US Government Printing Office, 1990–2000.

214. M. Killias, J. van Kesteren and M. Rindlisbacher, 'Guns, violent crime, and suicide in 21 countries', *Canadian Journal of Criminology* (2001) 43: 429–48.

215. UN Commission on Crime Prevention and Criminal Justice, 'Criminal justice reform and strengthening of legal institutions measures to regulate firearms', in Secretary-General Report E/CN.15/1997/4. Vienna: United Nations, 1997.

216. M. Miller, D. Hemenway and D. Azrael, 'State-level homicide victimization rates in the US in relation to survey measures of household firearm ownership, 2001–2003', *Social Science and Medicine* (2007) 64 (3): 656–64.

217. 'Behavioural Risk Factor Surveillance Survey. Survey Results 2001 for Nationwide: Firearms'. North Carolina State Center for Health Statistics. http://www.schs.state.nc.us/SCHS/brfss/2001/us/firearm3.html (accessed 9 September 2008).

218. D. Popenoe, *Life Without Father*. New York: Free Press, 1996.

219. H. B. Biller, *Fathers and Families: Paternal factors in child development*. Westport, CT: Auburn House, 1993.

220. S. R. Jaffee, T. E. Moffitt, A. Caspi and A. Taylor, 'Life with (or without) father: the benefits of living with two biological parents depend on the father's antisocial behavior', *Child Development* (2003) 74(1): 109–26.

221. M. Anderson, J. Kaufman, T. R. Simon, L. Barrios, L. Paulozzi, G. Ryan, R. Hammond, W. Modzeleski, T. Feucht and L. Potter, 'School-associated violent deaths in the United States, 1994–1999', *Journal of the American Medical Association* (2001) 286 (21): 2695–702.

222. M. R. Leary, R. M. Kowalski, L. Smith and S. Phillips, 'Teasing, rejection, and violence: case studies of the school shootings', *Aggressive Behavior* (2003) 29: 202–14.

223. C. Shaw and H. McKay, *Juvenile Delinquency and Urban Areas*. Chicago: University of Chicago Press, 1942.

224. R. Sampson, S. Raudenbush and F. Earls, 'Neighborhoods and violent crime: a multilevel study of collective efficacy', *Science* (1997) 277: 918–24.

225. W. J. Wilson, *The Truly Disadvantaged: The inner city, the underclass, and public policy*. Chicago: University of Chicago Press, 1987.

226. Federal Bureau of Investigation, *Crime in the United States 2006*. Washington, DC: US Government Printing Office, 2006.

227. H. Boonstra, *Teen Pregnancy: Trends and lessons learned.* Guttmacher Report on Public Policy. Washington, DC: Alan Guttmacher Institute, 2002.

228. B. E. Hamilton, J. A. Martin and S. J. Ventura, 'Births: preliminary data for 2006', *National Vital Statistics Report* (2007) 56 (7).

229. R. V. Burkhauser, S. Feng and S. P. Jenkins, 'Using the P90/P10 Index to Measure US Inequality Trends with Current Population Survey Data: A View from Inside the Census Bureau Vaults', IZA Discussion Paper No. 2839, available at Social Science Research Network: http://ssrn.com/abstract=998222 (accessed 9 September 2008).

230. C. Cantave, M. Vanouse and R. Harrison, *Trends in Poverty.* Washington, DC: Center for Political and Economic Studies, 1999.

231. Child Trends DataBank, *Children in Poverty.* Washington, DC: Child Trends, 2003.

232. A. Blumstein, F. P. Rivara and R. Rosenfeld, 'The rise and decline of homicide – and why', *Annual Review of Public Health* (2000) 21: 505–41.

233. Annie E. Casey Foundation, *KidsCount Databook.* Baltimore, MD. Annie E. Casey Foundation, 1995.

234. C. G. Colen, A. T. Geronimus and M. G. Phipps, 'Getting a piece of the pie? The economic boom of the 1990s and declining teen birth rates in the United States', *Social Science and Medicine* (2006) 63 (6): 1531–45.

235. D. Dorling, 'Prime suspect: murder in Britain', in P. Hillyard, C. Pantazis, S. Tombs, D. Gordon and D. Dorling (eds), *Criminal Obsessions: Why harm matters more than crime.* London: Crime and Society Foundation, 2005.

236. R. Walmsley. 'An overview of world imprisonment: global prison populations, trends and solutions', United Nations Programme Network Institutes Technical Assistance Workshop. Vienna, 2001.

237. R. Walmsley, *World Prison Population List* (6th and 7th editions). London: International Centre for Prison Studies, King's College, 2005 and 2006.

238. A. Blumstein and A. J. Beck, 'Population growth in US prisons, 1980–1996', *Crime and Justice* (1999) 26: 17–61.

239. E. Chemerinsky, 'Life in prison for shoplifting: cruel and unusual punishment', *Human Rights* (2004) 31: 11–13.

240. M. Hough, J. Jacobson and A. Millie, *The Decision to Imprison: Sentencing and the prison population. Rethinking crime and punishment.* London: Prison Reform Trust, 2003.

241. D. Downes, 'The buckling of the shields: Dutch penal policy 1985–1995', in R. P. Weiss and N. South (eds), *Comparing Prison Systems: Towards a comparative and international penology*. Amsterdam: Gordon & Breach Publishers, 1998.

242. M. Mauer, *Comparative International Rates of Incarceration: An examination of causes and trends*. Washington, DC: Sentencing Project, 2003.

243. US Department of Justice, Bureau of Justice Statistics, 'Incarceration rates for prisoners under State or Federal jurisdiction', File: corpop25.wk1. http://www.ojp.usdoj.gov/bjs/data/corpop25.wk1 (accessed 30 March 2006).

244. W. S. Wooden and A. O. Ballan, 'Adaptation strategies and transient niches of one middle-class inmate in prison', *Psychological Reports* (1996) 78 (3, Pt 1): 870.

245. The Sentencing Project, *State Rates of Incarceration by Race*. Washington, DC: Sentencing Project, 2004.

246. R. Councell and J. Olagundoye. *The Prison Population in 2001: A statistical review*. Home Office Findings 195. London: Home Office, 2003.

247. Annie E. Casey Foundation, *KidsCount Databook*. Baltimore, MD: Annie E. Casey Foundation, 2008.

248. Leadership Conference on Civil Rights and Leadership Conference on Civil Rights Education Fund, *Justice on Trial: Racial disparities in the American criminal justice system*. Washington, DC: LCCR/LCCREF, 2000.

249. E. H. Johnson. 'The Japanese experience: effects of decreasing resort to imprisonment', in R. P. Weiss and N. South (eds.), *Comparing Prison Systems: Towards a comparative and international penology*. Amsterdam: Gordon & Breach Publishers, 1998.

250. J. O. Haley, 'Confession, repentence and absolution', in: M. Wright and B. Galoway (eds), *Mediation and Criminal Justice*. Newbury Park, CA: Sage, 1989.

251. Amnesty International, *Annual Report – United States of America*. London: Amnesty International, 2004.

252. Human Rights Watch and Amnesty International, *The Rest of Their Lives: Life without parole for child offenders in the United States*. New York: Human Rights Watch, 2005.

253. Human Rights Watch, *Cold Storage: Super-maximum security confinement in Indiana*. New York: Human Rights Watch, 1997.

254. Human Rights Watch, *Red Onion State Prison: Super-maximum* *security confinement in Virginia*. New York: Human Rights Watch, 1999.

255. United Nations Committee against Torture, *Conclusions and Recommendations of the Committee against Torture: United States of America*. Geneva: United Nations, 2006.

256. J. Irwin, *The Warehouse Prison: Disposal of the new dangerous class*. Cary, NC: Roxbury Publishing Company, 2005.

257. Amnesty International, *Ill-treatment of Inmates in Maricopa County Jails, Arizona*. London: Amnesty International, 1997.

258. E. James, 'A life again', *Guardian*, 5 September 2005.

259. L. A. Rhodes. 'Can there be "best practices" in supermax?' in D. Jones (ed.), *Humane Prisons*. Oxford: Radcliffe Publishing, 2006.

260. The Commission on Safety and Abuse in America's Prisons, *Confronting Confinement*. New York: Vera Institute of Justice, 2006.

261. P. Carter. *Managing Offenders, Reducing Crime. Correctional Services Review*. London: Prime Minister's Strategy Unit, 2003.

262. Home Office, *Explaining Reconviction Rates: A critical analysis*. Home Office Research Study 136. London: Home Office, 1995.

263. S. Henry, 'On the Effectiveness of Prison as Punishment. Incarceration Nation: The warehousing of America's poor'. Ivy Tech State College, South Bend, Indiana: http://www.is.wayne.edu/stuarthenry/ Effectiveness_of_Punishment.htm, 2003.

264. E. Currie, *Crime and Punishment in America*. New York: Henry Holt & Co, 1998.

265. Youth Justice Board, *Anti-social Behaviour Orders* (B289). London: Youth Justice Board for England and Wales, 2006.

266. NCH, *Tackling Anti-social Behaviour: Have we got it right?* London: NCH Children's Charities, 2006.

267. K. Beckett and B. Western, 'Governing social marginality', in D. Garland (ed.), *Mass Imprisonment: Social causes and consequences*. London: Sage, 2001.

268. D. Downes and K. Hansen, *Welfare and Punishment: The relationship between welfare spending and imprisonment*. London: Crime and Society Foundation, 2006.

269. J. Silverman, 'Does prison work?' ESRC Society Today: Spotlights. http://www.esrc.ac.uk/ESRCInfoCentre/about/CI/CP/Our_Society_Today/ Spotlights–2006/prison.aspx?ComponentId=16448&SourcePageId=16475 (accessed 9 September 2008).

270. M. Tonry, 'Why are US incarceration rates so high?' *Crime and Delinquency* (1999) 45: 419–37.

271. J. Blanden, P. Gregg and S. Machin, *Intergenerational mobility in*

Europe and North America. London: Centre for Economic Performance, London School of Economics, 2005.

272. L. Mishel, J. Bernstein and S. Allegretto, *The State of Working America 2006/7.* An Economic Policy Institute Book. Ithaca, NY: ILR Press, an imprint of Cornell University Press, 2007.

273. OECD, *Education at a Glance 2003. OECD Indicators.* Paris: OECD, 2004.

274. D. S. Massey, 'The age of extremes: concentrated affluence and poverty in the twenty-first century', *Demography* (1996) 33: 395–412.

275. P. A. Jargowsky, 'Take the money and run: economic segregation in U.S. metropolitan areas', *American Sociological Review* (1996) 61 (6): 984–8.

276. P. A. Jargowsky, *Poverty and Place: Ghettos, barrios and the American city.* New York: Russell Sage Foundation, 1997.

277. P. A. Jargowsky, *Stunning Progress, Hidden Problems: The dramatic decline of concentrated poverty in the 1990s.* The Living Cities Census Series. Washington, DC: Brookings Institution Press, 2003.

278. D. Dorling, 'Why Trevor is wrong about race ghettos', *Observer*, 25 September 2005.

279. D. Dorling, *Human Geography of the UK.* London: Sage Publications, 2005.

280. D. Dorling and P. Rees, 'A nation still dividing: the British census and social polarization', *Environment and Planning* (2003) 35: 1287–313.

281. A. Berube, *Mixed Communities in England.* York: Joseph Rowntree Foundation, 2005.

282. I. Kawachi, 'Income inequality and economic residential segregation', *Journal of Epidemiology and Community Health* (2002) 56 (3): 165–6.

283. S. Mayer, *How the Growth in Income Inequality Increased Economic Segregation.* The Joint Center for Poverty Research Working Paper 235. Chicago: NorthWestern University/University of Chicago, 2001.

284. P. Lobmayer and R. G. Wilkinson, 'Inequality, residential segregation by income, and mortality in US cities', *Journal of Epidemiology and Community Health* (2002) 56 (3): 183–7.

285. N. J. Waitzman and K. R. Smith, 'Separate but lethal: the effects of economic segregation on mortality in metropolitan America', *Milbank Quarterly* (1998) 76 (3): 341–73.

286. P. Bourdieu, *Distinction: A social critique of the judgement of taste.* London: Routledge, 1984.

287. K. Fox, *Watching the English: The hidden rules of English behaviour.* London: Hodder & Stoughton, 2004.

288. J. Epstein, *Snobbery: The American version*. New York: Houghton Mifflin Company, 2002.

289. R. Sennett and J. Cobb, *The Hidden Injuries of Class*. New York: Alfred A. Knopf, 1972.

290. S. J. Charlesworth, P. Gilfillan and R. G. Wilkinson, 'Living inferiority', *British Medical Bulletin* (2004) 69: 49–60.

291. A. Marcus-Newhall, W. C. Pedersen, M. Carlson and N. Miller, 'Displaced aggression is alive and well: a meta-analytic review', *Journal of Personality and Social Psychology* (2000) 78 (4): 670–89.

292. R. A. Baron, J. H. Neumann and A. Geddes, 'Social and personal determinants of workplace aggression: evidence for the impact of perceived injustice and the Type A behavior pattern', *Aggressive Behavior* (1999) 25 (4): 281–96.

293. D. L. Horowitz, 'Direct, displaced and cumulative ethnic aggression', *Comparative Politics* (1973): 6 (1): 1–16.

294. H. Crawley, *Evidence on Attitudes to Asylum and Immigration: What we know, don't know and need to know*. Working Paper No. 23. Oxford: Centre on Migration, Policy and Society, University of Oxford, 2005.

295. J. L. Ireland, *Bullying among Prisoners: Evidence, research and intervention strategies*. Hove: Brunner-Routledge, 2002.

296. P. Earley, *The Hot House: Life inside Leavenworth prison*. New York: Bantam, 1992.

297. J. Sidanius and F. Pratto, *Social Dominance*. Cambridge: Cambridge University Press, 1999.

298. K. E. Pickett and R. G. Wilkinson, 'People like us: ethnic group density effects on health', *Ethnicity and Health* (2008) 13 (4): 321–34.

299. J. Boydell, J. van Os, K. McKenzie, J. Allardyce, R. Goel, R. G. McCreadie and R. M. Murray, 'Incidence of schizophrenia in ethnic minorities in London: ecological study into interactions with environment', *British Medical Journal* (2001) 323 (7325): 1336–8.

300. J. Neeleman and S. Wessely, 'Ethnic minority suicide: a small area geographical study in south London', *Psychological Medicine* (1999): 29 (2): 429–36.

301. J. Neeleman, C. Wilson-Jones and S. Wessely, 'Ethnic density and deliberate self-harm: a small area study in south east London', *Journal of Epidemiology and Community Health* (2001) 55: 85–90.

302. J. Fang, S. Madhavan, W. Bosworth and M. H. Alderman, 'Residential segregation and mortality in New York City', *Social Science and Medicine* (1998) 47 (4): 469–76.

303. L. Franzini and W. Spears, 'Contributions of social context to inequalities in years of life lost to heart disease in Texas, USA', *Social Science and Medicine* (2003) 57 (10): 1847–61.

304. C. M. Masi, L. C. Hawkley, Z. H. Piotrowski and K. E. Pickett, 'Neighborhood economic disadvantage, violent crime, group density, and pregnancy outcomes in a diverse, urban population', *Social Science and Medicine* (2007) 65 (12): 2440–57.

305. K. E. Pickett, J. W. Collins, Jr., C. M. Masi and R. G. Wilkinson, 'The effects of racial density and income incongruity on pregnancy outcomes', *Social Science and Medicine* (2005) 60 (10): 2229–38.

306. E. M. Roberts, 'Neighborhood social environments and the distribution of low birthweight in Chicago', *American Journal of Public Health* (1997) 87 (4): 597–603.

307. L. C. Vinikoor, J. S. Kaufman, R. F. MacLehose and B. A. Laraia, 'Effects of racial density and income incongruity on pregnancy outcomes in less segregated communities', *Social Science and Medicine* (2008) 66 (2): 255–9.

308. A. M. Jenny, K. C. Schoendorf and J. D. Parker, 'The association between community context and mortality among Mexican-American infants', *Ethnicity and Disease* (2001) 11 (4): 722–31.

309. J. R. Dunn, B. Burgess and N. A. Ross, 'Income distribution, public services expenditures, and all cause mortality in US States', *Journal of Epidemiology and Community Health* (2005) 59 (9): 768–74.

310. A. Deaton and D. Lubotsky, 'Mortality, inequality and race in American cities and states', *Social Science and Medicine* (2003) 56 (6): 1139–53.

311. D. K. McLaughlin and C. S. Stokes, 'Income inequality and mortality in US counties: does minority racial concentration matter?' *American Journal of Public Health* (2002) 92 (1): 99–104.

312. R. Ram, 'Income inequality, poverty, and population health: evidence from recent data for the United States', *Social Science and Medicine* (2005) 61 (12): 2568–76.

313. S. V. Subramanian and I. Kawachi, 'The association between state income inequality and worse health is not confounded by race', *International Journal of Epidemiology* (2003) 32 (6): 1022–8.

314. R. Ram, 'Further examination of the cross-country association between income inequality and population health', *Social Science and Medicine* (2006) 62 (3): 779–91.

315. J. Banks, M. Marmot, Z. Oldfield and J. P. Smith, 'Disease and disadvantage in the United States and in England', *Journal of the American Medical Association* (2006) 295 (17): 2037–45.

316. J. Banks, M. Marmot, Z. Oldfield and J. P. Smith, 'The SES Health Gradient on Both Sides of the Atlantic'. NBER Working Paper 12674. Cambridge, MA: National Bureau of Economic Research, 2007.

317. D. Vagero and O. Lundberg, 'Health inequalities in Britain and Sweden', *Lancet* (1989) 2 (8653): 35–6.

318. D. A. Leon, D. Vagero and P. O. Olausson, 'Social class differences in infant mortality in Sweden: comparison with England and Wales', *British Medical Journal* (1992) 305 (6855): 687–91.

319. S. V. Subramanian and I. Kawachi, 'Whose health is affected by income inequality? A multilevel interaction analysis of contemporaneous and lagged effects of state income inequality on individual self-rated health in the United States', *Health and Place* (2006) 12 (2): 141–56.

320. M. Wolfson, G. Kaplan, J. Lynch, N. Ross and E. Backlund, 'Relation between income inequality and mortality: empirical demonstration', *British Medical Journal* (1999) 319 (7215): 953–5.

321. S. J. Babones, 'Income inequality and population health: correlation and causality', *Social Science and Medicine* (2008) 66 (7): 1614–26.

322. C. A. Shively and T. B. Clarkson, 'Social status and coronary artery atherosclerosis in female monkeys', *Arteriosclerosis and Thrombosis* (1994) 14 (5): 721–6.

323. C. A. Shively and T. B. Clarkson, 'Regional obesity and coronary artery atherosclerosis in females: a non-human primate model', *Acta Medica Scandinavica*, Supplement (1988) 723: 71–8.

324. M. Sahlins, *Stone Age Economics*. London: Routledge, 2003.

325. T. Hobbes, *Leviathan*. Oxford: Oxford University Press, 1998.

326. K. Jensen, J. Call and M. Tomasello, 'Chimpanzees are rational maximisers in an ultimatum game', *Science* (2007) 318 (5847): 107–9.

327. J. Henrich, R. Boyd, S. Bowles, C. F. Camerer, E. Fehr, H. Gintis and R. McElreath, 'Overview and synthesis', in J. Henrich, R. Boyd, S. Bowles, C. F. Camerer, E. Fehr and H. Gintis (eds), *Foundations of Human Sociality*. Oxford: Oxford University Press, 2004.

328. F. B. de Waal and F. Lanting, *Bonobo: The forgotten ape*. Berkeley: University of California Press, 1997.

329. E. A. D. Hammock, L. J. Young, 'Microsatellite instability generates diversity in brain and sociobehavioral traits', *Science* (2005) 308 (5728): 1630–34.

330. J. B. Lassner, K. A. Matthews and C. M. Stoney, 'Are cardiovascular reactors to asocial stress also reactors to social stress?' *Journal of Personality and Social Psychology* (1994) 66 (1): 69–77.

331. R. I. M. Dunbar, 'Brains on two legs: group size and the evolution of intelligence', in F. B. de Waal (ed.), *Tree of Origin: What primate behavior can tell us about human social evolution.* Cambridge, MA: Harvard University Press, 2001.

332. C. Boehm, *Hierarchy in the Forest: The evolution of egalitarian behavior.* Cambridge, MA: Harvard University Press, 1999.

333. D. Erdal and A. Whiten, 'Egalitarianism and Machiavellian intelligence in human evolution', in P. Mellars and K. Gibson K. (eds), *Modelling the Early Human Mind.* Cambridge: McDonald Institute Monographs, 1996.

334. R. G. Wilkinson, *The Impact of Inequality.* New York: New Press, 2005.

335. J. Woodburn, 'Egalitarian societies', *Man* (1982) 17: 431–51.

336. I. C. G. Weaver, N. Cervoni, F. A. Champagne, A. C. d'Alessio, S. Sharma, J. R. Seckl, S. Dymov, M. Szyf and M. J. Meaney, 'Epigenetic programming by maternal behaviour', *Nature Neuroscience* (2004) 7: 847–54.

337. S. Morris, 'Women laughed as they forced toddlers to take part in "dog fight"', *Guardian*, 21 April 2007.

338. G. Rizzolatti and L. Craighero, 'The mirror-neuron system', *Annual Review of Neuroscience* (2004) 27: 169–72.

339. M. Kosfeld, M. Heinrichs, P. J. Zak, U. Fischbacher and E. Fehr, 'Oxytocin increases trust in humans', *Nature* (2005) 435: 673–6.

340. P. J. Zak, R. Kurzban and W. Matzner, 'The neurobiology of trust', *Annals of the New York Academy of Sciences* (2004) 1032: 224–7.

341. J. K. Rilling, G. A. Gutman, T. R. Zeh, G. Pagnoni, G. S. Berns and C. D. Kilts, 'A neural basis for social cooperation', *Neuron* (2002) 35: 395–405.

342. N. I. Eisenberger and M. D. Lieberman, 'Why rejection hurts', *Trends in Cognitive Science* (2004) 8: 294–300.

343. J. W. Ouwerkerk, P. A. M. van Lange and M. Gallucci, 'Avoiding the social death penalty: ostracism and cooperation in social dilemmas', in K. D. Williams, J. P. Forgas and W. von Hippel (eds), *The Social Outcast: Ostracism, social exclusion, rejection and bullying.* New York: Psychology Press, 2005.

344. World Bank, *World Development Indicators (WDI) September 2006.* Economic and Social Data Service International, Manchester: Mimas.

345. World Wildlife Fund, *Living Planet Report 2006.* Gland, Switzerland: WWF International, 2007.

346. R. M. Titmuss, *Essays on the Welfare State.* London: Unwin, 1958.

347. H. Daly, *Steady-state Economics*. Washington, DC: Island Press, 1991.

348. M. Bookchin, *The Ecology of Freedom*. Oakland, CA: AK Press, 2005.

349. R. G. Wilkinson, *Poverty and Progress*. London: Methuen, 1973.

350. H. C. Wallich, 'Zero growth', *Newsweek*, 24 January 1972.

351. R. H. Frank, *Falling Behind: How rising inequality harms the middle class*. Berkeley, CA: University of California Press, 2007.

352. S. Bowles and Y. Park, 'Emulation, inequality, and work hours: was Thorsten Veblen right?' *Economic Journal* (2005) 115: F397–F412.

353. D. Neumark and A. Postlethwaite, 'Relative income concerns and the rise in married women's employment', *Journal of Public Economics* (1998) 70: 157–83.

354. Y. Park, *Veblen Effects on Labor Supply: Male earnings inequality increases women's labor force participation*. New London, CT: Department of Economics, Connecticut College, 2004.

355. S. J. Solnick and D. Hemenway, 'Is more always better? A survey on positional concerns', *Journal of Economic Behavior & Organization* (1998) 37: 373–83.

356. T. Veblen, *The Theory of the Leisure Class*. Oxford: Oxford University Press, 2007.

357. Planet Ark, *The Recycling Olympic Report*. Sydney: Planet Ark Environmental Foundation, 2004.

358. Vision of Humanity, *Global Peace Index: Methodology, results and findings*. Cammeray, NSW: Vision of Humanity, 2007.

359. G. B. Shaw, *The Intelligent Woman's Guide to Socialism and Capitalism*. Edison, N J: Transaction Publishers, 2007.

360. M. Bloom, 'The performance effects of pay dispersion on individuals and organizations', *Academy of Management Journal* (1991) 42: 25–40.

361. J. P. Mackenbach, 'Socio-economic inequalities in health in Western Europe', in J. Siegrist and M. Marmot (eds), *Social Inequalities in Health*. Oxford: Oxford University Press, 2006.

362. OECD, *Social Expenditure – Aggregated Data*. Vol. 2008, OECD. Stat, 2001.

363. Tax Foundation, *State and Local Tax Burdens Compared to Other US States, 1970–2007*. Washington, DC: Tax Foundation, 2007.

364. Justice Policy Institute, *Cellblocks or Classrooms?* Washington, DC: Justice Policy Institute, 2002.

365. L. J. Schweinhart and D. P. Weikart, 'Success by empowerment:

REFERENCES

the High/Scope Perry Preschool Study through age 27', *Young Children* (1993) 49: 54–8.

366. World Bank, *The East Asian Miracle*. Oxford: Oxford University Press, 1993.

367. J. M. Page, 'The East Asian miracle: an introduction', *World Development* (1994) 22 (4): 615–25.

368. R. M. Titmuss, 'War and social policy', in R. M. Titmuss (ed.), *Essays on the Welfare State* (3rd edition). London: Unwin, 1976.

369. L. McCall and J. Brash, *What do Americans Think about Inequality?* Working Paper. New York: Demos, 2004.

370. J. Weeks, *Inequality Trends in Some Developed OECD Countries*. Working Paper No. 6. New York: United Nations Department of Economic and Social Affairs, 2005.

371. J. Benson, 'A typology of Japanese enterprise unions', *British Journal of Industrial Relations* (1996) 34: 371–86.

372. L. Osberg and T. Smeeding, '"Fair" inequality? Attitudes to pay differentials: The United States in comparative perspective', *American Sociological Review* (2006) 71: 450–73.

373. J. Finch, 'The boardroom bonanza', *Guardian*, 29 August 2007.

374. International Labour Organization, 'Income inequalities in the age of financial globalization', *World of Work Report 2008*. Geneva: ILO, 2008.

375. Institute for Policy Studies, *Annual CEO Compensation Survey*. Washington, DC: Institute for Policy Studies, 2007.

376. United Nations Conference on Trade and Development, 'Are transnationals bigger than countries?' Press release: TAD/INF/PR/47. Geneva: United Nations Conference on Trade and Development, 2002.

377. T. Paine, *The Rights of Man*. London: Penguin, 1984.

378. G. Alperovitz, *America beyond Capitalism*. Hoboken, NJ: Wiley, 2004.

379. W. Hutton. 'Let's get rid of our silly fears of public ownership', *Observer*, 6 April 2008.

380. M. J. Conyon and R. B. Freeman, *Shared Modes of Compensation and Firm Performance: UK Evidence*. NBER Working Paper W8448. Cambridge, MA: National Bureau of Economic Research, 2001.

381. A. Pendleton and C. Brewster, 'Portfolio workforce', *People Management* (2001) July: 38–40.

382. G. Gates, 'Holding your own: the case for employee capitalism', *Demos Quarterly* (1996) 8: 8–10.

383. P. M. Rooney, 'Worker participation in employee owned firms', *Journal of Economic Issues* (1988) XXII (2): 451–8.

384. J. L. Cotton, *Employee Involvement: Methods for improving performance and work attitudes*. Newbury Park, CA: Sage, 1993.

385. National Center for Employee Ownership, *Employee Ownership and Corporate Performance: A comprehensive review of the evidence*. Oakland, CA: National Center for Employee Ownership, 2004.

386. J. Blasi, D. Kruse and A. Bernstein, *In the Company of Owners*. New York: Basic Books, 2003.

387. P. A. Kardas, A. Scharf and J. Keogh, *Wealth and Income Consequences of Employee Ownership*. Olympia, WA: Washington State Department of Community, Trade and Economic Development, 1998.

388. R. Oakeshott, *Jobs and Fairness: The logic and experience of employee ownership*. Norwich: Michael Russell, 2000.

389. M. Quarrey and C. Rosen, 'How well is employee ownership working?' *Harvard Business Review* (1987) Sep.–Oct.: 126–32.

390. T. Theorell, 'Democracy at work and its relationship to health', in P. Perrewe and D. E. Ganster (eds), *Emotional and Physiological Processes and Intervention Strategies: Research in occupational stress and well being*, Volume 3. Greenwich, CT: JAI Press, 2003.

391. R. de Vogli, J. E. Ferrie, T. Chandola, M. Kivimaki and M. G. Marmot, 'Unfairness and health: evidence from the Whitehall II Study', *Journal of Epidemiology and Community Health* (2007) 61 (6): 513–18.

392. D. Erdal, *Local Heroes*. London: Viking, 2008.

393. D. Erdal, 'The Psychology of Sharing: An evolutionary approach'. Unpublished PhD thesis, St Andrews, 2000.

394. S. Milgram, *Obedience to Authority*. New York: Harper, 1969.

395. L. T. Hobhouse, *Liberalism*. London: Williams & Norgate, 1911.

396. D. Coyle, *The Weightless World*. Oxford: Capstone, 1997.

397. K. E. Kiernan, F. K. Mensah. 'Poverty, maternal depression, family status and children's cognitive and behavioural development in early childhood: A longitudinal study'. *Journal of Social Policy* 2009; doi: 10.1017/S0047279409003250: 1–20.

398. J. Bradshaw, N. Finch. *A Comparison of Child Benefit Packages in 22 Countries*. Table 2.2. London: Department for Work and Pensions, 2002.

399. OECD. *Society at a glance 2009: OECD Social Indicators*. OECD 2009.

400. I. Kawachi, B. P. Kennedy, K. Lochner, D. Prothrow-Stith. 'Social capital, income inequality, and mortality'. *Am J Public Health* 1997; 87(9): 1491–8.

401. E. Uslaner. *The moral foundations of trust*. Cambridge: Cambridge University Press, 2002.

402. F. J. Elgar, W. Craig, W. Boyce, A. Morgan, R. Vella-Zarb. 'Income inequality and school bullying: Multilevel study of adolescents in 37 countries'. *Journal of Adolescent Health* 2009; 45(4): 351–9.

403. World Intellectual Property Organization. *Intellectual property statistics, Publication A*. Geneva: WIPO, 2001.

404. Personal communication, R. De Vogli, D. Gimeno 2009.

405. R. G. Wilkinson, K. E. Pickett. *Equality and sustainability*. London: London Sustainable Development Commission, 2009.

406. J. Hills, T. Sefton, K. Stewart (eds). *Towards a more equal society? Poverty, inequality and policy since 1997*. Bristol: Policy Press, 2009.

407. P. Krugman. *The Conscience of a Liberal: Reclaiming America from the right*. London: Penguin, 2009.

408. L. Bamfield, T. Horton. *Understanding attitudes to tackling economic inequality*. York: Joseph Rowntree Foundation, 2009.

409. M. I. Norton, D. Ariely, 'Building a better America – one wealth quintile at a time', *Perspectives on Psychological Science:* in press.

410. D. Runciman, *London Review of Books* 2009, No. 29; 22 Oct. 2009.

411. J. H. Goldthorpe, 'Analysing Social Inequality: A Critique of Two Recent Contributions from Economics and Epidemiology', *European Sociological Review*, 2009; doi: 10.1093/esr/jcp046

412. N. Oreskes, E. M. Conway, *Merchants of Doubt: How a Handful of Scientists Obscured the Truth on Issues from Tobacco Smoke to Global Warming*. New York: Bloomsbury, 2010.

413. The Equality Trust. The authors respond to questions about *The Spirit Level*'s analysis. *http://www.equalitytrust.org.uk/resources/response-to-questions* 2010.

414. M. Daly and M. Wilson, 'Cultural inertia, economic incentives, and the persistence of "southern violence"', in *Evolution, culture, and the human mind*. Edited by M. Schaller, A. Norenzayan, S. Heine, T. Yamagishi and T. Kameda. New York: Psychology Press. (2010) Pp. 229–241.

415. F. J. Elgar, N. Aitken, 'Income inequality, trust and homicide in 33 countries', *European Journal of Public Health* 2010; doi:10.1093/eurpub/ckq068.

416. P. Saunders, *Beware of False Profits*, Policy Exchange, London 2010.

417. C. J. Snowdon, '*The Spirit Level Delusion*', Democracy Institute / Little Dice, London 2010.

418. S. Hales, P. Howden-Chapman, C. Salmond, A. Woodward, J. Mackenbach, 'National infant mortality rates in relation to gross national product and distribution of income', *Lancet* 1999; 354:2047.

419. N. A. Ross, M. C. Wolfson, J. R. Dunn, J. M. Berthelot, G. A. Kaplan, J. W. Lynch, 'Relation between income inequality and mortality in Canada and in the United States: cross sectional assessment using census data and vital statistics', *British Medical Journal* 2000; 320: 898–902.

420. P. Walberg, M. McKee, V. Shkolnikov, L. Chenet, D. A. Leon, 'Economic change, crime, and mortality crisis in Russia: regional analysis', *British Medical Journal* 1998; 317 (7154) : 312–8.

421. X. Pei , E. Rodriguez, 'Provincial income inequality and self-reported health status in China during 1991–7, *Journal of Epidemiology and Community Health* 2006; 60:1065–9.

422. Y. Ichida, K. Kondo, H. Hirai, T. Hanibuchi, G. Yoshikawa, C. Murata, 'Social capital, income inequality and self-rated health in Chita peninsula, Japan: a multilevel analysis of older people in 25 communities', *Social Science & Medicine* 2009; 69(4):489–99.

423. S. V. Subramanian, I. Delgado, L. Jadue, J. Vega, I. Kawachi, 'Income inequality and health: multilevel analysis of Chilean communities', *Journal of Epidemiology and Community Health* 2003;57(11):844–8.

424. K. E. Pickett, R. G. Wilkinson, 'Child wellbeing and income inequality in rich societies: ecological cross sectional study', *British Medical Journal* 2007; 335 (7629):1080.

425. K. E. Pickett, O. W. James, R. G. Wilkinson. Income inequality and the prevalence of mental illness: a preliminary international analysis. *J Epidemiol Community Health* 2006; 60(7): 646–7.

426. J. Blanden, 'How much can we learn from international comparisons of intergenerational mobility', London: Centre for the Economics of Education, London School of Economics, 2009.

427. S. J. Babones, 'Income inequality and population health: Correlation and causality', *Social Science & Medicine* 2008; 66(7): 1614–26.

428. D. Collison, C. Dey, G. Hannah, L. Stevenson, 'Income inequality and child mortality in wealthy nations', *Journal of Public Health* 2007; 29(2): 114–7.

429. F. J. Elgar, 'Income Inequality, trust, and population health in 33 countries', *American Journal of Public Health,* doi: 10.2105/AJPH.2009.189134.

430. V. Hildebrand, P. Van Kerm, 'Income inequality and self-rated health status: evidence from the European Community Household Panel', *Demography* 2009; 46(4): 805–25.

431. A. J. Idrovo, M. Ruiz-Rodriguez, A. P. Manzano-Patino, 'Beyond the income inequality hypothesis and human health: a worldwide exploration', *Revista Salude Publica* 2010; 44(4): 695–702.

432. M. H. Jen, K. Jones, R. Johnston, 'Compositional and contextual approaches to the study of health behaviour and outcomes: using multi-level modelling to evaluate Wilkinson's income inequality hypothesis', *Health & Place* 2009; 15(1):198–203.

433. M. H. Jen, K. Jones, R. Johnston, 'Global variations in health: evaluating Wilkinson's income inequality hypothesis using the World Values Survey', *Social Science & Medicine* 2009; 68(4): 643–53.

434. M. Karlsson, T. Nilsson, C. H. Lyttkens, G. Leeson, 'Income inequality and health: importance of a cross-country perspective', *Social Science & Medicine* 2010; 70(6): 875–85.

435. D. Kim, I. Kawachi, S. V. Hoorn, M. Ezzati, 'Is inequality at the heart of it? Cross-country associations of income inequality with cardiovascular diseases and risk factors', *Social Science & Medicine* 2008; 66(8): 1719–32.

436. A. Barford, D. Dorling, K. E. Pickett, 'Re-evaluating self evaluation: A commentary on Jen, Jones, and Johnston (68: 4, 2009). *Social Science & Medicine* 2010; 70(4): 496–7.

437. D. Dorling, A. Barford, 'The inequality hypothesis: thesis, antithesis, and a synthesis?' *Health & Place* 2009; 15(4): 1166–9.

438. N. Kondo, G. Sembajwe, I. Kawachi, R. M. van Dam, S. V. Subramanian, Z. Yamagata, 'Income inequality, mortality, and self rated health: meta-analysis of multilevel studies', *British Medical Journal* 2009; 339:b4471.

439. A. Clarkwest, 'Neo-materialist theory and the temporal relationship between income inequality and longevity change', *Social Science & Medicine* 2008; 66 (9): 1871–81.

440. J. Holt-Lunstad, T. B. Smith, J. B. Layton, 'Social relationships and mortality risk: a meta-analytic review'. *PLoS Medicine* 2010; 7(7):e1000316.

441. D. Dorling, 'Is more equal more green?' Lecture to the Royal Geographical Society; 2010; London. http://sasi.group.shef.ac.uk/presentations/rgs/.

442. R. G. Wilkinson, K. E. Pickett, R. De Vogli, 'A convenient truth', *British Medical Journal* in press.

443. J. T. Roberts, B. C. Parks, *Climate of Injustice: Global Inequality, North-South Politics and Climate Policy*. Boston: The MIT Press, 2006.

444. J-S. You, S. Khagram, 'Comparative study of inequality and corruption', *American Sociological Review* 2005; 70: 136–57.

445. I. Kawachi, B. P. Kennedy, 'Socioeconomic determinants of health : Health and social cohesion: why care about income inequality?' *British Medical Journal* 1997; 314: 1037.

446. B. Geysa, 'Explaining voter turnout: A review of aggregate-level research' Electoral Studies, 2006; 25(4): 637–663.

447. M. Iacoviello, 'Household debt and income inequality 1963 to 2003', *Journal of Money, Credit and Banking* 2008; 40:929–65.

448. OECD StatExtracts 2008, 2009 http://stats.oecd.org/Index.aspx? DataSetCode=SNA http://www.oecdwash.org/PUBS/ELECTRONIC/ SAMPLES/natac_vol3_guide.pdf

449. D. Sington, *The Flaw*: Dartmouth Films, 2010.

450. B. Milanovic, 'Income inequality and speculative investment by the rich and poor in America led to the financial meltdown', Two Views on the Cause of the Global Crisis – Part I. *YaleGlobal Online*, 4 May 2009.

451. D. Moss, 'An Ounce of Prevention: Financial Regulation, Moral Hazard, and the End of "Too Big to Fail"', *Harvard Magazine,* 2009; September–October 2009.

452. P. Krugman, 'Inequality and crises: coincidence or causation?' http://www.princeton.edu/~pkrugman/inequality_crises.pdf

453. D. Cameron, the *Guardian* Hugo Young Lecture, 10 November 2009.

454. E. Miliband, Victory speech, Labour Party Conference, Manchester 25 September 2010.

455. E. Miliband, BBC Radio 4, *Today*, 12 July 2010.

456. The Equality Trust. http://www.equalitytrust.org.uk/pledge/ signatories

Index

environmental issues *see* carbon
emissions; global warming
epidemiological transition 73
epidemiology xiii
epigenetic processes 211
Epstein, Joseph 164–5
equal/more equal societies 26,
173–7
achievement in 237–6
benefits for all inhabitants 84,
176, 179–80
and the environment 232, 235
inclusiveness and empathy in 168
international policies 235
poor people in 176
see also hunter gatherers
equality:
attainability 197, 213, 267–8
benefits from improving 29–30,
33, 62, 102, 175–82, 192
of conditions 50–51, 209
and counter-dominance
strategies 208
early societies and 200
and economic growth 226
and government changes
254–5
groups committed to xv, 242, 269
and human differences 237
as ideal 45, 197
of incomes 18, 55
and liberty 263
and merit 237
of opportunity *see* equality of
opportunity
responses to 236–7
routes to 184, 197, 213, 236–7
and sustainability 217–31
unstoppable trend 267–8
equality of opportunity 263, 267–8

ideology of/distant prospect 157,
164, 169
and social mobility 157, 169
Equality Trust xv, xxi, 269
Erdal, David 258, 260
ethnic differences 113, 150
ethnic minorities 143
discrimination and social
exclusion 185–6
exclusion from education and
employment 185
and group density effect 168–9
income differences 185–7
and inequality 185–6
and mental illness 68–9, 168
ethnicity:
and health 186
and inequality 179, 185–7
and status 185–7
and teenage births 124
Euripides 3
European and World Values
Survey 53
Evans, Gillian 115–17
evidence-based medicine/politics xiii
evolution *see* early human
evolution
exchange, forms of 202–3
executive incomes 249–51, 254,
259–60, 269–70
exercise/physical activity, lack of
75
and low status 75
and obesity 90, 95, 102
experiments 113–14, 194
economic 202–3, 209
in obedience 262
on students 113–15, 194, 215
in trust 214
Ezzati, Professor Majid 93n.

A NOTE ON THE AUTHORS

Richard Wilkinson has played a formative role in international research on the social determinants of health. He studied economic history at the London School of Economics before training in epidemiology and is Professor Emeritus at the University of Nottingham Medical School, Honorary Professor at University College London and Visiting Professor at the University of York.

Kate Pickett is Professor of Epidemiology at the University of York and a National Institute for Health Research Career Scientist. She studied physical anthropology at Cambridge, nutritional sciences at Cornell and epidemiology at the University of California – Berkeley.

They live in North Yorkshire.